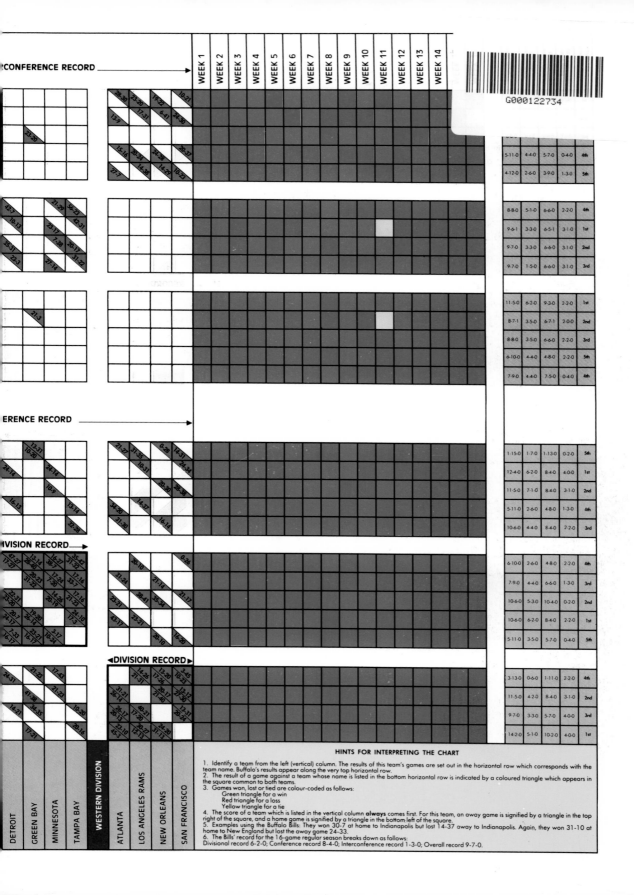

CONFERENCE RECORD ⟶

WEEK 1 · WEEK 2 · WEEK 3 · WEEK 4 · WEEK 5 · WEEK 6 · WEEK 7 · WEEK 8 · WEEK 9 · WEEK 10 · WEEK 11 · WEEK 12 · WEEK 13 · WEEK 14

G000122734

CONFERENCE RECORD ⟶

DIVISION RECORD ⟶

◄DIVISION RECORD►

DETROIT · GREEN BAY · MINNESOTA · TAMPA BAY · WESTERN DIVISION · ATLANTA · LOS ANGELES RAMS · NEW ORLEANS · SAN FRANCISCO

HINTS FOR INTERPRETING THE CHART

1. Identify a team from the left (vertical) column. The results of this team's games are set out in the horizontal row which corresponds with the team name. Buffalo's results appear along the very top horizontal row.

2. The result of a game against a team whose name is listed in the bottom horizontal row is indicated by a coloured triangle which appears in the square common to both teams.

3. Games won, lost or tied are colour-coded as follows:
    Green triangle for a win
    Red triangle for a loss
    Yellow triangle for a tie

4. The score of a team which is listed in the vertical column **always** comes first. For this team, an away game is signified by a triangle in the top right of the square, and a home game is signified by a triangle in the bottom left of the square.

5. Examples using the Buffalo Bills: They won 30-7 at home to Indianapolis but lost 14-37 away to Indianapolis. Again, they won 31-10 at home to New England but lost the away game 24-33.

6. The Bills' record for the 16-game regular season breaks down as follows:
Divisional record 6-2-0; Conference record 8-4-0; Interconference record 1-3-0; Overall record 9-7-0.

THE OFFICIAL CHANNEL FOUR
AMERICAN FOOTBALL
ANNUAL 1990-91

THE OFFICIAL CHANNEL FOUR
AMERICAN FOOTBALL
ANNUAL 1990-91

KEN THOMAS

Macdonald Queen Anne Press

In association with
Channel Four Television Company Limited

ACKNOWLEDGEMENTS

Last year I made reference to a list 'which continues to grow' and, twelve months on, that remains true. As usual, Roger Smith has turned up with a complete array of statistics, beautifully set out and double-checked, for which I am most grateful. I always point out that Roger was the very first British fan of the Dallas Cowboys, and he is good-humoured enough to see the funny side when I suggest that he may be the only one left! For major sections of the book I am indebted to Nick Wridgway, who, outside the United States, has no equal when it comes to a detailed knowledge of the twenty-eight NFL clubs. This year, Nick's speciality has been in compiling team rosters and discussing with me the many implications of the player movements resulting from the Plan-B free-agency system.

Over the years, many American experts who have given generously of their knowledge have become my good friends, and I am sure that the rest will not mind if I single out Beau Riffenburgh for special thanks. This is not to say that I take for granted the great help I receive from a host of others, including Larry Eldridge, Jr., who is the Assistant Director of Athletics at the University of Pittsburgh, and Linda Venzon, Pitt's Sports Information

Director. From the NFL office in New York, Pete Abitante and Leslie Hammond have kept up a continuous supply of information, often at great inconvenience to themselves. From NFL Creative Services Division in Los Angeles comes the photographic material, always on time and in perfect order thanks to the efficiency of Sharon Kuthe, Kevin Terrell and the imperturbable Stan James. John Herrera, a Senior Executive with the Los Angeles Raiders, has given freely of his football expertise. Ladies and gentlemen, I am extremely grateful.

Somehow, despite her increasing responsibilities with the Macdonald Publishing Group, Celia Kent manages to find the time to navigate this little project through the shoals, and it is to her skill rather than my proficiency that the publication deadline is met. In orchestrating matters, both Susanna Yager and her assistant, Sandy Holton, of Channel Four Television, have been no less considerate than Celia. To all three ladies I extend my gratitude.

Finally, Janie, whom readers of previous Annuals will know as my long-suffering wife, has been more tolerant than I have a right to expect. I really am grateful, love.

K.T., June 1990

A QUEEN ANNE PRESS BOOK

© Ken Thomas 1990

First published in Great Britain in 1990 by
Queen Anne Press, a division of
Macdonald & Co (Publishers) Ltd
Orbit House
1 New Fetter Lane
London EC4A 1AR

A member of Maxwell Macmillan Pergamon Publishing Corporation

Cover photographs – Front: Super Bowl XXIV
(All-Sport)
Back: Jerry Rice celebrates a touchdown
(All-Sport)

The Official Channel Four American Football Annual 1990-91 is associated with Channel Four Television's coverage of the sport

™ NFL Properties (UK) Ltd

British Library Cataloguing in Publication Data
Thomas, Ken
The official Channel 4 tv American football annual 1991. –
8th ed.
1. American football
I. Title
796.332

ISBN 0-356-19195-8

Typeset by SX Composing Ltd

Printed and bound in Great Britain by
BPCC Paulton Books Ltd

PHOTOGRAPHS
With the exception of the photographs on pages 3, 5, 6 which were supplied by All-Sport, all photographs have been supplied by courtesy of the NFL. The following photographers took the pictures on the pages indicated: Bill Amatucci 41R; John Biever 84; Vernon Biever 17, 21R, 125T; Clifton Boutelle 57, 65; Peter Brouillet 29R, 119; Dan Burns 103; Jimmy Cribb 27L, 29L, 49B; Dave Cross 28; Bill Cummings 70B; Scott Cunningham 15L, 70T, 83R; Brian Drake 72T; David Drapkin 38, 41L, 72L, 85; Malcolm Emmons 56, 107, 128; James Flores 60; Richard Gentile 12T, 139; Pete Groh 113, 127B, 129; Michael Heinz 35; Dan Honda 31, 47T, 153; Paul Jasienski 14, 47L 121, 151; Diane Johnson 12B, 111; Al Kooistra 72BR, 89L, 145; Don Lansu 34; Don Larson 11, 99; Laughead 9L; Amos Love 13; Richard Mackson 48L; Tak Makita 64; Robert Mayer 15R, 33; Rob McElroy 91; Al Messerschmidt 10, 22L, 24, 25L, 26, 45, 46, 93, 95, 97, 101, 117; Mike Moore 78, 86L, 137; William Pugliano 20; Richard Raphael 61; Kevin Reece 83L; Frank Rippon 58; Bob Rosato 19, 21L 42, 49T, 50, 51B, 79, 86R, 88, 135, 143, 147, 149; George Rose 27R, 36, 47BR, 87; Manny Rubio 39L, 82, 123; John Sandhaus 40; Chris Schwenk 28; Carl Skalak 59; Robert Smith 25R; Paul Spinelli 8, 43, 44, 45B, 89R, 94; Brian Spurlock 30, 115; Al Tielmans 18L; Tony Tomsic 62, 109, 141; Corky Trewin 51T, 74; Greg Trott 32, 157; Jim Turner 16, 22R, 105, 133; Ron Vesely 39R, 48R, 92; Fred Vuich 131; Michael Zagaris 37.

CONTENTS

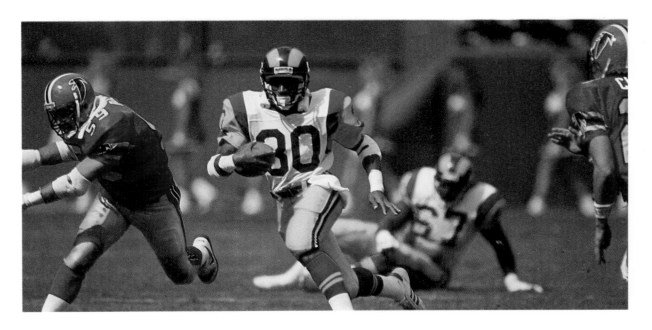

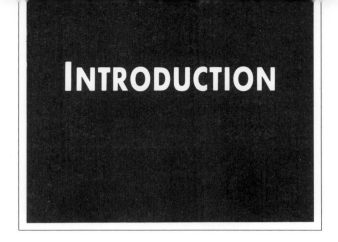

INTRODUCTION

If, at this stage last year, it was exciting to speculate on the prospect of the UK being involved in some kind of multi-national league of American Football, we can now sit back and savour the certainty that, though we shall not be hosting a full-status NFL team, at least we will be able to watch the next best thing playing in serious competition within these shores against foes from other nations. It began as a project speculatively titled the World American Football League, but, perhaps conscious of the potential impact of an acronym, the NFL eventually settled for World League of American Football. There will be twelve franchises, eight based in the Americas and one of the remaining four in London. Kickoff is scheduled for the Spring of 1991. What price a pair of tickets on the 50-yard line?

And that's not all. Now convinced that our lads are serious about playing the game, the NFL has assembled a help-programme from which nothing is excluded and, certainly, means that teams involved in our domestic competitions will be given the very best advice from visiting NFL coaches. Amongst other benefits, one will be the increased likelihood of a good prospect being 'spotted' by the NFL. My personal view is that the chances of British athletes being successful in the NFL are slim, not least for the fact that, each year, many outstanding American college football players fail the test. But, having been brought up in Rugby League country, for whose professionals I have an unqualified respect, I have seen enough talent to suggest that we could produce a specialist outside linebacker or perhaps a strong safety.

Apart from a chapter devoted to some members of the Pro Football Hall of Fame, very little is different in style from last year's Annual. Of course, writing it, sharing my love of the game, continues to be a privilege that I value greatly.

CONTENTS PAGE: Gaston Green should be ready to make his mark in the NFL.

LEFT: Tim Harris (#97) has become a towering force for Green Bay.

CHAPTER ONE

A REVIEW OF THE 1989 SEASON

Prologue

"No man in the history of professional sports and the awesome pressures commensurate with a commissionership ever acquitted himself more admirably than Pete Rozelle, who combined integrity, decency and fairness while being profoundly in love with a game that made him a household name."

John Steadman, Baltimore Morning Sun

Steadman was just one of the many sportswriters who felt moved to pen their respect when, on March 22nd, 1989, in his thirtieth year as commissioner, Pete Rozelle announced his intention to retire once a successor had been found. Under his leadership, the NFL had enjoyed a period of success unprecedented in American sports history. It would be a difficult act to follow and his replacement would not emerge for some time.

Back in 1960, Rozelle had welcomed into the NFL the newly formed Dallas Cowboys, who were to be coached by Tom Landry with Tex Schramm as general manager. Over the subsequent years, these two friends had fashioned one of pro football's historic powerhouses, with Landry becoming known as the 'Dean' of coaches while Schramm worked his magic in the front office. However, in the early months of 1989, both men would sever their formal connections with the club which, together, they had guided to two Super Bowl Championships and, despite a modest recent period, still was one of the most respected and feared opponents in the league.

New Cowboys owner Jimmy Jones, who purchased the Dallas franchise in late February, wanted a fresh start and preferred his long-time friend, Jimmy Johnson, to coach the team into the 1990s. It was with typical grace and dignity that Landry accepted his release. For Schramm, there was to emerge a challenge which would test even his managerial skills to the full. In the early Spring, the NFL confirmed its intention to form an international league, which, after a juggle with a variety of acronyms, was given the name, World

League of American Football (WLAF). Who better to run that show than Schramm, who resigned his post with Dallas in April and began his new job in earnest?

Johnson, who recently had been the hugely successful head coach of the University of Miami Hurricanes, was one of six head coaches, three in each conference, who would be entering their first full seasons with new teams. If Johnson had a job on his hands, the same was true of George Seifert, though for different reasons. Johnson's task was one of reconstruction from the bottom whereas Seifert, who took over in San Francisco following Bill Walsh's decision to begin a career

Commissioner Pete Rozelle welcomes top draftee Troy Aikman into the National Football League.

Commissioner Rozelle with head coach Tom Landry and general manager Tex Schramm of the expansion Dallas Cowboys in 1960.

The NFL's head coaches are all mates together at their annual preseason gathering.

in television, had been handed arguably the best squad in pro football. As an assistant for six years, he had played a large part in building the team, but now he was in sole charge and anything less than a Super Bowl repeat would be seen as failure. In Detroit, Wayne Fontes had proved to be an immensely popular and inspirational interim head coach over the final five games of the 1988 campaign, and the club ownership had not hesitated to offer him the permanent post.

In the AFC, Marty Schottenheimer, who had coached the Cleveland Browns to three successive division titles and a wild-card berth in the last four years, took his particular brand of charisma to Kansas City. His replacement in Cleveland, Bud Carson, brought the collective experience of 17 years as a highly praised assistant with Pittsburgh, the Rams, Baltimore, Kansas City and the Jets. Finally, for new Chargers head coach Dan Henning, the move to San Diego was a homecoming. Henning had played quarterback for the club in the mid-1960s, and, either side of a four-year term as the head coach of the Atlanta Falcons (1983-86), had been an assistant with Washington. The Chargers needed direction and he was the man with the compass.

Predictably, in the collegiate draft, the Cowboys had selected UCLA quarterback Troy Aikman with the first option overall. And it was not a surprise when Green Bay went for the destructive power of Michigan State tackle Tony Mandarich. Detroit took a chance on Oklahoma State running back Barry Sanders, who had ripped his way unchecked through the collegiate defenses all season and had been the comfortable winner of the Heisman Trophy. However, the sceptics questioned his ability to perform at that level in the

pros. More interesting for historians of the game, Sanders was the first true junior to enter the draft — it normally is open only to seniors — and there was speculation that, in future years, others might challenge a selection system that had continued essentially undisturbed since its inception in 1936. On draft day, the major trade was that of Pittsburgh linebacker Mike Merriweather, who went to the Minnesota Vikings in exchange for a first-round pick.

Recognising a need for greater player movement, the club owners introduced a plan in which all except the 37 so-called 'protected' players on each club would be free to seek contracts with other clubs, without the need for compensation payment. The 'Plan B' system, as it became known, resulted in 229 players moving to other teams, with Green Bay signing the largest number, 20, and the talent-rich Houston Oilers losing the most (15).

Turning to the prospects for the teams, the NFC entered the campaign having lifted the Vince Lombardi Trophy in seven of the previous nine years and for the last five in a row. Most fans recognised its superior strength in depth. However, AFC diehards could take comfort from the fact that, in each interconference series of games over the previous six seasons, the AFC either had won or tied. Still, when it came to picking a Super Bowl Champion, there was hardly an expert who didn't fancy San Francisco to become the first team to retain its title since the 1979 Pittsburgh Steelers. As usual, your writer took a different view. Indeed, he saw quite clearly that the Rams would find a way of beating Minnesota in the NFC Championship Game before holding off a good Houston team in the big one.

WEEK ONE

American Football Conference
Buffalo 27 at Miami 24
Cleveland 51 at Pittsburgh 0
Kansas City 20 at Denver 34
New England 27 at New York Jets 24
San Diego 14 at Los Angeles Raiders 40

National Football Conference
Dallas 0 at New Orleans 28
Los Angeles Rams 31 at Atlanta 21
New York Giants 27 at Washington 24
Phoenix 16 at Detroit 13
Tampa Bay 23 at Green Bay 21

Interconference Games
Cincinnati 14 at Chicago 17
Houston 7 at Minnesota 38
San Francisco 30 at Indianapolis 24
Seattle 7 at Philadelphia 31

Interconference Play
AFC 0 – NFC 4

'With one or two exceptions, much as anticipated,' might well have summed up the results on the opening weekend of the NFL's 70th season. But that is not to say that there was none of the drama that we have come to expect when the NFL's family of clubs begins its annual sort-out. First, though, the headlines. And they belonged to the Cleveland Browns, whose new 4-3 defense passed its initial test in Three Rivers Stadium. The unit recovered five fumbles, had three interceptions, logged six quarterback sacks and scored three touchdowns while handing the Steelers their biggest loss in the club's 57-year history. Elsewhere in the AFC, Buffalo quarterback Jim Kelly sparked a comeback with his late, 26-yard touchdown pass to wide receiver Flip Johnson, and then ran for a score as time expired to complete a rally against Miami. The Patriots, too, were in a tense finish, winning on a late touchdown from running back Reggie Dupard after having led 21-0 against the Jets. The Raiders surprised a few

OUTSTANDING INDIVIDUAL PERFORMANCES

100 Yards Rushing
Neal Anderson (Chicago) 21-146-35-0
Roger Craig (San Francisco) 24-131-27-2
Greg Bell (L.A. Rams) 26-128-16-2
Gerald Riggs (Washington) 24-111-17-0
Eric Dickerson (Indianapolis) 19-106-18-0

100 Yards Pass Receiving
Jerry Rice (San Francisco) 6-163-58t-1
Cedric Jones (New England) 8-148-36-0
Ricky Sanders (Washington) 6-143-48t-1
Mike Quick (Philadelphia) 6-140-40-1
Willie Gault (L.A. Raiders) 4-131-53-1
Anthony Carter (Minnesota) 7-123-32t-1
J.T. Smith (Phoenix) 10-121-24-0
Gary Clark (Washington) 6-101-28-0

Passing
Steve Beuerlein (L.A. Raiders) 22-15-206-0-43-2
Wade Wilson (Minnesota) 25-16-218-0-32t-2
Vinny Testaverde (Tampa Bay) 27-22-205-0-18-1
Mark Rypien (Washington) 32-22-349-1-48t-2
Bobby Hebert (New Orleans) 19-16-153-0-22-0
Chris Miller (Atlanta) 37-23-299-0-53t-2
Randall Cunningham (Philadelphia) 27-13-240-0-42-2
Joe Montana (San Francisco) 26-15-233-0-58t-1

Deion Sanders became the first man in history to score a major league home run and an NFL touchdown within the same week.

people with the ease of their victory over San Diego, though their elation was tempered by a serious knee injury to star wide receiver Tim Brown. Denver never looked back after taking advantage of early Kansas City errors to open up a 14-point lead.

In the NFC, of the clubs which have spent recent years wandering in the wilderness, Phoenix and Tampa Bay had narrow victories over Detroit and Green Bay respectively. The Rams, perennial contenders, had too much power for Atlanta, and New Orleans were never threatened in a clinical display against Dallas.

If you believed that the interconference series offered the best early indication of league-wide form, then there was only one possible conclusion. All four NFC teams won, with the Minnesota Vikings making the loudest statement when, after conceding the opening touchdown, they responded with 38 unanswered points against the physical Houston Oilers. Philadelphia dealt Seattle a similar blow after allowing the Seahawks to draw level on wide receiver Steve Largent's 98th career regular-season touchdown reception. Seeing running back Eric Dickerson reach 10,000 career rushing yards in just his 91st game, beating the previous NFL-best of 98 games by the great Jim Brown, was the Colts' one consolation in defeat by the reigning Super Bowl Champion 49ers. Joe Montana was virtually flawless, Roger Craig rushed for 131 yards and two touchdowns while Jerry Rice caught six passes for 163 yards and a touchdown. The demanding Chicago fans were not slow to voice their disapproval as quarterback

Mike Tomczak started poorly. But they were cheering at the end after Tomczak, who was replacing departed hero Jim McMahon, had thrown the game-winning touchdown pass to tight end James Thornton.

Just to round things off nicely, on Monday Night, the Giants' Raul Allegre kicked a 32-yard field goal to tie the Redskins, 24-24. Then, on the last play of the game, he split the uprights with a 52-yarder for the victory.

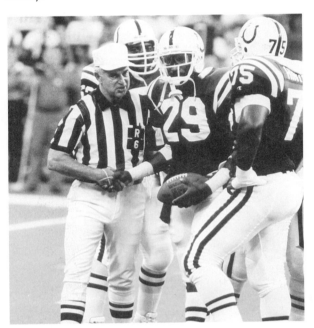

Eric Dickerson went beyond 10,000 career rushing yards.

STANDINGS

AFC East	W	L	T	PF	PA	NFC East	W	L	T	PF	PA
Buffalo	1	0	0	27	24	N.Y. Giants	1	0	0	27	24
New England	1	0	0	27	24	Philadelphia	1	0	0	31	7
Indianapolis	0	1	0	24	30	Phoenix	1	0	0	16	13
Miami	0	1	0	24	27	Dallas	0	1	0	0	28
N.Y. Jets	0	1	0	24	27	Washington	0	1	0	24	27
AFC Central						**NFC Central**					
Cleveland	1	0	0	51	0	Chicago	1	0	0	17	14
Cincinnati	0	1	0	14	17	Minnesota	1	0	0	38	7
Houston	0	1	0	7	38	Tampa Bay	1	0	0	23	21
Pittsburgh	0	1	0	0	51	Detroit	0	1	0	13	16
						Green Bay	0	1	0	21	23
AFC West						**NFC West**					
Denver	1	0	0	34	20	L.A. Rams	1	0	0	31	21
L.A. Raiders	1	0	0	40	14	New Orleans	1	0	0	28	0
Kansas City	0	1	0	14	40	San Francisco	1	0	0	30	24
San Diego	0	1	0	7	31	Atlanta	0	1	0	21	31
Seattle	0	1	0	7	31						

WEEK TWO

American Football Conference
Denver 28 at Buffalo 14
Houston 34 at San Diego 27
Los Angeles Raiders 19 at Kansas City 24
Miami 24 at New England 10
New York Jets 24 at Cleveland 38
Pittsburgh 10 at Cincinnati 41

National Football Conference
Dallas 21 at Atlanta 27
Detroit 14 at New York Giants 24
Minnesota 7 at Chicago 38
New Orleans 34 at Green Bay 35
Philadelphia 42 at Washington 37
San Francisco 20 at Tampa Bay 16

Interconference Games
Indianapolis 17 at Los Angeles Rams 31
Phoenix 34 at Seattle 24

Interconference Play
AFC 0 – NFC 6

On Week Two, both Philadelphia and Chicago delivered telling, if not mortal, blows to divisional rivals, while Denver made a point with a Buffalo club in what many felt could be a preview of the distant playoffs.

Despite losing possession on turnovers five times, the Redskins had used the power of running back Gerald Riggs, who would rush for the equal-sixth best single-game total since the 1970 merger, to establish a 37-35 lead. And with under two minutes left, his 58-yard gain appeared to have erased Philadelphia's faint hopes. But Riggs subsequently fumbled; Eagles safety Wes Hopkins returned the ball 77 yards and quarterback Randall Cunningham did the rest with a four-yard touchdown pass to tight end Keith Jackson. Against Minnesota, Chicago held a tenuous, three-point lead going into the final quarter, before exploding for four touchdowns, two of which were set up by interceptions with a third coming directly when reserve cornerback Lemuel Stinson returned his interception 29 yards into the end zone. Denver kept its 100% record at the expense of Buffalo, opening up a 21-point lead and absorbing a mini-rally before having the final say on rookie running back Bobby Humphrey's five-yard touchdown run.

In other games, the Cleveland defense was at it again, this time intercepting Jets quarterback Ken O'Brien four times in a 38-24 victory. For the Steelers, who had been routed a week earlier, the nightmare continued with a humiliating 41-10 loss to Cincinnati. Even allowing for the Bengals' firepower, two losses by a combined points total of 92-10 had to be worrying. There were signs of alarm, too, in Tampa, though the fear probably rested with the home fans. What else can you feel when, with your team leading by three points and 3:25 remaining, San Francisco's Joe Montana has

possession? True to form, Montana drove the 49ers 66 yards on nine plays before running four yards for the game-winning touchdown. Even in defeat, however, the Buccaneers showed that they could compete with any team in the league. Indeed, the quality of their victory over Green Bay the previous week was confirmed when the Packers outlasted New Orleans in a 35-34 shoot-out.

Philadelphia's Randall Cunningham passed for five touchdowns and a club-record 447 yards.

Derrick Thomas had eight tackles, 2.5 sacks and forced a fumble in Kansas City's win over the Raiders.

The Oilers, Chiefs, Falcons and Dolphins each opened their accounts. Houston needed to withstand a Chargers comeback led by Jim McMahon, while Kansas City capitalised on a series of Raiders penalties and Atlanta quarterback Chris Miller engineered a 17-point comeback against Dallas. Miami's victory over the Patriots was notable, not least for the fact that it was their first against an AFC East opponent following ten straight losses. In that win, Dolphins quarterback Dan Marino set an NFL record by passing for his 200th career touchdown in only his 89th game.

In the interconference series, the AFC still was without a victory as the Colts lost to an NFC West club for the second week in a row and Phoenix kept the Seahawks winless thanks to an inspirational, four-touchdown performance by quarterback Gary Hogeboom.

This Ernest Givins touchdown helped Houston to victory over San Diego.

OUTSTANDING INDIVIDUAL PERFORMANCES

100 Yards Rushing
Gerald Riggs (Washington) 29-221-58-1
Eric Dickerson (Indianapolis) 21-116-18-1
James Brooks (Cincinnati) 20-113-16-1
Brent Fullwood (Green Bay) 18-125-38-2

100 Yards Pass Receiving
Henry Ellard (L.A. Rams) 12-230-29t-3
Richard Johnson (Detroit) 9-172-71t-1
Roy Green (Phoenix) 8-166-59t-3
Anthony Miller (San Diego) 7-162-63t-2
Andre Reed (Buffalo) 13-157-23-0
Gary Clark (Washington) 4-153-80t-2
Brian Blades (Seattle) 9-146-28-1
Keith Byars (Philadelphia) 8-130-31-0
Keith Jackson (Philadelphia) 12-126-24-3
Louis Lipps (Pittsburgh) 5-122-40-0
Jerry Rice (San Francisco) 8-122-40-1
Michael Irvin (Dallas) 5-115-65t-1
Sterling Sharpe (Green Bay) 8-107-39-1
J.T. Smith (Phoenix) 7-104-25t-1
Tim McGee (Cincinnati) 6-100-27-0

Passing
Gary Hogeboom (Phoenix) 24-18-298-1-59t-4
Don Majkowski (Green Bay) 32-25-354-1-39-3
Randall Cunningham (Philadelphia) 46-34-447-1-35-5
Jim Everett (L.A. Rams) 35-28-368-1-39-3
Boomer Esiason (Cincinnati) 27-16-328-0-45-2
Phil Simms (N.Y. Giants) 26-20-218-0-25-2
Mark Rypien (Washington) 23-12-288-2-80t-4
Bobby Hebert (New Orleans) 32-23-282-1-32t-3
Jay Schroeder (L.A. Raiders) 21-14-192-1-29-2
Bernie Kosar (Cleveland) 30-15-196-0-36-3

STANDINGS

AFC East	W	L	T	PF	PA
Buffalo	1	1	0	41	52
Miami	1	1	0	48	37
New England	1	1	0	37	48
Indianapolis	0	2	0	41	61
N.Y. Jets	0	2	0	48	65
AFC Central					
Cleveland	2	0	0	89	24
Cincinnati	1	1	0	55	27
Houston	1	1	0	41	65
Pittsburgh	0	2	0	10	92
AFC West					
Denver	2	0	0	62	34
Kansas City	1	1	0	44	53
L.A. Raiders	1	1	0	59	38
San Diego	0	2	0	41	74
Seattle	0	2	0	31	65

NFC East	W	L	T	PF	PA
N.Y. Giants	2	0	0	51	38
Philadelphia	2	0	0	73	44
Phoenix	2	0	0	50	37
Dallas	0	2	0	21	55
Washington	0	2	0	61	69
NFC Central					
Chicago	2	0	0	55	21
Green Bay	1	1	0	56	57
Minnesota	1	1	0	45	45
Tampa Bay	1	1	0	39	41
Detroit	0	2	0	27	40
NFC West					
L.A. Rams	2	0	0	62	38
San Francisco	2	0	0	50	40
Atlanta	1	1	0	48	52
New Orleans	1	1	0	62	35

WEEK THREE

American Football Conference
Buffalo 47 at Houston 41 (OT)
Cleveland 14 at Cincinnati 21
Kansas City 6 at San Diego 21
Los Angeles Raiders 21 at Denver 31
New York Jets 40 at Miami 33
Seattle 24 at New England 3

National Football Conference
Chicago 47 at Detroit 27
Green Bay 38 at Los Angeles Rams 41
New Orleans 10 at Tampa Bay 20
Phoenix 7 at New York Giants 35
San Francisco 38 at Philadelphia 28
Washington 30 at Dallas 7

Interconference Games
Atlanta 9 at Indianapolis 13
Minnesota 14 at Pittsburgh 27

Interconference Play
AFC 2 – NFC 6

Though some elements of the form book appeared to be etched in position, there still was enough uncertainty around to make predicting as a business an even higher risk than usual.

Turning first to those games which went as expected, the 49ers beat Philadelphia, though they needed an astonishing spell from quarterback Joe Montana. With the Eagles holding a 21-10 lead, early in the final quarter, Montana, who would be sacked no fewer than eight times in the game, went on the rampage, completing 11 of 12 passes and throwing for touchdowns on four successive drives to round off the recovery. Again, when the Rams beat Green Bay, it was not a surprise, but a Packers rally – they outscored the Rams by 31 points to three in the second half – stalled only in the final moments when running back Brent Fullwood fumbled at the Rams' one. Chicago beat Detroit without too much bother while the NFC's other unbeaten team, the New York Giants, really came alive, intercepting quarterback Gary Hogeboom's fourth, fifth, seventh and eighth passes, recovering two Phoenix fumbles and logging five sacks as the Cardinals were dispatched. Washington vented the frustrations of back-to-back, last-minute losses with a victory over Dallas. Tampa Bay's victory over New Orleans was a surprise but only to the extent that, although the Buccaneers had looked good, they still hadn't rated up with the Saints.

Turning to the upset of the day, in Pittsburgh, the home team found new strength to put a dent in the Vikings' reputation. And it was no fluke. After trading early touchdowns, the Steelers gradually took control and, by the end, were showing a relaxed authority.

If, perhaps, the NFC clubs were falling into some

kind of order, that could not be said of the AFC, where a good deal of shuffling was going on. Denver had taken advantage of three Jay Schroeder fumbles in setting up a 28-point lead, before out-staying the Raiders to remain as the only unbeaten team in the conference. Cleveland suffered its first reverse at the hands of the dangerous Bengals, whose defense had collared Browns quarterback Bernie Kosar six times. With the Jets beating Miami and Indianapolis chalking up its first win, four clubs were tied at 1-2 behind the Eastern division leader, the Buffalo Bills, who, even with five touchdown passes from Jim Kelly, had needed the first overtime period of the season to shake off the tenacious Oilers. San Diego's first win of the campaign came at the expense of a club, Kansas City, which hadn't yet brought the full weight of its talent to bear. New England, in some discomfort following long-term injuries to several defensive starters, could not hold off Seattle, for whom running backs Curt Warner and John L. Williams were showing signs of form. The Seahawks had been slow out of the trap but, together with four others, they now were in a tie for second place in their division.

San Diego cornerback Gill Byrd halted two Kansas City drives with interceptions.

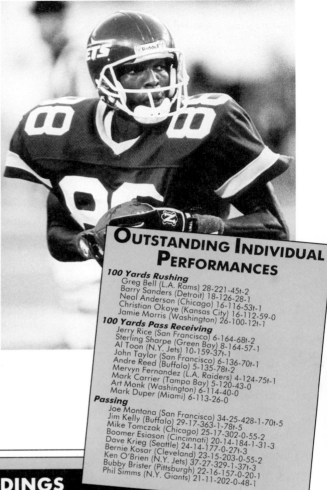

ABOVE: Even on a five-touchdown day, Joe Montana still takes advice from his coaches.

ABOVE RIGHT: Al Toon had ten catches for 159 yards and a touchdown as the Jets rallied to beat Miami.

OUTSTANDING INDIVIDUAL PERFORMANCES

100 Yards Rushing
Greg Bell (L.A. Rams) 28-221-45t-2
Barry Sanders (Detroit) 18-126-28-1
Neal Anderson (Chicago) 16-116-53t-1
Christian Okoye (Kansas City) 16-112-59-0
Jamie Morris (Washington) 26-100-12t-1

100 Yards Pass Receiving
Jerry Rice (San Francisco) 6-164-68t-2
Sterling Sharpe (Green Bay) 8-164-57-1
Al Toon (N.Y. Jets) 10-159-37t-1
John Taylor (San Francisco) 6-136-70t-1
Andre Reed (Buffalo) 5-135-78t-2
Mervyn Fernandez (L.A. Raiders) 4-124-75t-1
Mark Carrier (Tampa Bay) 5-120-43-0
Art Monk (Washington) 6-114-40-0
Mark Duper (Miami) 6-113-26-0

Passing
Joe Montana (San Francisco) 34-25-428-1-70t-5
Jim Kelly (Buffalo) 29-17-363-1-78t-5
Mike Tomczak (Chicago) 25-17-302-0-55-2
Boomer Esiason (Cincinnati) 20-14-184-1-31-3
Dave Krieg (Seattle) 24-14-177-0-27t-3
Bernie Kosar (Cleveland) 23-15-203-0-55-2
Ken O'Brien (N.Y. Jets) 37-27-329-1-37t-3
Bubby Brister (Pittsburgh) 22-16-157-0-20-1
Phil Simms (N.Y. Giants) 21-11-202-0-48-1

STANDINGS

AFC East	W	L	T	PF	PA	NFC East	W	L	T	PF	PA
Buffalo	2	1	0	88	93	N.Y. Giants	3	0	0	86	45
Indianapolis	1	2	0	54	70	Philadelphia	2	1	0	101	82
Miami	1	2	0	81	77	Phoenix	2	1	0	57	72
New England	1	2	0	40	72	Washington	1	2	0	91	76
N.Y. Jets	1	2	0	88	98	Dallas	0	3	0	28	85
AFC Central						**NFC Central**					
Cincinnati	2	1	0	76	41	Chicago	3	0	0	102	48
Cleveland	2	1	0	103	45	Tampa Bay	2	1	0	59	51
Houston	1	2	0	82	112	Green Bay	1	2	0	94	98
Pittsburgh	1	2	0	37	106	Minnesota	1	2	0	59	72
						Detroit	0	3	0	54	87
AFC West						**NFC West**					
Denver	3	0	0	93	55	L.A. Rams	3	0	0	103	76
Kansas City	1	2	0	50	74	San Francisco	3	0	0	88	68
L.A. Raiders	1	2	0	80	69	Atlanta	1	2	0	57	65
San Diego	1	2	0	62	80	New Orleans	1	2	0	72	55
Seattle	1	2	0	55	68						

WEEK FOUR

American Football Conference
Cincinnati 21 at Kansas City 17
Denver 13 at Cleveland 16
Indianapolis 17 at New York Jets 10
Miami 7 at Houston 39
New England 10 at Buffalo 31
Seattle 24 at Los Angeles Raiders 20

National Football Conference
Atlanta 21 v Green Bay 23 (at Milwaukee)
Los Angeles Rams 13 at San Francisco 12
New York Giants 30 at Dallas 13
Philadelphia 13 at Chicago 27
Tampa Bay 3 at Minnesota 17
Washington 16 at New Orleans 14

Interconference Games
Pittsburgh 23 at Detroit 3
San Diego 24 at Phoenix 13

Interconference Play
AFC 4 – NFC 6

It was important enough when San Francisco entertained the Rams and Denver travelled to Cleveland, but the teams can not have known that, down the line, there would be much more at stake – they would meet in their respective conference title games. For the moment, there were three unbeaten records to protect and, in the Browns' case, there was the small matter of ending a sequence which had seen them lose ten straight games to Denver. Coincidentally, the scores in both games were remarkably similar and, in each case, the results were decided by placekickers.

For the Rams, Mike Lansford has made a habit of kicking last-minute, game-winning field goals – he had five to his credit over his career. And against the 49ers he made it six with a 26-yarder to give the Rams a one-point win and the undisputed lead in the NFC West. Against Cleveland, with the scores tied at 13-13, the Broncos had driven into a potential game-winning position at the Browns' 16-yard line, only to see Cleveland linebacker Mike Johnson strip the ball from the arms of Broncos running back Sammy Winder. Browns quarterback Bernie Kosar swiftly moved the ball 54 yards to set up Matt Bahr's 48-yard field goal attempt, which found its mark as time expired.

The other unbeaten clubs, Chicago and the New York Giants, cruised smoothly on. The Bears' defense sacked Philadelphia quarterback Randall Cunningham five times and pressured him into throwing four pass interceptions. Against Dallas, Giants quarterback Phil Simms had similar trouble, being intercepted three times. But his team had little difficulty in keeping the Cowboys winless, an indignity they now shared only with Detroit in the entire NFL. The Lions had been handled easily enough by a Steelers club which rapidly had erased the memory of its two early losses and now stood only one game behind the leaders in the AFC Central. Completing a winning day for that division, both Cincinnati and Houston showed signs of running into their best form. With quarterback Boomer Esiason playing despite an injury, the Bengals remained in touch with Kansas City thanks to three interceptions by safety David Fulcher and went ahead to stay when linebacker Leon White returned a loose ball 22 yards for a

Bill Brooks' 55-yard touchdown reception gave Indianapolis the lead.

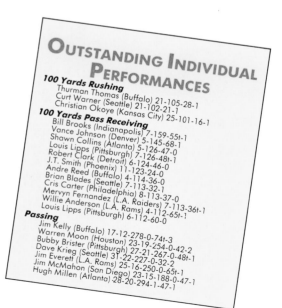

OUTSTANDING INDIVIDUAL PERFORMANCES

100 Yards Rushing
Thurman Thomas (Buffalo) 21-105-28-1
Curt Warner (Seattle) 21-102-21-1
Christian Okoye (Kansas City) 25-101-16-1

100 Yards Pass Receiving
Bill Brooks (Indianapolis) 7-159-55t-1
Vance Johnson (Denver) 5-145-68-1
Shawn Collins (Atlanta) 5-126-47-0
Louis Lipps (Pittsburgh) 7-126-48t-1
Robert Clark (Detroit) 6-124-46-0
J.T. Smith (Phoenix) 11-123-24-0
Andre Reed (Buffalo) 4-114-36-0
Brian Blades (Seattle) 7-113-32-1
Cris Carter (Philadelphia) 8-113-37-0
Mervyn Fernandez (L.A. Raiders) 7-113-36t-1
Willie Anderson (L.A. Rams) 4-112-65t-1
Louis Lipps (Pittsburgh) 6-112-60-0

Passing
Jim Kelly (Buffalo) 17-12-278-0-74t-3
Warren Moon (Houston) 23-19-254-0-42-2
Bubby Brister (Pittsburgh) 27-21-267-0-48t-1
Dave Krieg (Seattle) 31-22-227-0-32-2
Jim Everett (L.A. Rams) 25-16-250-0-65t-1
Jim McMahon (San Diego) 23-15-188-0-47-1
Hugh Millen (Atlanta) 28-20-294-1-47-1

16

Tim Harris had four sacks as Green Bay rallied for victory against Atlanta.

touchdown. The Oilers opened up with their entire armoury against an out-of-touch Miami team, whose one moment of defiance came in the final quarter when Marc Logan returned a kickoff 97 yards for a touchdown.

Denver's loss gave their AFC West competitors an opportunity and when the Seahawks grabbed theirs it was at the expense of the Raiders. Hardly a massacre, it was nonetheless too much for Raiders principal owner Al Davis, who fired head coach Mike Shanahan. For Shanahan's replacement, Davis stayed in the family, promoting offensive line coach Art Shell, a former Raiders tackle who recently had been inducted into the Pro Football Hall of Fame. Now, one felt, we might just see the real Raiders.

STANDINGS

AFC East	W	L	T	PF	PA	NFC East	W	L	T	PF	PA
Buffalo	3	1	0	119	103	N.Y. Giants	4	0	0	116	58
Indianapolis	2	2	0	71	80	Philadelphia	2	2	0	114	109
Miami	1	3	0	88	116	Phoenix	2	2	0	70	96
New England	1	3	0	50	103	Washington	2	2	0	107	90
N.Y. Jets	1	3	0	98	115	Dallas	0	4	0	41	115
AFC Central						**NFC Central**					
Cincinnati	3	1	0	97	58	Chicago	4	0	0	129	61
Cleveland	3	1	0	119	58	Green Bay	2	2	0	117	119
Houston	2	2	0	121	119	Minnesota	2	2	0	76	75
Pittsburgh	2	2	0	60	109	Tampa Bay	2	2	0	62	68
						Detroit	0	4	0	57	110
AFC West						**NFC West**					
Denver	3	1	0	106	71	L.A. Rams	4	0	0	116	88
San Diego	2	2	0	86	93	San Francisco	3	1	0	100	81
Seattle	2	2	0	79	88	Atlanta	1	3	0	78	88
Kansas City	1	3	0	67	95	New Orleans	1	3	0	86	71
L.A. Raiders	1	3	0	100	93						

WEEK FIVE

American Football Conference
Buffalo 14 at Indianapolis 37
Cincinnati 26 at Pittsburgh 16
Cleveland 10 at Miami 13 (OT)
Houston 13 at New England 23
Kansas City 20 at Seattle 16
Los Angeles Raiders 14 at New York Jets 7
San Diego 10 at Denver 16

National Football Conference
Atlanta 14 at Los Angeles Rams 26
Chicago 35 at Tampa Bay 42
Dallas 13 at Green Bay 31
Detroit 17 at Minnesota 24
New York Giants 19 at Philadelphia 21
Phoenix 28 at Washington 30
San Francisco 24 at New Orleans 20

Interconference Play
AFC 4 – NFC 6

Under new head coach Art Shell, the Raiders were hardly dominant — in fact they were shoved around by a modest Jets team. But two big plays, a 73-yard touchdown bomb from Jay Schroeder to wide receiver Mervyn Fernandez and Eddie Anderson's 87-yard interception return for a touchdown, took them to a 14-7

victory. It would be a happy 'plane trip home.

In other games there were six upsets of varying magnitude and almost a seventh as the New Orleans Saints came close to dealing San Francisco a second consecutive loss. In that game, the 49ers rallied with a pair of touchdowns, one of which was hotly disputed and another which was questioned. First, wide receiver Jerry Rice appeared to lose possession before entering the end zone and then there was a possibility that the other wide receiver, John Taylor, may have had the ball stripped free short of the goal line. The Saints' complaints fell on deaf ears and the 49ers were once again back in business.

The biggest surprise came in Tampa, where the home team jumped out to a 21-point lead before keeping the Bears at arm's length in a stunning victory which halted Tampa Bay's sequence of 12 straight losses to the team from the 'Windy City'. Bucs quarterback Vinny Testaverde completed 11 of his first 12 passes and went on to throw for three touchdowns. The NFC Eastern division-leading New York Giants lost their unbeaten record as Philadelphia, driven by quarterback Randall Cunningham, came from behind to win on Anthony Toney's two-yard touchdown run. Only the Rams, who beat Atlanta despite a career-best performance by

Falcons quarterback Chris Miller, now remained undefeated.

There were interesting developments in the AFC, particularly in the East but with consequences for the Central. With superstar running back Eric Dickerson slowed by nagging injuries, the Colts used turnovers to halt the division-leading Bills. For Buffalo, more worrying than the loss was the knowledge that, for the next month or so, they'd have to do without starting quarterback Jim Kelly, who separated a shoulder. If the Colts' win had been unexpected, how about Miami's overtime victory against the heavily favoured Cleveland Browns? In that game, Pete Stoyanovich made up for a field goal miss late in regulation time by chipping the winner from 35 yards in the extra period. And it was similarly surprising that New England, a team ravaged by injuries, handled the Oilers. The Patriots converted a pair of Houston turnovers into touchdowns but a share of the credit had to go to sometime-starting quarterback Doug Flutie, who extended his record in starts at Sullivan Stadium to 11-0 (including five victories in college). In the AFC West, Denver rediscovered the winning formula at the expense of San Diego and Kansas City avenged its earlier loss to Seattle. It meant that four teams now were tied for second place in that division.

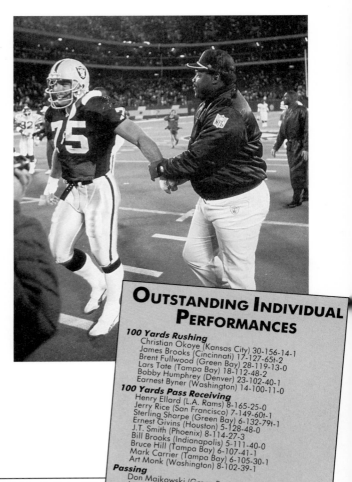

LEFT: Philadelphia's Randall Cunningham passed for five touchdowns and a club-record 447 yards.

RIGHT: Raiders new head coach Art Shell walks off the field a happy man after his first NFL win.

OUTSTANDING INDIVIDUAL PERFORMANCES

100 Yards Rushing
Christian Okoye (Kansas City) 30-156-14-1
James Brooks (Cincinnati) 17-127-65t-2
Brent Fullwood (Green Bay) 28-119-13-0
Lars Tate (Tampa Bay) 18-112-48-2
Bobby Humphrey (Denver) 23-102-40-1
Earnest Byner (Washington) 14-100-11-0

100 Yards Pass Receiving
Henry Ellard (L.A. Rams) 8-165-25-0
Jerry Rice (San Francisco) 7-149-60t-1
Sterling Sharpe (Green Bay) 6-132-79t-1
Ernest Givins (Houston) 5-128-48-0
J.T. Smith (Phoenix) 8-114-27-3
Bill Brooks (Indianapolis) 5-111-40-0
Bruce Hill (Tampa Bay) 6-107-41-1
Mark Carrier (Tampa Bay) 6-105-30-1
Art Monk (Washington) 8-102-39-1

Passing
Don Majkowski (Green Bay) 32-21-313-0-79t-4
Joe Montana (San Francisco) 29-21-291-0-60t-3
Tommy Kramer (Minnesota) 18-11-146-0-27-1
Jim Everett (L.A. Rams) 28-16-290-1-48-2
Ron Jaworski (Kansas City) 18-12-104-0-21-1

STANDINGS

AFC East	W	L	T	PF	PA
Buffalo	3	2	0	133	140
Indianapolis	3	2	0	108	94
Miami	2	3	0	101	126
New England	2	3	0	73	116
N.Y. Jets	1	4	0	105	129
AFC Central					
Cincinnati	4	1	0	123	74
Cleveland	3	2	0	129	71
Houston	2	3	0	134	142
Pittsburgh	2	3	0	76	135
AFC West					
Denver	4	1	0	122	81
Kansas City	2	3	0	87	111
L.A. Raiders	2	3	0	114	100
San Diego	2	3	0	96	109
Seattle	2	3	0	95	108

NFC East	W	L	T	PF	PA
N.Y. Giants	4	1	0	135	79
Philadelphia	3	2	0	135	128
Washington	3	2	0	137	118
Phoenix	2	3	0	98	126
Dallas	0	5	0	54	146
NFC Central					
Chicago	4	1	0	164	103
Green Bay	3	2	0	148	132
Minnesota	3	2	0	100	92
Tampa Bay	3	2	0	104	103
Detroit	0	5	0	74	134
NFC West					
L.A. Rams	5	0	0	142	102
San Francisco	4	1	0	124	101
Atlanta	1	4	0	92	114
New Orleans	1	4	0	106	95

Week Six

American Football Conference
Indianapolis 3 at Denver 14
Kansas City 14 at Los Angeles Raiders 20
Miami 20 at Cincinnati 13
Pittsburgh 17 at Cleveland 7
Seattle 17 at San Diego 16

National Football Conference
Detroit 17 at Tampa Bay 16
Green Bay 14 at Minnesota 26
Philadelphia 17 at Phoenix 5
San Francisco 31 at Dallas 14
Washington 17 at New York Giants 20

Interconference Games
Houston 33 at Chicago 28
Los Angeles Rams 20 at Buffalo 23
New England 15 at Atlanta 16
New York Jets 14 at New Orleans 29

Interconference Play
AFC 6 – NFC 8

Running back Herschel Walker opened his account for his new club by rushing for 148 yards on 18 carries.

'Would the 1989 season ever settle down to some kind of normality?' one wondered as, yet again, favoured teams were knocked over. Pittsburgh, which had been mauled by Cleveland on opening day, went into the rematch without injured starting quarterback Bubby Brister. But seven Cleveland turnovers, four of which came on interceptions of Bernie Kosar passes, helped the Steelers to a morale-boosting victory and ended a seven-game losing sequence against their long-time rival. That victory, coupled with Houston's win over Chicago and Cincinnati's upset at the hands of Miami, left three teams sharing second place in the AFC Central, one game behind the division-leading Bengals. In the absence of Jim Kelly, reserve quarterback Frank Reich made his first start for Buffalo and he would be facing the big-city Rams complete with their fabulous array of talent and a 5-0 record on the season. However, with support from running back Thurman Thomas and a defense which controlled Rams running back Greg Bell, Reich kept the Bills in contention before settling the issue with a late, eight-yard touchdown pass to wide receiver Andre Reed.

In the AFC West, the Broncos galloped on while, behind them, the Raiders and Seattle saw off domestic rivals Kansas City and San Diego respectively. The Raiders were boosted by the return of major league baseball star Bo Jackson, who quickly slipped into gear, rushing for a touchdown and setting up another with one 45-yard explosion from scrimmage.

In the days leading up to Week Six, a trade of immense proportions had taken running back Herschel Walker from Dallas to Minnesota. The expectation was that the Vikings, who already had shown themselves to be serious contenders, now would become little short of lethal. And Walker could hardly have given his new club a better start. With his first touch of the ball, he returned a kickoff just over 50 yards. A penalty took half of that gain away but, shortly afterwards, on his very first run from scrimmage, he bounded 47 yards on the way to rushing for a game total of 148. Defensive tackle Keith Millard had four of the Vikings' eight sacks and cornerback Reggie Rutland had a pair of interceptions as the Packers were soundly beaten. In the lower reaches of the NFC Central division, the Lions were stirring. Barry Sanders had been an instant success but, on this day, in his absence, it was rookie quarterback Rodney Peete who sparked the team to its first win at the expense of Tampa Bay. Peete, who passed for 268 yards and a touchdown, also rushed for 78 yards, the last five of which took him into the end zone for the game-winning touchdown on fourth down with 23 seconds to play. There were hints of revival at the bottom of the NFC West, too, with Atlanta and New Orleans ending three- and four-game losing streaks respectively.

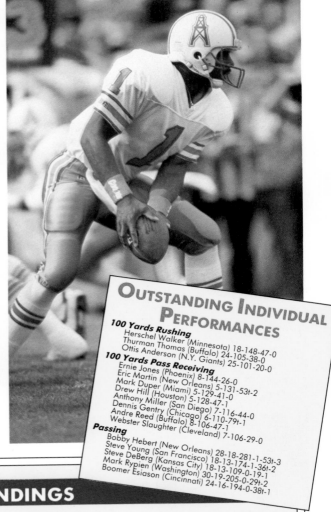

ABOVE: Lions quarterback Rodney Peete has the composure of a veteran.

RIGHT: Warren Moon rallied Houston for the win against Chicago.

STANDINGS

AFC East	W	L	T	PF	PA
Buffalo	4	2	0	156	160
Indianapolis	3	3	0	111	108
Miami	3	3	0	121	139
New England	2	4	0	88	132
N.Y. Jets	1	5	0	119	158
AFC Central					
Cincinnati	4	2	0	136	94
Cleveland	3	3	0	136	88
Houston	3	3	0	167	170
Pittsburgh	3	3	0	93	142
AFC West					
Denver	5	1	0	136	84
L.A. Raiders	3	3	0	134	114
Seattle	3	3	0	112	124
Kansas City	2	4	0	101	131
San Diego	2	4	0	112	126

NFC East	W	L	T	PF	PA
N.Y. Giants	5	1	0	155	96
Philadelphia	4	2	0	152	133
Washington	3	3	0	154	138
Phoenix	2	4	0	103	143
Dallas	0	6	0	68	177
NFC Central					
Chicago	4	2	0	192	136
Minnesota	4	2	0	126	106
Green Bay	3	3	0	162	158
Tampa Bay	3	3	0	120	120
Detroit	1	5	0	91	150
NFC West					
L.A. Rams	5	1	0	162	125
San Francisco	5	1	0	155	115
Atlanta	2	4	0	108	129
New Orleans	2	4	0	135	109

WEEK SEVEN

American Football Conference
Denver 24 at Seattle 21 (OT)
Indianapolis 23 at Cincinnati 12
New York Jets 3 at Buffalo 34
Pittsburgh 0 at Houston 27

National Football Conference
Atlanta 20 at Phoenix 34
Minnesota 20 at Detroit 7
New Orleans 40 at Los Angeles Rams 21
Tampa Bay 28 at Washington 32

Interconference Games
Chicago 7 at Cleveland 27
Dallas 28 at Kansas City 36
Green Bay 20 at Miami 23
Los Angeles Raiders 7 at Philadelphia 10
New England 20 v San Francisco 37 (at Stanford Stadium)
New York Giants 20 at San Diego 13

Interconference Play
AFC 9-NFC 11

By no means were the Broncos rolling over their opponents but the wins were still coming and, with the latest, in overtime against Seattle, they opened up a three-game lead in the AFC West. Two other teams, San Francisco and the Giants, also ended the day at 6-1. Late in the week preceding San Francisco's meeting with New England, Candlestick Park had sustained some damage during a major earthquake which rocked the Bay area and, as a precaution, the 'home' game was relocated to Stanford Stadium. In what turned out to be a comfortable victory, the 49ers suffered damage themselves, losing starting safety Jeff Fuller with serious neck injuries, starting linebacker Jim Fahnhorst with a broken foot, reserve running back Harry Sydney with a broken arm and Joe Montana with a sprained knee. Coming on to replace Montana, Steve Young, who had started the previous week, completed 11 of 12 passes for 188 yards and three touchdowns. The Giants were nothing like as deep as San Francisco but they, too, had come up with solid backups where it mattered. And that was never more true than in the offensive backfield, where Ottis Anderson, who had been the Cardinals' franchise running back for the first seven of his years as a pro, had stepped in for the injured Joe Morris and now was established as the unquestioned starter. In six previous games he had rushed for a total of 447 yards and now, against San Diego, he added another 96 and scored a pair of touchdowns. The Giants' obvious challenger in the NFC East, Philadelphia, burst the Raiders' bubble, and the team third in that division, Washington, held off a Tampa Bay rally to stay in touch.

Other teams on the move included the Colts, who were helped to a 23-12 victory against Cincinnati by Eric Dickerson's best outing of the campaign, while another running back, Kansas City's 260-pound Christian Okoye, trampled all over the Cowboys in the

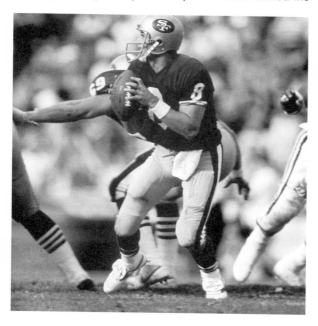

ABOVE: Steve Young approached perfection against New England.

RIGHT: Mike Merriweather was a one-man defense against Detroit.

Chiefs' 36-28 win. Warren Moon passed for three touchdowns as Houston blanked Pittsburgh, and a three-touchdown performance by reserve Frank Reich helped the Bills to stay one game clear on top of the AFC East. In Miami, Pete Stoyanovich kicked a late, 33-yard field goal to extend the Dolphins' sequence of victories to three.

Cleveland handed Chicago a third straight loss and Minnesota took advantage to go one game clear on top of the NFC Central. For the Vikings, Herschel Walker gained 96 combined yards and scored a touchdown but linebacker Mike Merriweather had done the most damage with two sacks, two forced fumbles, one fumble recovery and an interception as the Lions were put in their place.

But things didn't go so well for the Rams. Following their first loss of the season, they were treated with little respect by the Saints, for whom running back Dalton Hilliard scored three touchdowns in a surprisingly easy victory.

Bills quarterback Frank Reich passed for three touchdowns.

OUTSTANDING INDIVIDUAL PERFORMANCES

100 Yards Rushing
Christian Okoye (Kansas City) 33-170-23-2
Eric Dickerson (Indianapolis) 31-152-21t-1

100 Yards Pass Receiving
Webster Slaughter (Cleveland) 8-186-97t-1
Michael Young (Denver) 6-137-47-0
Eric Martin (New Orleans) 5-116-51-1
Jerry Rice (San Francisco) 6-112-50t-2
Mark Carrier (Tampa Bay) 8-106-37-1
Tom Rathman (San Francisco) 11-103-22-0
Irving Fryar (New England) 5-102-52-0

Passing
Steve Young (San Francisco) 12-11-188-0-50t-3
Bobby Hebert (New Orleans) 22-15-276-1-54t-3
Frank Reich (Buffalo) 20-13-145-0-20t-3
Bernie Kosar (Cleveland) 29-22-281-0-97t-2
Warren Moon (Houston) 29-17-229-0-51t-3
Joe Montana (San Francisco) 22-16-178-0-32-1
Steve DeBerg (Kansas City) 22-17-237-0-25-0
John Elway (Denver) 35-18-344-0-54t-2

STANDINGS

AFC East	W	L	T	PF	PA
Buffalo	5	2	0	190	163
Indianapolis	4	3	0	134	120
Miami	4	3	0	144	159
New England	2	5	0	108	169
N.Y. Jets	1	6	0	122	192
AFC Central					
Cincinnati	4	3	0	148	117
Cleveland	4	3	0	163	95
Houston	4	3	0	194	170
Pittsburgh	3	4	0	93	169
AFC West					
Denver	6	1	0	160	105
Kansas City	3	4	0	137	159
L.A. Raiders	3	4	0	141	124
Seattle	3	4	0	133	148
San Diego	2	5	0	125	146

NFC East	W	L	T	PF	PA
N.Y. Giants	6	1	0	175	109
Philadelphia	5	2	0	162	140
Washington	4	3	0	186	166
Phoenix	3	4	0	137	163
Dallas	0	7	0	96	213
NFC Central					
Minnesota	5	2	0	146	113
Chicago	4	3	0	199	163
Green Bay	3	4	0	182	181
Tampa Bay	3	4	0	148	152
Detroit	1	6	0	98	170
NFC West					
San Francisco	6	1	0	192	135
L.A. Rams	5	2	0	183	165
New Orleans	3	4	0	175	130
Atlanta	2	5	0	128	163

WEEK EIGHT

American Football Conference
Houston 17 at Cleveland 28
Kansas City 17 at Pittsburgh 23
Miami 17 at Buffalo 31
New England 23 at Indianapolis 20 (OT)
San Diego 7 at Seattle 10

National Football Conference
Atlanta 13 at New Orleans 20
Detroit 20 v Green Bay 23 (OT) (at Milwaukee)
Los Angeles Rams 10 at Chicago 20
Minnesota 14 at New York Giants 24
Phoenix 19 at Dallas 10

Interconference Games
Philadelphia 28 at Denver 24
San Francisco 23 at New York Jets 10
Tampa Bay 23 at Cincinnati 56
Washington 24 at Los Angeles Raiders 37

Interconference Play
AFC 11 – NFC 13

Webster Slaughter caught touchdown passes of 80 and 77 yards.

The Miami Dolphins have a reputation for discipline – it is not unusual for them to lead the league in fewest penalties conceded – and they entered Week Eight not having given up a quarterback sack for an NFL-record 19 regular-season games. However, that sequence finally came to an end when Buffalo backup nose tackle Jeff Wright earned his spot in league history by sending Dan Marino to the turf. Miami's defense against the rush was exposed by Buffalo running backs Thurman Thomas and Larry Kinnebrew, each of whom rushed for over 100 yards. And though reserve quarterback Frank Reich passed only sparingly, he could feel well pleased that, as a stand-in for injured starter Jim Kelly, he had won all three games. In Cleveland, one of the NFL's better individual streaks was halted when the Browns' great veteran tight end, Ozzie Newsome, who had caught at least one pass in his previous 150 regular-season games, sprained his ankle in the early going and came up empty-handed. But his team had the satisfaction of overcoming a 10-point deficit to beat Houston. Wide receiver Webster Slaughter, who had caught eight passes for 186 yards, including a 97-yard touchdown, on Week Seven, followed up with four receptions for 184 yards, scoring touchdowns on plays covering 80 and 77 yards.

There were signs of a Bears revival when, with quarterback Mike Tomczak ineffective, backup Jim Harbaugh came off the bench to engineer a victory over the slumping Rams. If the Rams were fading, the New Orleans Saints were clawing their way back after a poor start to the campaign. A classy, dual-purpose performance from running back Dalton Hilliard, who rushed for 93 yards, caught seven passes for 97 yards and scored touchdowns in each role, had helped the Saints to a third straight win. The Giants won their third game in a row, halting the Vikings' four-game charge. The Giants scored touchdowns after recovering fumbles by Minnesota's Alfred Anderson on successive kickoff returns to set up a game-winning lead.

In the interconference series, the AFC ended the day two wins adrift of the NFC but at least they had split the four games. Philadelphia handed Denver a loss after nine consecutive home wins, while the 49ers sacked Jets quarterback Ken O'Brien nine times in a 23-10 stroll. However, two AFC teams won in fine style. The Bengals had gone off the boil, scoring only 25 points in two successive home defeats but, against Tampa Bay, quarterback Boomer Esiason passed for five touchdowns as Cincinnati rolled up 56 points. The Raiders, too, seemed to be running into their best form as they logged seven sacks and forced eight Washington turnovers. Best of all, Bo Jackson rushed for 144 yards, including a 73-yard, tackle-breaking touchdown run, as the Redskins were beaten more easily than the 37-24 scoreline suggests.

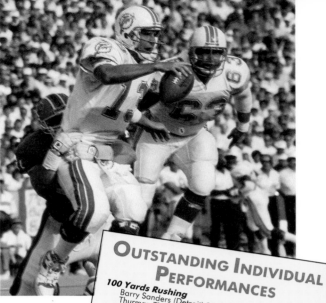

ABOVE: Saints linebacker Pat Swilling had three sacks for the second week in a row.

RIGHT: Dan Marino is sacked for the first time in 20 consecutive games.

OUTSTANDING INDIVIDUAL PERFORMANCES

100 Yards Rushing
Barry Sanders (Detroit) 30-184-31-0
Thurman Thomas (Buffalo) 27-148-30t-1
Bo Jackson (L.A. Raiders) 19-144-73t-1
James Brooks (Cincinnati) 17-131-41-1
Larry Kinnebrew (Buffalo) 21-121-25-1
Christian Okoye (Kansas City) 23-101-19-0

100 Yards Pass Receiving
Webster Slaughter (Cleveland) 4-184-80t-2
Stephone Paige (Kansas City) 7-163-50-0
Ricky Sanders (Washington) 12-158-51-1
Vance Johnson (Denver) 9-148-33-1
Gary Clark (Washington) 8-145-35-1
Louis Lipps (Pittsburgh) 7-130-64t-2
Andre Rison (Indianapolis) 6-129-30-1
Tim McGee (Cincinnati) 5-127-46t-2
Mark Clayton (Miami) 7-125-53-2
Bruce Hill (Tampa Bay) 7-122-44t-1
Brian Blades (Seattle) 10-117-21t-1
Eric Sievers (New England) 7-113-46-0
Andre Brown (Miami) 5-105-44t-1
Sterling Sharpe (Green Bay) 7-105-28-1
Mark Carrier (Tampa Bay) 7-100-26-1
Henry Ellard (L.A. Rams) 5-100-44-0

Passing
Boomer Esiason (Cincinnati) 28-17-197-0-30-5
Bubby Brister (Pittsburgh) 27-17-253-0-64t-2
Jim Harbaugh (Chicago) 13-10-157-0-41-0
Bernie Kosar (Cleveland) 19-14-262-2-80t-2
Steve Young (San Francisco) 20-13-182-0-41-1
Randall Cunningham (Philadelphia) 20-11-126-0-66t-2
Warren Moon (Houston) 25-15-241-0-55-1

STANDINGS

AFC East	W	L	T	PF	PA
Buffalo	6	2	0	221	180
Indianapolis	4	4	0	154	143
Miami	4	4	0	161	190
New England	3	5	0	131	189
N.Y. Jets	1	7	0	132	215
AFC Central					
Cincinnati	5	3	0	204	140
Cleveland	5	3	0	191	112
Houston	4	4	0	211	198
Pittsburgh	4	4	0	116	186
AFC West					
Denver	6	2	0	184	133
L.A. Raiders	4	4	0	178	148
Seattle	4	4	0	143	155
Kansas City	3	5	0	154	182
San Diego	2	6	0	132	156

NFC East	W	L	T	PF	PA
N.Y. Giants	7	1	0	199	123
Philadelphia	6	2	0	190	164
Phoenix	4	4	0	156	173
Washington	4	4	0	210	203
Dallas	0	8	0	106	232
NFC Central					
Chicago	5	3	0	219	173
Minnesota	5	3	0	160	137
Green Bay	4	4	0	205	201
Tampa Bay	3	5	0	171	208
Detroit	1	7	0	118	193
NFC West					
San Francisco	7	1	0	215	145
L.A. Rams	5	3	0	193	185
New Orleans	4	4	0	195	143
Atlanta	2	6	0	141	183

WEEK NINE

On what was a wild day all round, let's give pride of place to the Cowboys, Chargers, Falcons and the Jets, all of whom brought off upsets. And the biggest took place in Washington, where the Redskins were restricted to just three points as Dallas scored its first win of the campaign. Cowboys running back Paul Palmer rushed for 110 yards, including the 47-yard gain which set up his own two-yard touchdown plunge. The Falcons' triumph over Buffalo was only slightly less sensational and even more dramatic. In a crazy final 82 seconds, the lead changed hands three times. Atlanta's Keith Jones scored a touchdown with 1:22 remaining but Buffalo rookie Don Beebe returned the ensuing kickoff 85 yards to the Atlanta eight, setting up Larry Kinnebrew's one-yard touchdown run. Trailing by one point and with only 29 seconds left, Falcons quarterback Chris Miller heaved a 41-yard completion to wide receiver Stacey Bailey, and placekicker Paul McFadden completed the job from 50 yards out with the clock showing two seconds. Only one second remained when Pat Leahy's 23-yard field goal brought victory for the Jets. Little over a minute earlier, Patriots quarterback Marc Wilson, who had replaced the injured Steve Grogan, had thrown an 11-yard touchdown pass to give New England a 26-24 lead. In contrast to those late victories by Atlanta and the Jets, San Diego's winning points came with plenty to spare — four seconds remained! Yet it owed even more to timing. With seconds left and the teams tied at 17-17, Chris Bahr's 44-yard field goal attempt failed. However, moments before the snap, San Diego tackle James FitzPatrick had jumped offside. The key phrase here was 'before the snap', for it meant that the kick had to be retaken but with a five-yard penalty added to the distance. Given his second

bite at the cherry from 49 yards out, Bahr made no mistake.

Green Bay fans love the instant replay camera but that may not be true of the Bears, who felt that they had held off a late Packers surge when quarterback Don Majkowski's fourth-down 'touchdown pass' to wide receiver Sterling Sharpe was nullified because, it was adjudged, Majkowski apparently had passed from beyond the line of scrimmage. But after a four-minute scrutiny of the instant replay, the touchdown pass was validated, leaving Chris Jacke the opportunity to chip the game-winning extra point.

Elsewhere, Vikings placekicker Rich Karlis equalled the NFL single-game record with seven field goals in regulation time, but the deciding points came on an overtime safety by Mike Merriweather as the Rams were handed their fourth straight loss. With Bo Jackson rushing for 159 yards, including a club-record, 92-yard touchdown run, the Raiders continued their revival. And there was a growing confidence in the way that all four of San Francisco, the New York Giants, Cleveland and Denver asserted their authority.

Vikings placekicker Rich Karlis kicked seven field goals to equal the NFL single-game record.

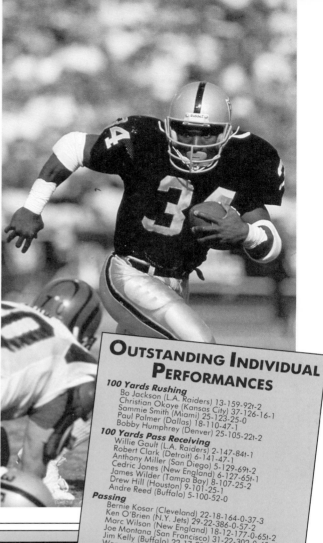

ABOVE: Quarterback Jim Kelly returned from a three-week absence and had a big day – but the Bills lost.

RIGHT: Bo Jackson rushed for 159 yards and led the Raiders' domination of the injury-riddled Bengals.

OUTSTANDING INDIVIDUAL PERFORMANCES

100 Yards Rushing
Bo Jackson (L.A. Raiders) 13-159-92t-2
Christian Okoye (Kansas City) 37-126-16-1
Sammie Smith (Miami) 25-123-25-0
Paul Palmer (Dallas) 18-110-47-1
Bobby Humphrey (Denver) 25-105-22t-2

100 Yards Pass Receiving
Willie Gault (L.A. Raiders) 2-147-84t-1
Robert Clark (Detroit) 6-141-47-1
Anthony Miller (San Diego) 5-129-69t-2
Cedric Jones (New England) 6-127-65t-1
James Wilder (Tampa Bay) 8-107-25-2
Drew Hill (Houston) 9-101-25-1
Andre Reed (Buffalo) 5-100-52-0

Passing
Bernie Kosar (Cleveland) 22-18-164-0-37-3
Ken O'Brien (N.Y. Jets) 29-22-386-0-57-2
Marc Wilson (New England) 18-12-177-0-65t-2
Joe Montana (San Francisco) 31-22-302-0-45t-3
Jim Kelly (Buffalo) 22-17-231-1-52-2
Warren Moon (Houston) 38-30-345-1-32-2

STANDINGS

AFC East	W	L	T	PF	PA
Buffalo	6	3	0	249	210
Miami	5	4	0	180	203
Indianapolis	4	5	0	167	162
New England	3	6	0	157	216
N.Y. Jets	2	7	0	159	241
AFC Central					
Cleveland	6	3	0	233	143
Cincinnati	5	4	0	211	168
Houston	5	4	0	246	229
Pittsburgh	4	5	0	123	220
AFC West					
Denver	7	2	0	218	140
L.A. Raiders	5	4	0	206	155
Kansas City	4	5	0	174	192
Seattle	4	5	0	153	175
San Diego	3	6	0	152	173

NFC East	W	L	T	PF	PA
N.Y. Giants	8	1	0	219	136
Philadelphia	6	3	0	207	184
Phoenix	4	5	0	169	193
Washington	4	5	0	213	216
Dallas	1	8	0	119	235
NFC Central					
Minnesota	6	3	0	183	158
Chicago	5	4	0	232	187
Green Bay	5	4	0	219	214
Tampa Bay	3	6	0	202	250
Detroit	1	8	0	149	228
NFC West					
San Francisco	8	1	0	246	158
L.A. Rams	5	4	0	214	208
New Orleans	4	5	0	208	174
Atlanta	3	6	0	171	211

WEEK TEN

Pete Stoyanovich's (Miami) 59-yard field goal equalled the third-longest in NFL history.

Week Ten saw five of the six division leaders continue their progress, the one exception being the Giants who were well beaten by a Rams team that had regrouped for its playoff bid. The key period came with the Rams holding a 10-3 lead. Quarterback Jim Everett passed 51 yards for a touchdown to wide receiver Aaron Cox and then punished a Giants fumble on the ensuing kick-off with a 21-yard touchdown pass to wide receiver Willie (Flipper) Anderson. Of the other front-runners, all but Denver had a smooth passage. Even in the absence of power back Christian Okoye and despite the loss of starting nose tackle Bill Maas with a broken arm, Kansas City hung on grimly and succumbed only to a last-second, 26-yard field goal by David Tread-well. Behind Denver, the Raiders must have fancied their chances against San Diego and, although not able to score a touchdown, moved steadily to a 12-0 lead. But immediately following Jeff Jaeger's fourth field goal, San Diego's Anthony Miller returned the kickoff 91 yards for a touchdown and, in the fourth quarter, running back Tim Spencer capitalized on a partially blocked punt to score the game-winning touchdown.

In the AFC Central confrontation between Houston and Cincinnati, the lead changed hands five times in the final quarter, with the Oilers having the final say as the Bengals slipped to their fourth loss in a five-week period. By contrast, the Miami Dolphins swept to their fifth win in six weeks, though at one time in the second quarter they had trailed the Jets by the score of 20-3. With the defense repeatedly holding firm on key third- and fourth-down plays, quarterback Dan Marino passed for three touchdowns in a 28-point rally to which the Jets could respond with just a field goal.

Turning to the NFC chasers, the Eagles missed an opportunity to make ground on the Giants when they were stifled by Washington. Sacked three times by Redskins defensive end Dexter Manley, Philadelphia quarterback Randall Cunningham was no more suc-cessful rushing the ball – he was held to zero yards on four carries. The Redskins, then, hovered in the back-ground, three games off the pace in company with the Cardinals, who had emerged from a mini shoot-out with Dallas. For the Cowboys, quarterback Troy Aik-man returned from injury to pass for 379 yards and a pair of touchdowns, including a 75-yarder to wide receiver James Dixon. However, Cardinals reserve quarterback Tom Tupa responded with a 72-yard touchdown bomb to wide receiver Ernie Jones to secure the win with just 58 seconds remaining. New Orleans jumped out to a 28-point lead against New England and held on in the face of a Steve Grogan-led rally. And it was good for the race in the NFC Central that Chicago hinted at a return to form with a victory over a Pittsburgh team that suffered its third shut-out of the campaign.

OUTSTANDING INDIVIDUAL PERFORMANCES

100 Yards Rushing
James Brooks (Cincinnati) 19-141-58t-1
Thurman Thomas (Buffalo) 29-127-16-0
Roger Craig (San Francisco) 17-109-21-0
Dalton Hilliard (New Orleans) 28-106-11-2
Bo Jackson (L.A. Raiders) 21-103-20-0

100 Yards Pass Receiving
James Dixon (Dallas) 6-203-75t-1
Ernie Jones (Phoenix) 3-139-72t-2
Mark Clayton (Miami) 4-125-78t-1
Louis Lipps (Pittsburgh) 4-112-60-0
Scott Schwedes (Miami) 3-107-65t-1
Robert Awalt (Phoenix) 6-105-28-0
Hart Lee Dykes (New England) 5-105-34-1

Passing
Joe Montana (San Francisco) 19-16-270-0-78-3
Tom Tupa (Phoenix) 22-14-245-0-72t-2
Boomer Esiason (Cincinnati) 19-11-209-0-73t-1

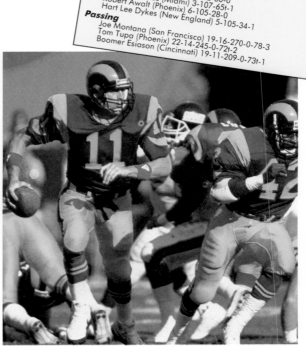

ABOVE: In his first game since breaking a finger, Dallas wide receiver James Dixon caught six passes for 203 yards and a touchdown.

RIGHT: Jim Everett had 18 consecutive pass completions as the Rams halted a four-game losing streak.

STANDINGS

AFC East	W	L	T	PF	PA
Buffalo	7	3	0	279	217
Miami	6	4	0	211	226
Indianapolis	4	6	0	174	192
New England	3	7	0	181	244
N.Y. Jets	2	8	0	182	272
AFC Central					
Cleveland	7	3	0	250	150
Houston	6	4	0	272	253
Cincinnati	5	5	0	235	194
Pittsburgh	4	6	0	123	240
AFC West					
Denver	8	2	0	234	153
L.A. Raiders	5	5	0	218	169
Kansas City	4	6	0	187	208
San Diego	4	6	0	166	185
Seattle	4	6	0	160	192

NFC East	W	L	T	PF	PA
N.Y. Giants	8	2	0	229	167
Philadelphia	6	4	0	210	194
Phoenix	5	5	0	193	213
Washington	5	5	0	223	219
Dallas	1	9	0	139	259
NFC Central					
Minnesota	7	3	0	207	168
Chicago	6	4	0	252	187
Green Bay	5	5	0	241	245
Tampa Bay	3	7	0	212	274
Detroit	2	8	0	180	250
NFC West					
San Francisco	9	1	0	291	161
L.A. Rams	6	4	0	245	218
New Orleans	5	5	0	236	198
Atlanta	3	7	0	174	256

WEEK ELEVEN

American Football Conference
Buffalo 24 at New England 33
Kansas City 10 at Cleveland 10 (OT)
Los Angeles Raiders 7 at Houston 23
New York Jets 10 at Indianapolis 27
San Diego 17 at Pittsburgh 20

National Football Conference
Green Bay 21 at San Francisco 17
Minnesota 9 at Philadelphia 10
New Orleans 26 at Atlanta 17
Phoenix 14 at Los Angeles Rams 37
Tampa Bay 32 at Chicago 31

Interconference Games
Denver 14 at Washington 10
Detroit 7 at Cincinnati 42
Miami 17 at Dallas 14
Seattle 3 at New York Giants 15

Interconference Play
AFC 17 – NFC 17

Tim McGee caught a Bengals-record 11 passes as Cincinnati overwhelmed Detroit.

OUTSTANDING INDIVIDUAL PERFORMANCES

100 Yards Rushing
Dalton Hilliard (New Orleans) 29-158-24-1
Eric Dickerson (Indianapolis) 31-131-19-1
John Stephens (New England) 23-126-26-0
Barry Sanders (Detroit) 18-114-29-1
Bobby Humphrey (Denver) 31-110-13-0
Neal Anderson (Chicago) 15-100-59†-1

100 Yards Pass Receiving
Tim McGee (Cincinnati) 11-194-55-1
Mark Carrier (Tampa Bay) 6-164-78†-1
Henry Ellard (L.A. Rams) 5-163-49†-2
Andre Rison (Indianapolis) 5-108-61-0
Andre Reed (New England) 6-107-48-0
Jerry Rice (San Francisco) 9-106-20-1
Anthony Miller (San Diego) 7-104-21-2
Mervyn Fernandez (L.A. Raiders) 5-102-38-0

Passing
Jim Everett (L.A. Rams) 24-15-308-0-49†-2
Boomer Esiason (Cincinnati) 39-30-399-1-55-3
Jack Trudeau (Indianapolis) 28-17-255-0-61-1
Warren Moon (Houston) 30-20-249-1-42-2
Phil Simms (N.Y. Giants) 26-17-194-0-27-1

On Week Eleven, the San Francisco 49ers reminded us that they were human after all. They gave up penalties, made mistakes and allowed Joe Montana to be sacked six times. Nonetheless, they appeared to have done enough to defeat Green Bay when safety Chet Brooks returned an interception of Don Majkowski's pass 94 yards for a touchdown. But that apparent score was nullified on one of three 49ers penalties in the space of four plays. With the unexpected possession, Majkowski re-established the momentum, rounding off a 73-yard drive with his second touchdown run of the game to give the Packers a seven-point lead to which the 49ers could respond only with a field goal. With Jim Everett passing for 308 yards, including touchdown bombs of 49 and 42 yards to wide receiver Henry Ellard, the Rams beat Phoenix easily to move within two games of the 49ers. The following day, Cardinals head coach Gene Stallings, who had indicated that he did not wish to renew his contract, was replaced by running backs coach Hank Kuhlmann for the final five games. The other NFC favourite to come a cropper was Chicago, which lost its second game of the campaign to Tampa Bay on a last-second, Donald Igwebuike field goal. By way of small consolation, Bears placekicker Kevin Butler landed his 23rd consecutive field goal to equal the NFL record held by the retired Mark Moseley.

In the AFC there was an upset of some magnitude when Buffalo was tripped by New England. With the Bills leading by the score of 24-13 and under nine minutes left, Patriots quarterback Steve Grogan cut loose, directing a rally which produced 20 unanswered points. Miami took full advantage of the opportunity, moving into a share of first place against the luckless Dallas Cowboys. It was a surprise that the Cleveland Browns, who had won their previous four games, were held to a 10-10 tie by Kansas City. And the Browns may consider themselves lucky not to have lost, for Chiefs placekicker Nick Lowery missed a 39-yard field goal attempt late in regulation time and then failed with a 47-yarder in overtime. Behind the Browns, all three AFC Central teams won. Houston was too strong for a listless Raiders team, restricting Bo Jackson to just 54 yards rushing and intercepting quarterback Steve Beuerlein three times. In Cincinnati's runaway win over Detroit, Bengals wide receiver Tim McGee caught a club-record 11 passes for 194 yards and a touchdown, while Pittsburgh's Rod Woodson returned a kickoff 84 yards for a touchdown and Merril Hoge scored on a fourth-down plunge as the Steelers slipped past San Diego. On what was a dismal day for four AFC West clubs, none of which won, Denver held off the Redskins to open up a near-unassailable, four-game lead on top of that division.

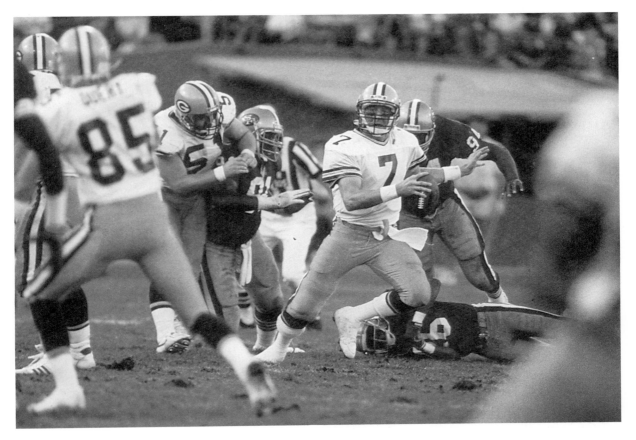

Don Majkowski overcame injuries to lead Green Bay past San Francisco.

STANDINGS

AFC East	W	L	T	PF	PA	NFC East	W	L	T	PF	PA
Buffalo	7	4	0	303	250	N.Y. Giants	9	2	0	244	170
Miami	7	4	0	228	240	Philadelphia	7	4	0	220	203
Indianapolis	5	6	0	201	202	Washington	5	6	0	233	233
New England	4	7	0	214	268	Phoenix	5	6	0	207	250
N.Y. Jets	2	9	0	192	299	Dallas	1	10	0	153	276
AFC Central						**NFC Central**					
Cleveland	7	3	1	260	160	Minnesota	7	4	0	216	178
Houston	7	4	0	295	260	Chicago	6	5	0	283	219
Cincinnati	6	5	0	277	201	Green Bay	6	5	0	262	262
Pittsburgh	5	6	0	143	257	Tampa Bay	4	7	0	244	305
						Detroit	2	9	0	187	292
AFC West						**NFC West**					
Denver	9	2	0	248	163						
L.A. Raiders	5	6	0	225	192	San Francisco	9	2	0	308	182
Kansas City	4	6	1	197	218	L.A. Rams	7	4	0	282	232
San Diego	4	7	0	183	205	New Orleans	6	5	0	262	215
Seattle	4	7	0	163	207	Atlanta	3	8	0	191	282

WEEK TWELVE

American Football Conference
Cincinnati 7 at Buffalo 24
Houston 0 at Kansas City 34
New England 21 at Los Angeles Raiders 24
Pittsburgh 34 at Miami 14
San Diego 6 at Indianapolis 10
Seattle 14 at Denver 41

National Football Conference
Chicago 14 at Washington 38
Los Angeles Rams 20 at New Orleans 17 (OT)
Minnesota 19 v Green Bay 20 (at Milwaukee)
New York Giants 24 at San Francisco 34
Philadelphia 27 at Dallas 0
Tampa Bay 14 at Phoenix 13

Interconference Games
Atlanta 7 at New York Jets 27
Cleveland 10 at Detroit 13

Interconference Play
AFC 18 – NFC 18

Willie Anderson set an NFL single-game record with 336 yards receiving against New Orleans.

OUTSTANDING INDIVIDUAL PERFORMANCES

100 Yards Rushing
Barry Sanders (Detroit) 28-145-23-0
Dalton Hilliard (New Orleans) 24-112-40-0
James Brooks (Cincinnati) 20-105-30-0
Thurman Thomas (Buffalo) 26-100-14-0

100 Yards Pass Receiving
Willie Anderson (L.A. Rams) 15-336-50-1
Sterling Sharpe (Green Bay) 10-157-34t-2
Vance Johnson (Denver) 6-154-69-2
Art Monk (Washington) 9-152-42-2
Gary Clark (Washington) 8-124-26-1
Brian Blades (Seattle) 8-122-24-0
Jerry Rice (San Francisco) 7-117-37-1
Stephone Paige (Kansas City) 7-114-42-0
Eric Martin (New Orleans) 5-107-35t-2
Anthony Carter (Minnesota) 6-103-25-0
Bill Brooks (Indianapolis) 8-101-25t-1

Passing
John Elway (Denver) 19-10-217-0-69-4
Jim Kelly (Buffalo) 15-10-123-0-42t-3
Joe Montana (San Francisco) 33-27-292-0-37-3
Mark Rypien (Washington) 47-30-401-1-42-4
Steve Beuerlein (L.A. Raiders) 25-15-169-0-28-2
Randall Cunningham (Philadelphia) 33-21-234-0-36-2
Don Majkowski (Green Bay) 35-26-276-1-34t-2
Steve DeBerg (Kansas City) 25-15-224-0-44-1

On Thanksgiving Day, the Detroit Lions certainly were not in a giving mood as they stunned the title-chasing Cleveland Browns by the score of 13-10. Before this game, Lions running back Barry Sanders had established himself as a player of the very highest class, and now he began to make his mark in the record book, rushing for 145 yards, despite being bothered by an ankle injury, and crashing through the 1,000-yard barrier. The Browns faced an anxious wait for the weekend's results but, as it turned out, the damage wasn't too great. The Chiefs' defense and special teams either scored or set up 17 points as Kansas City shut out the Oilers 34-0. Similarly, the Bengals were hardly a factor against the Buffalo Bills, who rediscovered their touch in a 24-7 win. However, Pittsburgh did win, despite, or perhaps because of, a Florida rainstorm. With Miami waterlogged, the Steelers rode the surf to a 34-14 victory and now were only one and a half games out of first place in the division. Buffalo's win, coupled with Miami's loss, left the Bills one game clear on top of the AFC East and the feeling was that they'd have to keep an eye on the Colts, who were only two games adrift following their 10-6 victory over San Diego.

One divisional race was decided, when the Broncos stampeded over Seattle to become only the second team ever to clinch a division title in the first 12 games of a 16-game season, matching the feat of Buffalo in 1988. Quarterback John Elway threw four touchdown passes in the first half before withdrawing to the sideline.

The big clash in the NFC saw the 49ers beat the Giants, but it had not been easy and they had needed to find a second wind after a pair of Phil Simms touchdown passes had brought the Giants into a 24-24 tie. Philadelphia's Thanksgiving Day shutout of Dallas trimmed the Giants' lead on top of the NFC East to just one game. In the NFC Central, the Green Bay Packers, conquerors of the 49ers on Week Eleven, dodged a few bullets against the Vikings and held out for the one-point victory which, for the first time in the campaign, gave them a share of first place.

In the NFC West, though trailing San Francisco by two games, the Rams still could win the title and there was a second meeting with the NFL Champions to come. However, before then, they had to take care of a potential threat from New Orleans, who trailed Los Angeles by one game but had beaten them on Week Seven. It was a close one. Rams wide receiver Willie (Flipper) Anderson caught 15 passes for an NFL single-game record 336 yards and a touchdown, but it took an overtime field goal by Mike Lansford to resolve a tense struggle.

Tim Worley ran and leapt for 95 yards as Pittsburgh beat Miami.

STANDINGS

AFC East	W	L	T	PF	PA	NFC East	W	L	T	PF	PA
Buffalo	8	4	0	327	257	N.Y. Giants	9	3	0	268	204
Miami	7	5	0	242	274	Philadelphia	8	4	0	247	203
Indianapolis	6	6	0	211	208	Washington	6	6	0	271	247
New England	4	8	0	235	292	Phoenix	5	7	0	220	264
N.Y. Jets	3	9	0	219	306	Dallas	1	11	0	153	303
AFC Central						**NFC Central**					
Cleveland	7	4	1	270	173	Green Bay	7	5	0	282	281
Houston	7	5	0	295	294	Minnesota	7	5	0	235	198
Cincinnati	6	6	0	284	225	Chicago	6	6	0	297	257
Pittsburgh	6	6	0	177	271	Tampa Bay	5	7	0	258	318
						Detroit	3	9	0	200	302
AFC West											
Denver†	10	2	0	289	177	**NFC West**					
L.A. Raiders	6	6	0	249	213	San Francisco	10	2	0	342	206
Kansas City	5	6	1	231	218	L.A. Rams	8	4	0	302	249
San Diego	4	8	0	189	215	New Orleans	6	6	0	279	235
Seattle	4	8	0	177	248	Atlanta	3	9	0	198	309

†Division Champion

WEEK THIRTEEN

American Football Conference
Buffalo 16 at Seattle 17
Cincinnati 21 at Cleveland 0
Denver 13 at Los Angeles Raiders 16 (OT)
Houston 23 at Pittsburgh 16
Indianapolis 16 at New England 22
Miami 21 at Kansas City 26
New York Jets 20 at San Diego 17

National Football Conference
Chicago 16 at Minnesota 27
Green Bay 17 at Tampa Bay 16
Los Angeles Rams 35 at Dallas 31
New Orleans 14 at Detroit 21
Philadelphia 24 at New York Giants 17
San Francisco 23 at Atlanta 10
Washington 29 at Phoenix 10

Interconference Play
AFC 18 – NFC 18

On Week Thirteen, interconference rivalries were set aside as the clubs focused on domestic matters. And there was no race closer than that in the AFC Central, which was thrown into turmoil by victories for both Cincinnati and Houston. The Bengals took advantage of

Cleveland's few errors to gather 21 points while holding the Browns scoreless, and, despite having won only three of their last eight games, now stood just one off the lead. The new front-runner was Houston, for whom quarterback Warren Moon threw two touchdown passes while Lorenzo White had his best single-game rushing total as a pro. White's one-yard touchdown run broke a 16-16 tie in the bitter cold of Pittsburgh's Three Rivers Stadium. The Buffalo Bills went into the Monday Night Game knowing that a victory would take them two games clear of Miami and three ahead of the Colts, both of whom had lost. Yet the Bills failed to grasp their opportunity, going down to their fourth straight away defeat on a 51-yard touchdown pass from Seattle quarterback Dave Krieg to running back John L. Williams. With the title in the AFC West already having been secured by Denver, both the Raiders and Kansas City enhanced their prospects of competing for a wild card spot with victories over the Broncos and Miami respectively. For the Raiders, first-year tight end Mike Dyal had his best day as a pro, catching a 67-yard touchdown pass and setting up Jeff Jaeger's overtime field goal with clutch receptions of 26 and 15 yards. In the Chiefs' victory over Miami, Christian Okoye rushed for over 100 yards for the seventh time in the season.

In the NFC's feature game, Philadelphia scored all its points following turnovers, intercepting two passes and recovering two Phil Simms fumbles. The game-winning score, Keith Byars' two-yard touchdown run, was set up when a harrassed Simms fumbled after being placed inbetween a rock and a hard place by quarterback Randall Cunningham's 91-yard punt (it was the third-longest in league history). The result meant that Philadelphia and the Giants shared first place in the East but, having beaten the Giants twice, Philadelphia was guaranteed the advantage in the event of a two-way tie-breaker. In the NFC Central, Minnesota broke a two-game losing sequence and handed the Bears their third straight loss. For Chicago, placekicker Kevin Butler set a new NFL record with his 24th consecutive field goal but his sequence came to an end when, on his next attempt, he failed from 44 yards out. Green Bay kept pace, snatching victory from the jaws of defeat in a hair-raising encounter with Tampa Bay. After a Buccaneers penalty had allowed the Packers to retain possession following a fourth-down pass incompletion, quarterback Don Majkowski nudged his team into position for Chris Jacke's 47-yard field goal attempt which limped over the crossbar with just one second left. As a prelude to the clash of the titans on Week Fourteen, both the Rams and the 49ers won handily.

Kevin Butler set an NFL record with his 24th consecutive field goal.

Cincinnati defenders smothered Eric Metcalf as the Browns were blanked.

STANDINGS

AFC East	W	L	T	PF	PA	NFC East	W	L	T	PF	PA
Buffalo	8	5	0	343	274	N.Y. Giants	9	4	0	285	228
Miami	7	6	0	263	300	Philadelphia	9	4	0	271	220
Indianapolis	6	7	0	227	230	Washington	7	6	0	300	257
New England	5	8	0	257	308	Phoenix	5	8	0	230	293
N.Y. Jets	4	9	0	239	323	Dallas	1	12	0	184	338
AFC Central						**NFC Central**					
Houston	8	5	0	318	310	Green Bay	8	5	0	299	297
Cleveland	7	5	1	270	194	Minnesota	8	5	0	262	214
Cincinnati	7	6	0	305	225	Chicago	6	7	0	313	284
Pittsburgh	6	7	0	193	294	Tampa Bay	5	8	0	274	335
						Detroit	4	9	0	221	316
AFC West											
Denver†	10	3	0	302	193	**NFC West**					
L.A. Raiders	7	6	0	265	226	San Francisco	11	2	0	365	216
Kansas City	6	6	1	257	239	L.A. Rams	9	4	0	337	280
Seattle	5	8	0	194	264	New Orleans	6	7	0	293	256
San Diego	4	9	0	206	235	Atlanta	3	10	0	208	332

†Division Champion

WEEK FOURTEEN

American Football Conference
Cleveland 17 at Indianapolis 23 (OT)
New England 10 at Miami 31
Pittsburgh 13 at New York Jets 0
Seattle 24 at Cincinnati 17

National Football Conference
Atlanta 17 at Minnesota 43
Dallas 10 at Philadelphia 20
Detroit 27 at Chicago 17
San Francisco 30 at Los Angeles Rams 27

Interconference Games
Kansas City 21 at Green Bay 3
New Orleans 22 at Buffalo 19
New York Giants 14 at Denver 7
Phoenix 14 at Los Angeles Raiders 16
San Diego 21 at Washington 26
Tampa Bay 17 at Houston 20

Interconference Play
AFC 21 – NFC 21

In the much anticipated rematch between the Rams and San Francisco, the Rams were on the verge of putting the game away before crumbling under the irresistible force of a 49ers rally which saw them lift the title in the

Marcus Allen returned after an absence of nine games through injury to help the Raiders beat Phoenix.

NFC West. Leading by the score of 27-17 and standing at second-and-goal on the San Francisco four-yard line, the Rams contrived to muff the snap; 49ers linebacker Matt Millen recovered possession and the great fightback began. On the very next play, wide receiver John Taylor, who earlier had caught a 92-yard touchdown pass, scored on a 95-yard reception. Rams returner Ron Brown fumbled the ensuing kickoff; the 49ers recovered possession yet again and running back Roger Craig punched into the end zone for the winning score with 3:42 remaining. Defeat left the Rams chasing a wild card berth and, in this, they could not afford another slip. One of the two available spots seemed certain to go to either Philadelphia or the Giants, both of whom won to stay locked in a tie for first place in the NFC East. In the NFC Central, Minnesota took time to shake off a tenacious Atlanta outfit, but, once in the clear, they coasted to their best single-game points total of the campaign. Against Kansas City, Green Bay had been unable to stop quarterback Steve DeBerg and could generate only three points as they slipped one game behind the division leader

In the AFC Central, Houston took advantage of most surprising losses by both Cincinnati and Cleveland to end the day needing one victory to secure the division title. After leading Tampa Bay by the score of 20-3, the Oilers killed off a Buccaneers resurgence when rookie safety Bubba McDowell recovered James Wilder's fumble at the Houston 18. Pittsburgh, meanwhile, had confirmed its entry into the race for a playoff berth by stifling the Jets. The Steelers joined a field which, instead of shedding plodders, was gathering strength, with the Raiders' prospects looking distinctly promising. Against Phoenix, running back Marcus Allen had climaxed a late Raiders rally with a one-yard touchdown run. The Chiefs, who halted the Packers' three-game charge, also had an outside chance of playoff contention. The AFC East picture showed no real signs of clearing. Buffalo lost to a solid New Orleans team, leaving open a door for both Miami and Indianapolis. Against New England, the Miami offense was at its best while the Colts used a combination of Eric Dickerson and entrepreneurial defense, together with a little help from the Browns. Dickerson rushed for 137 yards and nickel back Keith Taylor returned an interception 77 yards to set up the game-tying score. However, Browns placekicker Matt Bahr failed on potential game-winning field goal attempts of 39 yards in regulation time and 35 yards in overtime. The deadlock was broken when Indianapolis free safety Mike Prior returned an interception 58 yards for a touchdown. If momentum counted for anything, then both Miami and the Colts had to be fancied to reach the playoffs.

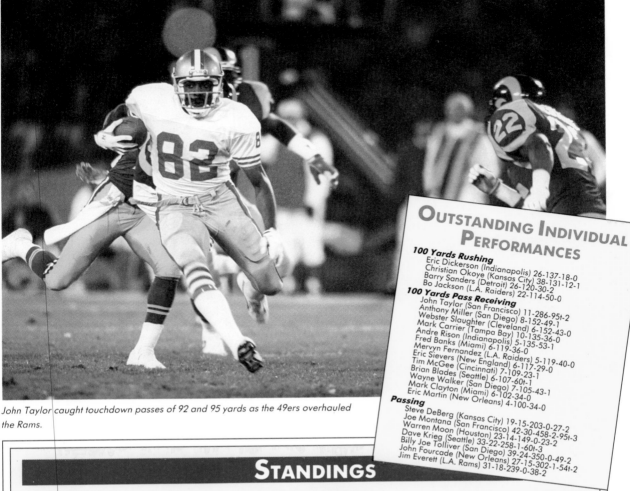

John Taylor caught touchdown passes of 92 and 95 yards as the 49ers overhauled the Rams.

OUTSTANDING INDIVIDUAL PERFORMANCES

100 Yards Rushing
Eric Dickerson (Indianapolis) 26-137-18-0
Christian Okoye (Kansas City) 38-131-12-1
Barry Sanders (Detroit) 26-120-30-2
Bo Jackson (L.A. Raiders) 22-114-50-0

100 Yards Pass Receiving
John Taylor (San Francisco) 11-286-95t-2
Anthony Miller (San Diego) 8-152-49-1
Webster Slaughter (Cleveland) 6-152-43-0
Mark Carrier (Tampa Bay) 10-135-36-0
Andre Rison (Indianapolis) 5-135-53-1
Fred Banks (Miami) 6-119-36-0
Mervyn Fernandez (L.A. Raiders) 5-119-40-0
Eric Sievers (New England) 6-117-29-0
Tim McGee (Cincinnati) 7-109-23-1
Brian Blades (Seattle) 6-107-60t-1
Wayne Walker (San Diego) 7-105-43-1
Mark Clayton (Miami) 6-102-34-0
Eric Martin (New Orleans) 4-100-34-0

Passing
Steve DeBerg (Kansas City) 19-15-203-0-27-2
Joe Montana (San Francisco) 42-30-458-2-95t-3
Warren Moon (Houston) 23-14-149-0-23-2
Dave Krieg (Seattle) 33-22-258-1-60t-3
Billy Joe Tolliver (San Diego) 39-24-350-0-49-2
John Fourcade (New Orleans) 27-15-302-1-54t-2
Jim Everett (L.A. Rams) 31-18-239-0-38-2

STANDINGS

AFC East	W	L	T	PF	PA
Buffalo	8	6	0	362	296
Miami	8	6	0	294	310
Indianapolis	7	7	0	250	247
New England	5	9	0	267	339
N.Y. Jets	4	10	0	239	336

AFC Central	W	L	T	PF	PA
Houston	9	5	0	338	327
Cleveland	7	6	1	287	217
Cincinnati	7	7	0	322	249
Pittsburgh	7	7	0	206	294

AFC West	W	L	T	PF	PA
Denver†	10	4	0	309	207
L.A. Raiders	8	6	0	281	240
Kansas City	7	6	1	278	242
Seattle	6	8	0	218	281
San Diego	4	10	0	227	261

NFC East	W	L	T	PF	PA
Philadelphia	10	4	0	291	230
N.Y. Giants	10	4	0	299	235
Washington	8	6	0	326	278
Phoenix	5	9	0	244	309
Dallas	1	13	0	194	358

NFC Central	W	L	T	PF	PA
Minnesota	9	5	0	305	231
Green Bay	8	6	0	302	318
Chicago	6	8	0	330	311
Detroit	5	9	0	248	333
Tampa Bay	5	9	0	291	355

NFC West	W	L	T	PF	PA
San Francisco†	12	2	0	395	243
L.A. Rams	9	5	0	364	310
New Orleans	7	7	0	315	275
Atlanta	3	11	0	225	375

†Division Champion

WEEK FIFTEEN

American Football Conference
Houston 7 at Cincinnati 61
Los Angeles Raiders 17 at Seattle 23
Miami 13 at Indianapolis 42
New England 10 at Pittsburgh 28
San Diego 20 at Kansas City 13

National Football Conference
Dallas 0 at New York Giants 15
Green Bay 40 at Chicago 28
Philadelphia 20 at New Orleans 30
Tampa Bay 7 at Detroit 33
Washington 31 at Atlanta 30

Interconference Games
Buffalo 10 at San Francisco 21
Denver 37 at Phoenix 0
Minnesota 17 at Cleveland 23 (OT)
New York Jets 14 at Los Angeles Rams 38

Interconference Play
AFC 23 – NFC 23

OUTSTANDING INDIVIDUAL PERFORMANCES

100 Yards Rushing
Marion Butts (San Diego) 39-176-17-0
Bobby Humphrey (Denver) 23-128-22-0
Neal Anderson (Chicago) 12-119-73-0
Keith Woodside (Green Bay) 10-116-68t-1
Eric Dickerson (Indianapolis) 21-107-17-2
Roger Craig (San Francisco) 25-105-14-1
Barry Sanders (Detroit) 21-104-34-1
Tim Worley (Pittsburgh) 19-104-22-1

100 Yards Pass Receiving
Michael Haynes (Atlanta) 6-190-72t-2
Ricky Sanders (Washington) 7-167-68-0
Tim McGee (Cincinnati) 6-147-74t-1
Reginald Langhorne (Cleveland) 6-140-62t-1
Mark Carrier (Tampa Bay) 4-131-69t-1
Art Monk (Washington) 6-131-60t-2
Hart Lee Dykes (New England) 10-130-21-0
John L. Williams (Seattle) 12-129-36-1
Eric Martin (New Orleans) 9-120-20t-2
Jason Phillips (Detroit) 10-115-55t-1
Andre Reed (Buffalo) 10-115-37-0
Keith Byars (Philadelphia) 6-109-60-0
Eddie Brown (Cincinnati) 6-107-35t-2

Passing
Boomer Esiason (Cincinnati) 27-20-326-0-74t-4
Jim Everett (L.A. Rams) 26-16-273-0-43t-2
Dave Krieg (Seattle) 34-25-270-0-36-2
Jack Trudeau (Indianapolis) 35-23-195-1-30-4

One team, the New York Giants, made certain of reaching the playoffs but, in many cases, it was a weekend of missed opportunities. The Giants were in cautious mood, keeping the Cowboys under pressure and taking the points on three Bjorn Nittmo field goals before running back Ottis Anderson eased them to relative safety with a one-yard touchdown run. In the Monday Night Game, Philadelphia surrendered the initiative by losing to a New Orleans team which took advantage of Eagles errors, notably a pair of Randall Cunningham fumbles and an interception. Failing a Raiders victory over New York on the final weekend, it meant that the Eagles would be in a scramble for a wild-card spot. The name of Brett Faryniarz does not come instantly to mind but, in the Rams' 38-14 win over the Jets, the second-year linebacker had three sacks, recovered two fumbles, forced a third, made three other tackles and set up two touchdowns. The odds now were heavily in favour of the Rams reaching the playoffs as a wild card.

Green Bay rebounded from its defeat on Week Fourteen, and though the Packers were slightly flattered by the margin of victory over Chicago, they moved into a tie for first place in the NFC Central. The Minnesota Vikings, who had led that division entering Week Fifteen, lost in an overtime thriller when a win would have given them the title. For Cleveland, the victory meant a new lease of life, as there had been a shocking result involving its Central division rivals. Oilers head coach Jerry Glanville had won few friends by his approach to reinvigorating a club which was well stocked with talent but had lacked a little fire. His team now overtly adopted a verbal and physical approach which, some opponents felt, went too far. It was with some satisfaction for Bengals head coach Sam Wyche, then, that his team just kept on scoring, even to the point of taking an onside kick at 45-0 and chipping a field goal when the score was already 58-7 in Cincinnati's favour. Some rather extreme events would have to take place for the Oilers not to reach the playoffs, but their loss, coupled with Pittsburgh's win, ensured that this race would go down to the wire. The same was true in the AFC East, where the result of the day was the Colts' thumping win over Miami. Buffalo's loss to San Francisco meant that all three of the Bills, Dolphins and Colts were locked at 8-7 going into the final weekend. In the AFC West, both the Raiders and Kansas City were beaten by divisional opponents, meaning that they now faced almost insurmountable odds if they were to qualify as wild cards. The Raiders were held at arm's length by Seattle, but the Chiefs squandered a 13-0 lead over San Diego.

Boomer Esiason passed for four touchdowns to lead the Bengals' rout of Houston.

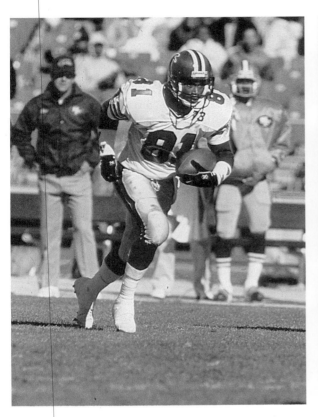

Atlanta's Michael Haynes caught six passes for 190 yards and two touchdowns in a losing cause.

Keith Woodside rushed for 116 yards as Green Bay beat Chicago for the second time in the season.

STANDINGS

AFC East	W	L	T	PF	PA	NFC East	W	L	T	PF	PA
Buffalo	8	7	0	372	317	N.Y. Giants*	11	4	0	314	235
Indianapolis	8	7	0	292	260	Philadelphia	10	5	0	311	260
Miami	8	7	0	307	352	Washington	9	6	0	357	308
New England	5	10	0	277	367	Phoenix	5	10	0	244	346
N.Y. Jets	4	11	0	253	374	Dallas	1	14	0	194	373
AFC Central						**NFC Central**					
Houston	9	6	0	345	388	Green Bay	9	6	0	342	346
Cleveland	8	6	1	310	234	Minnesota	9	6	0	322	254
Cincinnati	8	7	0	383	256	Chicago	6	9	0	358	351
Pittsburgh	8	7	0	234	304	Detroit	6	9	0	281	340
						Tampa Bay	5	10	0	298	388
AFC West						**NFC West**					
Denver†	11	4	0	346	207						
L.A. Raiders	8	7	0	298	263	San Francisco†	13	2	0	416	253
Kansas City	7	7	1	291	262	L.A. Rams	10	5	0	402	324
Seattle	7	8	0	241	298	New Orleans	8	7	0	345	295
San Diego	5	10	0	247	274	Atlanta	3	12	0	255	406

†Division Champion   *Clinched Playoff Spot

WEEK SIXTEEN

American Football Conference
Buffalo 37 at New York Jets 0
Cleveland 24 at Houston 20
Denver 16 at San Diego 19
Kansas City 27 at Miami 24

National Football Conference
Chicago 0 at San Francisco 26
Detroit 31 at Atlanta 24
Green Bay 20 at Dallas 10
Phoenix 14 at Philadelphia 31

Interconference Games
Cincinnati 21 at Minnesota 29
Indianapolis 6 at New Orleans 41
Los Angeles Raiders 17 at New York Giants 34
Los Angeles Rams 24 at New England 20
Pittsburgh 31 at Tampa Bay 22
Washington 29 at Seattle 0

Interconference Play
AFC 24 – NFC 28

Before the day dawned on the final Sunday, the sun had broken through the clouds for both the Buffalo Bills and the Cleveland Browns, who already had secured their respective division titles. In the first of Saturday's three games, Buffalo had hardly raised a sweat against a Jets team which could not muster a single point. Subsequently, Jets head coach Joe Walton was released. The Browns-Oilers game, that same evening, was a wholly different affair, with the Browns moving out to a steady, 17-0 lead, only to fall behind to a Warren Moon-led rally which gave Houston a 20-17 edge with just 4:46 remaining. The go-ahead touchdown had come after a tragically botched lateral by Cleveland linebacker Clay Matthews. However, there were 39 seconds to spare when Browns running back Kevin Mack finished off a 58-yard drive with the title-clinching, four-yard touchdown run. Between those games, Washington, which could not reach the playoffs under any circumstances, had eliminated Seattle with ease.

The Pittsburgh Steelers made their bid the following day and used a big performance from wide receiver Louis Lipps in slipping past a Tampa Bay club which always posed a threat. The day's results meant that, despite having lost, the Oilers would enter the playoffs. However, for Pittsburgh to join them, all three of the Raiders, Indianapolis and Cincinnati had to lose. The pieces were falling into place but the Steelers faced a nervous wait until late on Christmas Day. Sunday's thriller came in Foxboro, Massachusetts, where a tough New England team did everything but ruin the Rams' hopes of a wild-card spot. Although Rams running back Greg Bell would rush for 210 yards, it was only with 1:55 to go that Bell's three-yard touchdown run gave the Rams a 24-20 lead. Even then the drama wasn't over, for veteran quarterback Steve Grogan took the Patriots on a furious drive down to the Rams' four-yard line before throwing three incompletions in the final nine seconds.

The title in the NFC East duly went to the Giants, who, at half time, had been tied 17-17 with the Raiders before accelerating into the distance. In defeat, the Raiders were eliminated from contention. Against Phoenix, the Philadelphia Eagles turned on their best rushing display of the campaign to crush the Cardinals and take a wild card spot. Their bonus was that they would have the home-field advantage over the Rams. Much depended on the Monday Night Game when victory for Minnesota would earn the title in the NFC Central and eliminate Green Bay from the playoffs. A Vikings loss would leave them out in the cold. A win would give Cincinnati a wild card spot. In the event, an aerial bombardment featuring quarterbacks Boomer Esiason and Wade Wilson was decided when the Vikings' defense finally played up to its best to protect an eight-point lead after seeing the Bengals rally to within a point. The final pieces were in place.

OUTSTANDING INDIVIDUAL PERFORMANCES

100 Yards Rushing
Greg Bell (L.A. Rams) 26-210-47-1
Barry Sanders (Detroit) 20-158-25t-3

100 Yards Pass Receiving
Gary Clark (Washington) 9-149-44t-1
Drew Hill (Houston) 10-141-37-2
Louis Lipps (Pittsburgh) 4-137-79t-2
Richard Johnson (Detroit) 7-135-35-1
Mervyn Fernandez (L.A. Raiders) 6-125-39-1
Anthony Carter (Minnesota) 7-118-26-0
Henry Ellard (L.A. Rams) 4-111-53-0
Eddie Brown (Cincinnati) 6-109-34t-1
Hart Lee Dykes (New England) 8-108-25-0
Mark Clayton (Miami) 6-102-35-1
Mark Carrier (Tampa Bay) 6-101-39t-2
Jerry Rice (San Francisco) 4-101-45-1

Passing
John Fourcade (New Orleans) 28-21-291-1-38-2
Don Majkowski (Green Bay) 32-21-232-0-38-2
Jim Kelly (Buffalo) 21-13-208-1-31-2
Wade Wilson (Minnesota) 35-19-303-0-50-2

Greg Bell rushed for 210 yards and scored a late touchdown to carry the Rams into the playoffs.

An aerial display by Wade Wilson earned Minnesota a playoff spot.

Louis Lipps caught four passes for 137 yards, including touchdowns of 79 and 12 yards, as Pittsburgh earned a wild-card spot.

STANDINGS

AFC East	W	L	T	PF	PA	NFC East	W	L	T	PF	PA
Buffalo†	9	7	0	409	317	N.Y. Giants†	12	4	0	348	252
Indianapolis	8	8	0	298	301	Philadelphia*	11	5	0	342	274
Miami	8	8	0	331	379	Washington	10	6	0	386	308
New England	5	11	0	297	391	Phoenix	5	11	0	258	377
N.Y. Jets	4	12	0	253	411	Dallas	1	15	0	204	393
AFC Central						**NFC Central**					
Cleveland†	9	6	1	334	254	Minnesota†	10	6	0	351	275
Houston*	9	7	0	365	412	Green Bay	10	6	0	362	356
Pittsburgh*	9	7	0	265	326	Detroit	7	9	0	312	364
Cincinnati	8	8	0	404	285	Chicago	6	10	0	358	377
						Tampa Bay	5	11	0	320	419
AFC West						**NFC West**					
Denver†	11	5	0	362	226	San Francisco†	14	2	0	442	253
Kansas City	8	7	1	318	286	L.A. Rams*	11	5	0	426	344
L.A. Raiders	8	8	0	315	297	New Orleans	9	7	0	386	301
Seattle	7	9	0	241	327	Atlanta	3	13	0	279	437
San Diego	6	10	0	266	290						

†Division Champion   *Wild Card

WEEK SEVENTEEN
WILD CARD WEEKEND
AFC   Pittsburgh 26 at Houston 23 (OT)

It was as much a conflict between two head coaches as a battle between their teams when Pittsburgh travelled to meet Houston in the AFC Wild Card Game. And it was a decision by Chuck Noll which gave the Steelers an early boost, setting the tone for much of the way. With Pittsburgh in point-blank field goal range at the Houston nine, but on fourth down, Noll sent in a rushing play and rookie Tim Worley obliged by sweeping into the end zone for the opening touchdown. There followed a kicking duel which would see each of Houston's Tony Zendejas and the Steelers' Gary Anderson successful on three field goal attempts as Pittsburgh protected its seven-point advantage in the final quarter.

Yet in quick succession, either side of an inconsequential, four-play Steelers drive, Houston wide receiver Ernest Givins caught touchdown passes of 18 and nine yards, leaving the Oilers needing to protect a seven-point lead for barely more than six minutes. However, back came Pittsburgh, not with the reckless abandon of a mob in panic, but with the cool, calculating confidence of a team which knew it could do the job. Ten plays, including a 22-yard reverse by wide receiver Dwight Stone, set up Merril Hoge's game-tying, two-yard touchdown run with 46 seconds left in regulation time. In the extra period, the end came quickly. The Oilers did have an opportunity, taking over possession just inside Pittsburgh territory after forcing a short punt. But Steelers cornerback Rod Woodson stripped the ball free from Houston running back Lorenzo White and made the fumble recovery. When the return drive stalled, Anderson calmly hit the game-winning, 50-yard field goal.

Pittsburgh's Gary Anderson kicks the game-winning field goal.

Henry Ellard's 39-yard touchdown reception set the Rams on their way to victory against Philadelphia.

NFC Los Angeles Rams 21 at Philadelphia 7

Philadelphia's Veterans Stadium is not the most hospitable place — the fans have been known to register disapproval in the most expressive manner, even for the home team — and the cold, driving rain did nothing to help the hot-house Rams. But it might have been any other day of practice in sunny Southern California as Los Angeles drove unchecked to a 14-point lead with their first two possessions. Quarterback Jim Everett completed seven of 11 passes during that opening spell, hitting wide receiver Henry Ellard and tight end Damone Johnson with touchdown passes of 39 and four yards. The Rams could have made the score 21-0 had not running back Greg Bell fumbled at the Philadelphia five from a position set up by Willie (Flipper) Anderson's 55-yard pass reception.

Inevitably, the pace had to slacken, but if the Rams were unable to make headway neither could the Eagles, who failed to unravel the mysteries of the Rams' novel defensive system which used five linebackers and six defensive backs every time a pass was likely. It was only in the fourth quarter that Philadelphia opened its account after having been sparked to an 80-yard drive by running back Heath Sherman's 23-yard carry. Trailing by just seven points, the Eagles could not take advantage of an interception by linebacker Seth Joyner on the Rams' return drive. And it turned out to have been their last real chance. With 6:34 left, Bell became the first back to rush for over 100 yards against Philadelphia all season when he scythed for a 54-yard gain. Two plays later, he ran into the end zone from seven yards out to seal the victory.

WEEK EIGHTEEN

DIVISIONAL PLAYOFFS

American Football Conference

Buffalo 30 at Cleveland 34

In a high-scoring game, quarterback Jim Kelly only just failed to round off a late drive which could have brought the Bills an heroic victory. Kelly opened the scoring with a 72-yard touchdown pass to wide receiver Andre Reed, sparking a series of exchanges which included a pair of touchdown bombs from Cleveland quarterback Bernie Kosar to wide receiver Webster Slaughter and a 90-yard kickoff return by rookie Eric Metcalf, the latter which gave the Browns a 31-21 lead. A trade of field goals left the Bills facing the same deficit with 6:50 left. With running back Thurman Thomas moving towards a playoff-record-tying total of 13 pass receptions on his second touchdown catch, the Bills drew to within four points. Tragically, placekicker Scott Norwood missed the extra point and this would be a crucial factor in the end game. For with Buffalo again pressing as time ran out, only a touchdown would do. Bills running back Ronnie Harmon couldn't quite hold on to a pass in the end zone and, with just three seconds left, Kelly's final attempt, bound for Thomas, was intercepted at the goal line by Browns linebacker Clay Matthews.

Pittsburgh 23 at Denver 24

Pittsburgh had its heroes, running back Merril Hoge, quarterback Bubby Brister and placekicker Gary Anderson, but Denver had John Elway, the man who made the difference. With the Steelers heading comfortably into half time, sitting on a deserved 17-7 lead, Elway used two quick plays, pass completions of 26 and 15 yards, to set up a David Treadwell field goal which came as the second quarter expired. Shortly after the resumption, he passed 37 yards for a touchdown to wide receiver Vance Johnson immediately after Steelers running back Tim Worley had fumbled. Yet the Steelers simply would not stand aside and, though they were twice stopped short of the Denver end zone, Anderson confidently chipped them into a six-point lead with field goals of 35 and 32 yards. But those did no more than set the scene for the kind of drive for which Elway is famed. An 18-yard pass to Mark Jackson was followed by a cheeky 36-yarder to Johnson. Rookie running back Bobby Humphrey ran nine, five and seven yards down to the Pittsburgh two, setting up Melvin Bratton's one-yard touchdown run which clinched a place in the AFC Championship Game.

In a losing cause, Merril Hoge had a career-best day.

National Football Conference

Los Angeles Rams 19 at New York Giants 13 (OT)

With veteran running back Ottis Anderson rushing for 120 yards, the Giants held the upper hand for much of the way, yet just two errors, one of which was unforced and the other hotly disputed, brought their downfall. The first came close to half time, with the Giants deep in their own territory. Quarterback Phil Simms attempted a pass which was tipped into the hands of Rams safety Michael Stewart. On the very next play, wide receiver Willie (Flipper) Anderson caught a 20-yard touchdown pass to send the Rams into the break with a 7-6 lead. An 82-yard march culminating in Ottis Anderson's two-yard touchdown run saw the Giants regain the lead, but it was on merit that the resurgent Rams drew level on field goals of 31 and 22 yards from Mike Lansford. In overtime, the end came quickly. With quarterback Jim Everett completing passes of 12 and 13 yards, the Rams moved smoothly, but the big gain came as the result of a 27-yard pass interference penalty called on Giants cornerback Sheldon White. Instant replay showed the decision to be sound. Shortly afterwards, Everett hit the flying (Flipper) Anderson with the game-winning, 30-yard touchdown pass.

Quarterback Jim Kelly almost pulled it off for Buffalo.

Minnesota 13 at San Francisco 41

Minnesota drew first blood with Rich Karlis's 38-yard field goal, but, by early in the second quarter, the pattern had been established. Wide receiver Jerry Rice had caught a 72-yard touchdown pass and tight end Brent Jones had done likewise with an eight-yarder. Touchdown receptions by wide receiver John Taylor and Rice's second took the 49ers into half time with a 27-3 lead. The Vikings did generate a response with Karlis's 44-yard field goal, the only scoring play of the third quarter. But if that encouraged hopes of a recovery, they were dashed as pressure from the San Francisco defense brought its rewards in the shape of fourth-quarter interceptions by safety Ronnie Lott and cornerback Tim McKyer. Lott returned his theft 58 yards for a touchdown while McKyer's 41-yard return set up a score for running back Roger Craig. At the heart of it all had been Mr. Cool, quarterback Joe Montana, carrying on from what had been a record-breaking regular season with a show of consummate authority.

The Browns celebrate Clay Matthews' game-saving pass interception.

WEEK NINETEEN

CONFERENCE CHAMPIONSHIPS

American Football Conference

Cleveland 21 at Denver 37

It is a measure of the consistency of these two teams that, for the third time in the last four years, they were matched in the AFC Championship Game. In the previous two encounters, Denver quarterback John Elway had been at the top of his form as the Broncos came away with victories by three and five points. And Denver entered this game favoured to win after having swept through the regular season with the AFC's best record and reaching the playoffs in equal-record time. As often happens in such cases, the Broncos had gone off the boil with losses in three of the final four games. However, in the divisional playoffs, they'd been shaken back to reality by a Pittsburgh team which almost brought off a famous upset.

The Browns had been forced to fight all the way in the AFC's toughest division and in a late-season, four-week spell, when they tied one and then lost three straight games, they appeared to have spurned their chance. It was by the margin of the tied game that they won the division title. The squad was more mature than the one which had suffered those disappointing Championship Game losses in 1986 and 1987. As before, though, the main question surrounded their ability to control Elway.

There are games when you wonder if Elway ever could make a mistake, and this one started out along those lines as he quickly had the Broncos in front, building on David Treadwell's field goal with a 70-yard touchdown pass to wide receiver Michael Young. After the Browns had made their opening statement, Elway answered by simply upping the pace with two more touchdowns, the first of these being set up by his 53-yard completion to Young. A brief flurry by Bernie Kosar saw the Browns re-enter the contest and when, following a Denver fumble, Cleveland running back Tim Manoa scored from two yards out, the Browns trailed by only three points. But that merely stung Elway to greater heights. He fired a 39-yard scoring strike to Sammy Winder before easing into semi-automatic pilot to drive the offense for two more field goals, as Denver earned its fourth trip to the Super Bowl.

Injury replacement Sammy Winder scored touchdowns on a seven-yard run and a 39-yard reception.

National Football Conference

Los Angeles Rams 3 at San Francisco 30

After the manner of the 49ers' victory over Minnesota in the divisional playoffs, in particular that their slightly suspect offensive line had kept the ferocious Vikings' defense at bay, it was difficult for an opponent to sniff out the slightest weakness. The Rams, too, had come good at the best possible time. Even their most begrudging critic had to extend some praise for having subdued the wild-card Eagles in Philadelphia and, subsequently, overcoming a solid Giants team. In that divisional playoff game, the Rams had run up 316 yards in the second half against the NFL's fifth-best defense. The fine-tuning was complete and there remained only the intangibles, the mental adjustments that any team has to make in going up against the best. Moreover, there were strong indications that, planned or otherwise, the Rams might have a system which the 49ers found tricky. After all, the Rams had held them without a touchdown in that 13-12 victory on Week Four. And hadn't the Rams been on the verge of putting the game away before San Francisco rallied for a 30-27 win in the rematch?

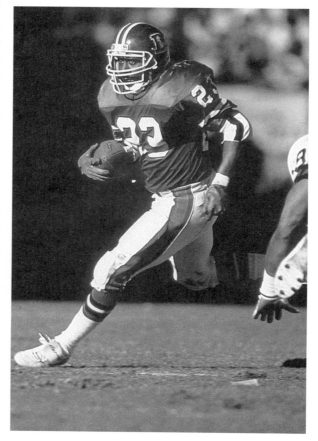

The early sparring suggested that the Rams might be ready to do battle. After forcing the 49ers to punt on the initial possession and, with quarterback Jim Everett looking supremely confident, they drove deep into San Francisco territory for the opening field goal. Shortly afterwards, with a bonus possession following a 49ers fumble near midfield, what seemed a certain touchdown play evaporated as Everett delayed just a little and his bomb to wide receiver (Flipper) Anderson was batted away by San Francisco safety Ronnie Lott, who made a sensational play look routine. And then the 49ers machine began its inexorable progress for the first touchdown as a 13-play drive culminated in tight end Brent Jones' 20-yard scoring catch. Four minutes later, Roger Craig capitalised on an interception by cornerback Tim McKyer and, with nine seconds to go before half time, wide receiver John Taylor took the score to 21-3 with his 18-yard touchdown reception. Thankfully, with the 49ers opting for ball control throughout the second half, a well-beaten Rams team did not have to suffer humiliation.

ABOVE: Willie (Flipper) Anderson was closely marked by 49ers cornerback Tim McKyer.

LEFT: John Elway took Denver to its third Super Bowl in the last four years.

BELOW: San Francisco's Tom Rathman accounted for 111 combined yards as the Rams were smothered.

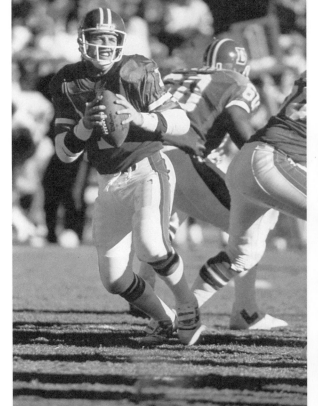

47

SUPER BOWL XXIV

Denver 10 – San Francisco 55

Louisiana Superdome, New Orleans, Louisiana, January 28, 1990

There had been significant changes to the Denver squad which suffered heavy defeats in both Super Bowls XXI and XXII. On the offensive line, four new starters had joined right tackle Ken Lanier and there was an exciting rookie pairing at running back in Bobby Humphrey and Melvin Bratton. Humphrey had the potential for a big gain every time he carried the ball while Bratton was easing back to full pace after suffering a serious knee injury late in his college career. Behind them hovered the vastly experienced Sammy Winder. Running the show was quarterback John Elway, a multi-talented, inspirational leader whose flamboyance had been tempered by the bitterness of defeat and probably never would reach the heights expected when the Colts made him the first pick in the 1983 draft. But on his day he could murder the opposition in a flash. Elway would have a choice of targets, with wide receiver Vance Johnson the most likely to do the damage.

For the defense, Denver had done well, acquiring

John Elway had started in two losing Super Bowls.

veteran starting defensive ends Ron Holmes and Alphonso Carreker, who originally were first-round picks of Tampa Bay and Green Bay respectively. The secondary had been boosted by the arrival of first-round draftee free safety Steve Atwater, and it was reassuring that strong safety Dennis Smith had returned to something approaching his best. The cornerbacks were known to be vulnerable, but Tyrone Braxton had intercepted a team-leading six passes during the regular season and could not be taken lightly.

Even before this game, the San Francisco 49ers were widely accepted as the team of the decade, but some still needed to see them equal the Pittsburgh Steelers who had gained four Super Bowl Championships in the 1970s, twice winning in consecutive years.

Without question, San Francisco had an offense more potent even than those awesome Steelers, if, perhaps, there was little to choose between the defenses. The cornerstone throughout the 49ers' remarkable period of success had been Joe Montana, the outstanding quarterback in pro football, whose passer rating of 112.4 in the 1989 regular season had established a new NFL record. Montana's partnership with Jerry Rice and John Taylor was the most feared in the game, each of the wide receivers having caught passes for over 1,000 yards and Rice having led the league with 1,483. At running back, the combination of halfback Roger Craig and fullback Tom Rathman approached perfection.

Joe Montana was seeking his fourth Super Bowl victory.

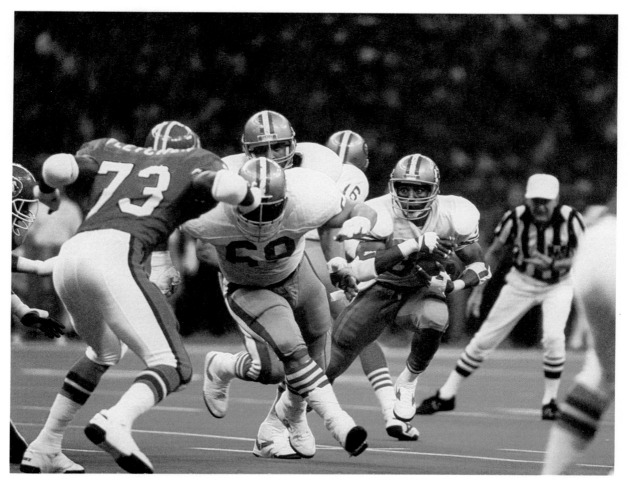

ABOVE: 49ers running back Roger Craig (#33) was given excellent blocking.

BELOW: Occasionally, the 49ers' rushing game was stopped.

The defense had gathered strength as the season wore on. It was a system of great sophistication; one which seemed to have an instant response to its opponent's every statement. There was abundant speed in pass rushers Pierce Holt, Kevin Fagan and Charles Haley, and a mix of hard-nosed veterans jammed up the running lanes. Once the ball was in the air, a secondary led by the legendary Ronnie Lott hovered ready for the kill. Green Bay and the Rams had shown that San Francisco could be beaten, but that was of little comfort to the Broncos.

Going into the game, you had to have a heart of stone not to feel for the underdog Broncos just a little. If not at that stage, certainly after the 49ers' opening possession, with which they went 66 yards in ten plays for the first touchdown. 'Would this be all over by eleven o'clock?' we wondered. But wait a minute. The Broncos answered immediately with a solid, 49-yard march for

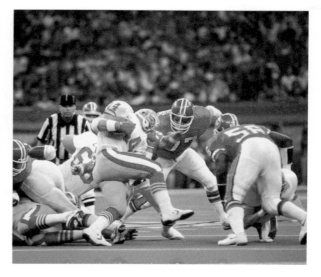

ABOVE: Running back Bobby Humphrey gave Denver early hopes.

BELOW: Jerry Rice lopes in for one of his Super Bowl-record three touchdown receptions.

David Treadwell's 42-yard field goal. And then the unthinkable happened as Denver held the 49ers to four yards in three downs, forcing a punt. Now we had a game. 'A Denver touchdown or even a field goal might just rattle the 49ers enough to induce the odd mistake and then who knows?' went the reasoning. But on the very next play from scrimmage, Broncos running back Bobby Humphrey fumbled; 49ers strong safety Chet Brooks recovered and the 49ers took the bonus possession 54 yards for a second touchdown. The kick failed but it mattered little, since, before the final gun, Mike Cofer would be given six more opportunities for redemption as San Francisco moved unchecked for a Super Bowl-best 55 points. Montana was voted Super Bowl MVP for a record third time on the day that he bettered no fewer than eight previous Super Bowl marks.

To the Denver Broncos organisation went a share of the disappointment at being the losing team in four Super Bowls, that sentiment previously belonging exclusively to the Minnesota Vikings. However, it bears consideration that the Broncos earned their most recent tilt while still in the early stages of reconstruction. They'll be a more dangerous prospect in 1990.

THE GAME

Scoring By Quarters

1st Quarter
San Francisco: Rice, 20-yard pass from Montana; Cofer kick (4:54)
San Francisco 7 – Denver 0
Denver: Treadwell, 42-yard field goal (8:13)
San Francisco 7 – Denver 3
San Francisco: Jones, 7-yard pass from Montana; kick failed (14:57)
San Francisco 13 – Denver 3

2nd Quarter
San Francisco: Rathman, 1-yard run; Cofer kick (7:45)
San Francisco 20 – Denver 3
San Francisco: Rice, 38-yard pass from Montana; Cofer kick (14:26)
San Francisco 27 – Denver 3

3rd Quarter
San Francisco: Rice, 28-yard pass from Montana; Cofer kick (2:12)
San Francisco 34 – Denver 3
San Francisco: Taylor, 35-yard pass from Montana; Cofer kick (5:16)
San Francisco 41 – Denver 3
Denver: Elway, 3-yard run; Treadwell kick (8:07)
San Francisco 41 – Denver 10

4th Quarter
San Francisco: Rathman, 4-yard run; Cofer kick (0:03)
San Francisco 48 – Denver 10
San Francisco: Craig, 1-yard run; Cofer kick (1:13)
San Francisco 55 – Denver 10

ABOVE: Roger Craig was yet again at his best in Super Bowl play.

ABOVE: George Seifert savours his first Super Bowl victory as a head coach.

51

ANATOMY OF SUPER BOWL XXIV

1st Quarter

FIRST DOWNS
8
3

YARDS RUSHING
42
25

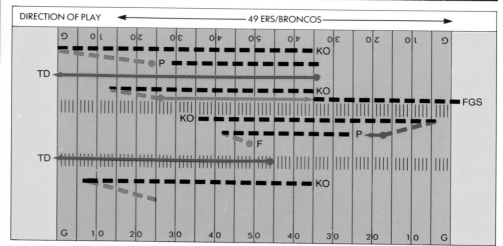

DIRECTION OF PLAY ← 49 ERS/BRONCOS →

YARDS PASSING
92
27

THIRD DOWN CONVERSIONS
60%
33.3%

TIME OF POSSESSION
10:36
4:24

SCORE AFTER FIRST QUARTER
49ers 13
Broncos 3

2nd Quarter

FIRST DOWNS
8
2

YARDS RUSHING
38
−1

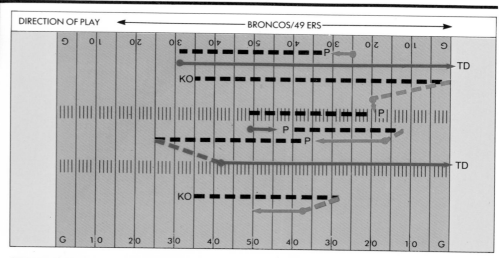

DIRECTION OF PLAY ← BRONCOS/49 ERS →

YARDS PASSING
97
37

THIRD DOWN CONVERSIONS
50%
0%

TIME OF POSSESSION
10:19
4:41

SCORE AFTER SECOND QUARTER
49ers 27
Broncos 3

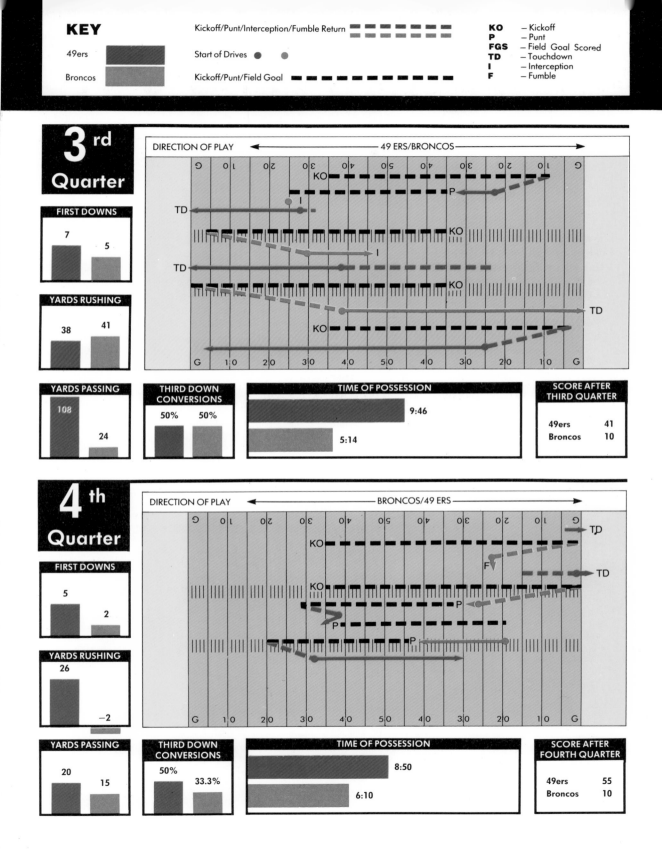

KEY

49ers

Broncos

Kickoff/Punt/Interception/Fumble Return

Start of Drives ●   ●

Kickoff/Punt/Field Goal

KO	– Kickoff
P	– Punt
FGS	– Field Goal Scored
TD	– Touchdown
I	– Interception
F	– Fumble

3rd Quarter

DIRECTION OF PLAY ◄——— 49 ERS/BRONCOS ———►

KO
P
I
TD
KO
I
TD
KO
TD
KO

FIRST DOWNS
7 5

YARDS RUSHING
38 41

YARDS PASSING
108 24

THIRD DOWN CONVERSIONS
50% 50%

TIME OF POSSESSION
9:46
5:14

SCORE AFTER THIRD QUARTER

49ers	41
Broncos	10

4th Quarter

DIRECTION OF PLAY ◄——— BRONCOS/49 ERS ———►

KO
TD
F
TD
KO
P
P
P

FIRST DOWNS
5 2

YARDS RUSHING
26 −2

YARDS PASSING
20 15

THIRD DOWN CONVERSIONS
50% 33.3%

TIME OF POSSESSION
8:50
6:10

SCORE AFTER FOURTH QUARTER

49ers	55
Broncos	10

HALL OF FAME

Of the many thousands of players, owners and administrators who have graced the game since the inception of professional football, only 155 have achieved the ultimate accolade, enshrinement in the Pro Football Hall of Fame.

BRONKO NAGURSKI (Minnesota); Fullback: 6-2, 225; Chicago Bears (1930-37 and 1943)

Career Rushing

Year	Att.	Yds.	Avg.	TDs
1930*	51	254	5.0	0
1931*	79	401	5.1	2
1932	111	496	4.5	4
1933	128	533	4.2	1
1934	123	586	4.8	7
1935	37	137	3.7	1
1936	122	529	4.3	3
1937	73	343	4.7	1
1943	16	84	5.3	1
Totals**	**610**	**2,708**	**4.4**	**18**

* Unofficial statistics (for six games only in 1930 and nine in 1931)
** Excluding unofficial statistics

On the subject of who really was the NFL's first truly great running back, the arguments may begin and end with Jim Thorpe, who, in a wider sense than football, was regarded as America's finest athlete. But by 1920, the year which saw the birth of the NFL, Thorpe's powers were on the wane. Many would choose Red Grange, the 'Galloping Ghost', who only rarely reproduced his collegiate form but whose very presence on the field drew crowds of more than 70,000 and helped save the NFL in its time of need. Others might opt for Ernie Nevers, a scoring machine who was described by the legendary Glenn (Pop) Warner as 'the greatest player I ever coached'. But in discussions of who was the first great power back, there is no dispute. That honour belongs to the indestructible Bronko Nagurski, who set the standards by which others have been

Bronko Nagurski veers left with determination.

measured over the 50 years since he thundered across the gridiron.

Far more than just a punishing fullback, Nagurski also was a shuddering blocker, even to the effect that, while he was selected to some collegiate All-America teams in the fullback position, officially he was All-America at tackle. In partnership with Grange, he gave the Bears the best rushing game in the NFL. In addition, he could pass the ball. It was his disputed forward pass for a touchdown to Grange which brought the Bears the NFL Championship in their 1932 playoff with the Portsmouth Spartans. The following year, he threw a touchdown pass to Bill Karr in the Bears' 23-21 title game victory over the New York Giants.

In 1943, with many of Chicago's players in the armed services, Nagurski, who had retired in 1937 to take up pro wrestling, came back to help out. After playing at tackle all season, he reverted to fullback for the final regular-season game. In the last NFL game of his career, the championship confrontation with Washington, his three-yard touchdown run gave the Bears a lead they would not relinquish.

STEVE VAN BUREN (Louisiana State); Halfback: 6-1, 200; Philadelphia Eagles (1944-51)

Career Rushing

Year	Att.	Yds.	Avg.	TDs
1944	80	444	5.6	5
1945	143	832	5.8	15
1946	116	529	4.6	5
1947	217	1,008	4.6	13
1948	201	945	4.7	10
1949	263	1,146	4.4	11
1950	188	629	3.3	4
1951	112	327	2.9	6
Totals	**1,320**	**5,860**	**4.4**	**69**

Career Kickoff Returns

Year	Att.	Yds.	Avg.	TDs
1944	8	266	33.3	1
1945	13	373	28.7	1
1946	11	319	29.0	0
1947	13	382	29.4	1
1948	14	292	20.9	0
1949	12	288	24.0	0
1950	5	110	22.0	0
Totals	**76**	**2,030**	**26.7**	**3**

Steve Van Buren slides out of a tackle versus Washington in 1947.

Blessed with the speed of a halfback and fullback strength, Steve Van Buren was a giant in his time. Before he joined Philadelphia as a rookie in 1944, the Eagles had never had a net winning season (other than as the hybrid formed with Pittsburgh for 1943 only), had never finished higher than equal-third in their division and usually finished last.

With Van Buren at halfback, over the next eight years, Philadelphia would be competitive and at times dominant as they won the NFL Championship in both 1948 and 1949.

Van Buren's impact was immediate and sustained as, in his first three seasons, the Eagles finished second in their division and followed up with three straight divisional titles, the final two of which led to the NFL Championship.

Van Buren's tally of personal honours began as a rookie, when he led the league in punt return average as a prelude to a remarkable treble of individual titles for rushing, kickoff returns and scoring, all in 1945. In his eight-year career, he was the NFL leading rusher four times, three times consecutively. Five times he was voted All-Pro.

In 1934, Chicago rookie Beattie Feathers had become the first man to rush for 1,000 yards in a season. Regarded as barely credible at the time, some statisticians still doubt the validity of what, nonetheless, is an official NFL statistic. However, there was no doubting the authenticity of the second 1,000-yards-rushing season, by Van Buren, who powered for 1,008 yards in 1947 and, two years later, to a new mark of 1,146 yards,

a total which survived as the NFL single-season record until the emergence of Cleveland's Jim Brown in 1958. He retired in 1951, having rushed for a (then) NFL career record 5,860 yards.

DON MAYNARD (Texas Western); Wide Receiver: 6-1, 180; New York Giants (1958), New York Titans-New York Jets (1960-72); St Louis Cardinals (1973)

Career Pass Receiving

Year	No.	Yds.	Avg.	TDs
1958	5	84	16.8	0
1959		Not in NFL		
1960	72	1,265	17.6	6
1961	43	629	14.6	8
1962	56	1,041	18.6	8
1963	38	780	20.5	9
1964	46	847	18.4	8
1965	68	1,218	17.9	14
1966	48	840	17.5	5
1967	71	1,434	20.2	10
1968	57	1,297	22.8	10
1969	47	938	20.0	6
1970	31	525	16.9	0
1971	21	408	19.4	2
1972	29	510	17.6	2
1973	1	18	18.0	0
Totals	**633**	**11,834**	**18.7**	**88**

With sideburns and cowboy boots to match, Don Maynard hardly cut the figure of a typical pro wide receiver. But then, Maynard was much more than a typical wide receiver. In fact, taking his 15-year career as a whole,

Don Maynard cradles the ball under double coverage.

he was the most productive of his era. Yet his individual honours were few. He never won a league receiving title (though he led the AFL in yards receiving in 1967), but then, he played in a league which could boast the class of wide receivers such as Otis Taylor, Art Powell, Lance Alworth and even his teammate with the Jets, George Sauer. A somewhat shy, retiring sort, he just kept ringing up the numbers, catching passes for more than 1,000 yards in a season five times, a figure exceeded only by Steve Largent (8) and Alworth (7). Interestingly, he had four-figure receiving campaigns in combination with three different Jets starting quarterbacks, Al Dorow, Johnny Green and, of course, Joe Namath.

Though not the fastest and lacking a great move, he had an uncanny knack of finding an open space and this he coupled with an amazing ability to adjust to passes which were less than perfect. Even now, 17 years after his retirement, he still ranks sixth in receptions, third in yards receiving, third in touchdown receptions and first in 100-yards-receiving games (50).

Many remember his great contributions in the 1968 postseason. In the AFL Championship Game against the Raiders, he caught six passes, including one for the game-winning touchdown. Two weeks later in Super Bowl III, he was carrying a leg injury but the Colts were not to know. He didn't catch a pass in that game but, ironically, the one he almost caught – it was a 60-yard bomb from Namath – meant that the Colts could not ignore his potential threat.

KEN HOUSTON (Prairie View A&M); Strong Safety: 6-3, 198; Houston Oilers (1967-72), Washington Redskins (1973-80)

Career Interceptions

Year	No.	Yds.	Avg.	TDs
1967	4	151	37.8	2
1968	5	160	32.0	2
1969	4	87	21.8	1
1970	3	32	10.7	0
1971	9	220	24.4	4
1972	0	0	0.0	0
1973	6	32	5.3	0
1974	2	40	20.0	0
1975	4	33	8.3	0
1976	4	25	6.3	0
1977	5	69	13.8	0
1978	2	29	14.5	0
1979	1	20	20.0	0
1980	0	0	0.0	0
Totals	**49**	**898**	**18.3**	**9**

With great speed, super hands and a flowing style of running, Ken Houston might well have become a wide receiver. But add to these the instincts of a linebacker and there emerged one of the finest strong safeties of all time.

Houston had played linebacker at modest Prairie

Ken Houston was one of the finest strong safeties of all time.

View A&M but was mostly overlooked, and it was only in the 1967 ninth round that the AFL's Houston Oilers selected him. They had seen a potential safety and he quickly confirmed their judgement in the fifth game (it was his third as a starter) of his rookie season when he ran 45 yards for a touchdown following a blocked field goal and, later, returned an interception 43 yards for another score.

After only five years in the pros, he had established the still-existing career record with nine touchdowns on interception returns, including a single-season record four in 1971.

Naturally, he was coveted by most head coaches, including the Redskins' George Allen, who obtained him in a 1973 trade which sent five Washington players (three became starters) to the Oilers. It was in his very first season in Washington that he delivered a sensational hit – some call it 'the hit' – which ranks amongst the very best ever. With Washington leading Dallas by seven points and 16 seconds remaining in a Monday Night Game, Cowboys power back Walt Garrison had a full head of steam and seemed certain to blast into the end zone just one yard away. But the explosion came from a different direction as Garrison was brought to a shuddering halt by a missile called Houston.

Houston would repay the Redskins' faith over eight years, extending his sequence of Pro Bowl selections to 12, a total bettered only by the great Merlin Olsen. He was named All-Pro five times.

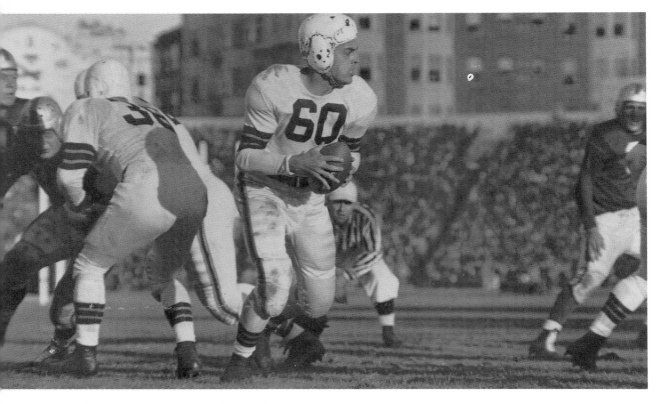

Otto Graham took his team to a league championship game in ten consecutive seasons.

OTTO GRAHAM (Northwestern); Quarterback: 6-1, 195; Cleveland Browns AAFC (1946-49), Cleveland Browns NFL (1950-55)

Career Passing

Year	Att.	Comp.	Pct.	Yds.	Int.	TDs
1946	174	95	54.6	1,834	5	17
1947	269	163	60.6	2,753	11	25
1948	333	173	52.0	2,713	15	25
1949	285	161	56.5	2,785	10	19
1950	253	137	54.2	1,943	20	14
1951	265	147	55.5	2,205	16	17
1952	364	181	49.7	2,816	24	20
1953	258	167	64.7	2,722	9	11
1954	240	142	59.2	2,092	17	11
1955	185	98	53.0	1,721	8	15
Totals	**2,626**	**1,464**	**55.8**	**23,584**	**135**	**174**

If winning is any measure of individual greatness, then Otto Graham would have to be ranked as the best quarterback ever. For in all ten of the seasons he was at the helm, the Cleveland Browns contested league championship games, winning seven.

A music major in college, where he was accomplished in all three of the cornet, French horn and the violin, Graham showed himself to be a fine passer but he was overlooked by the NFL team scouts. Playing for Northwestern, Graham had been a Single-Wing tail-back but Paul Brown, who was the head coach of the newly formed AAFC Cleveland club, knew what he wanted and did not hesitate to install this cool, accurate passer as his T-formation quarterback. In the brief lifetime of the AAFC, each year Graham directed his team to the championship, winning all four individual passing titles. The Browns organization was one of three AAFC clubs invited to join the NFL when the rival league folded at the end of the 1949 season. Not many people expected the AAFC teams to compete with the established NFL powerhouses, but the Browns fired off an early warning when they defeated the reigning NFL Champion Philadelphia Eagles in the season opener and then, with Graham throwing four touchdown passes, they climaxed their inaugural season by beating the mighty Los Angeles Rams in the NFL Championship Game.

At the end of his ninth year, after passing for three touchdowns and running for three in the Browns' 56-10 rout of Detroit in the 1954 NFL title game, Graham retired. But he was persuaded to return for one more year, in which he was voted all-league for the ninth time in a career which, fittingly, ended with his passing for two touchdowns and rushing for two more in Cleveland's 38-14 championship game defeat of the Rams.

JOE GREENE (North Texas State); Defensive Tackle: 6-4, 260; Pittsburgh Steelers (1969-81)

More than being in at the start, Joe Greene is credited by many historians as having been *the* start of a Steelers charge which faltered only after they had won four Super Bowl Championships in the space of six seasons. Before Greene's arrival, Pittsburgh had never won a title of any kind, and there were more than a few Steelers fans who doubted the wisdom of using the club's priceless first-round option (it was the fourth overall) to select a defensive tackle from North Texas State, a small college which does not normally rank amongst the nation's leaders. A couple of veterans on the team were of similar mind, and they intended to

Joe Greene was the inspirational force which catalysed the Steelers to greatness in the 1970s.

express that view in the first practice. Tackling Greene both high and low at the same time, they felt, would be a lovely way to welcome him into the NFL. But they hadn't anticipated being tossed around like a pair of rag dolls, and they could only watch helplessly as he collared the quarterback.

An instant success, Greene was named NFL Defensive Rookie of the Year and was voted to the first of his ten Pro Bowls. Even as a rookie he was able to assert the kind of dominance which, at times, enabled him singlehandedly to dictate the course of a game. 'All of a sudden we had a player who was head and shoulders above everyone,' said Pittsburgh center Ray Mansfield. 'It was like having a big brother around when the bullies were coming to fight you.'

In 1972 against the Houston Oilers in a late-season game which was critical to the Steelers' hopes of a first divisional title, Greene took control when both starting quarterback Terry Bradshaw and backup Terry Hanratty were injured. With the teams tied at 3-3 and knowing that the defense simply had to prevent Houston from scoring another point, he set the example by logging six unassisted tackles, blocking a field goal attempt and forcing two fumbles, one of which he recovered to set up a Pittsburgh field goal. On the Oilers' last possession, with the Steelers protecting a 9-3 lead, on first, third and fourth down he sacked quarterback Dante Pastorini to secure the win. Greene was that kind of player.

WILLIE LANIER (Morgan State); Middle Linebacker: 6-1, 245; Kansas City Chiefs (1967-77)

Career Interceptions

Year	No.	Yds.	Avg.	TDs
1967	0	0	0.0	0
1968	4	120	30.0	1
1969	4	70	17.5	0
1970	2	2	1.0	0
1971	2	38	19.0	0
1972	2	2	1.0	0
1973	3	47	15.7	1
1974	2	28	14.0	0
1975	5	105	21.0	0
1976	3	28	9.3	0
1977	0	0	0.0	0
Totals	**27**	**440**	**16.3**	**2**

In the turbulence at the line of scrimmage, the play of the middle linebacker often can go unnoticed. His job begins before the ball is snapped as he reads the offense, sizing up the options. At the snap of the ball there is a moment of suspended electricity as he identifies the point of attack before, in the space of two or three seconds, a discharge of pent-up energy engulfs the running back. Only when the bodies unpile is the enforcer's number revealed, and, over an 11-year period at Kansas City's Arrowhead Stadium, that

number usually was the 63 worn by Willie Lanier.

Good-looking and with an easy charm off the field, on the gridiron Lanier was transformed into a man driven to a point of fury, fearless and with an almost reckless abandon. As a rookie, his ferocious style of play brought him several concussions and led to his wearing a helmet fitted with extra padding.

An added feature which separated Lanier from the other top-class middle linebackers of the day was his ability to cover a receiver. It was a role in which, remarkably, he intercepted 27 passes.

But it is those fearsome collisions – euphemistically, he was nicknamed 'Contact' – for which he will be remembered. And never was his charismatic leadership more important than in a critical series of downs during the Chiefs' 1969 playoff game with the New York Jets. Bolstered by his near fanatical urging, twice the Chiefs defense repelled Jets runners at the one-yard line before, in desperation, Jets quarterback Joe Namath underthrew a third-down pass. The Jets were held to a field goal in what turned out to be a 13-6 victory for Kansas City. Two weeks later, with Lanier the focal point of the defense, the Chiefs beat Minnesota in Super Bowl IV.

LARRY CSONKA (Syracuse); Fullback: 6-3, 235; Miami Dolphins (1968-74 and 1979), New York Giants (1976-78)

Career Rushing

Year	Att.	Yds.	Avg.	TDs
1968	138	540	3.9	6
1969	131	566	4.3	2
1970	193	874	4.5	6
1971	195	1,051	5.4	7
1972	213	1,117	5.2	6
1973	219	1,003	4.6	5
1974	197	749	3.8	9
1975		Not in NFL		
1976	160	569	3.6	4
1977	134	464	3.5	1
1978	91	311	3.4	6
1979	220	837	3.8	12
Totals	**1,891**	**8,081**	**4.3**	**64**

Short-legged, barrel-bodied and snub-nosed, Larry Csonka was the blunt instrument of a Miami Dolphins offense which, at its height, ruled the NFL. Week after week, Csonka pounded out the message. Defenses knew he was coming but Csonka knew where he was going. The outcome was predictable.

With Csonka leading the way, Miami marched to three straight AFC Championships, beating first the powerful Baltimore Colts, then a Pittsburgh club on the rise and, finally, overpowering the mighty Oakland Raiders. In 1972, the Miami Dolphins had the only

modern-day perfect season when they went 17-0, rounding off with victory in Super Bowl VII.

The AFC title game victory over the Raiders in December 1973, came during what perhaps was Csonka's most dominant period. On that afternoon in Miami, the likes of Otis Sistrunk, Dan Conners, Phil Villapiano and Jack Tatum were helpless in the face of a demoralising performance which saw Csonka crash his way to 117 yards and three touchdowns on a load-carrying 29 rushes. Two weeks later, in Super Bowl VIII, the awesome Minnesota Vikings were beaten into submission by Csonka's then-Super Bowl, single-game record rushing total of 145 yards on 33 back-breaking carries, two of which took the ball into the end zone.

It is a disappointment that much of Csonka's force was dissipated during his one-year term in the ill-fated World Football League though, in his three subsequent campaigns with the New York Giants followed by one last hurrah with Miami, he still was a solid player. But the memory of those early years remains.

"This ball is mine and I'm going places," Larry Csonka might be saying.

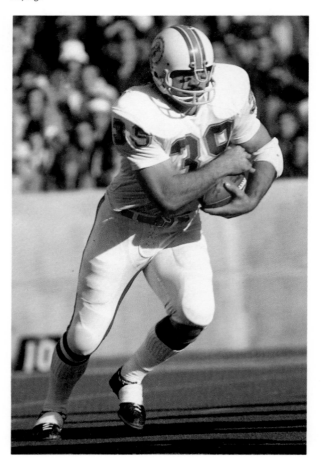

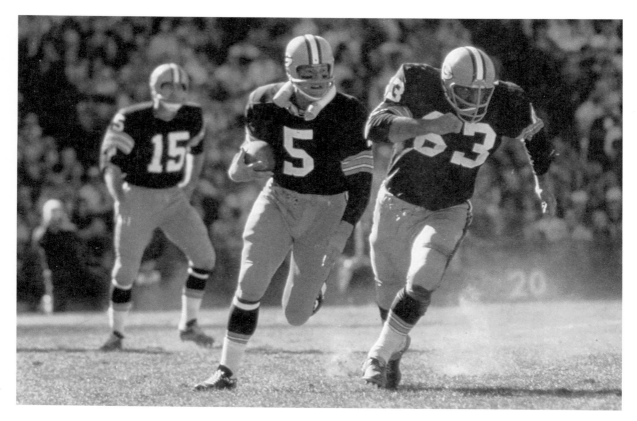

Paul Hornung (#5) follows his blocker around right end.

PAUL HORNUNG (Notre Dame); Halfback/Placekicker: 6-2, 220; Green Bay Packers (1957-62 and 1964-66)

Career Rushing

Year	Att.	Yds.	Avg.	TDs
1957	60	319	5.3	3
1958	69	310	4.5	2
1959	152	681	4.5	7
1960	160	671	4.2	13
1961	127	597	4.7	8
1962	57	219	3.8	5
1963		Suspended		
1964	103	415	4.0	5
1965	89	299	3.4	5
1966	76	200	2.6	2
Totals	**893**	**3,711**	**4.2**	**50**

Career Scoring

Year	TDs	PATs	FG	Pts.
1957	3	0	0	18
1958	2	22	11	67
1959	7	31	7	94
1960	15	41	15	176
1961	10	41	15	146
1962	7	14	6	74
1963		Suspended		
1964	5	41	12	107
1965	8	0	0	48
1966	5	0	0	30
Totals	**62**	**190**	**66**	**760**

Even before he played a down in the NFL, with the Heisman Trophy as the final statement on a glittering collegiate career at storied Notre Dame, Paul Hornung was assured of his place in football history. A running quarterback, he was the bonus draft pick of a Green Bay Packers club in the doldrums and, for two years, as the Packers continued without success, he could not find a role which suited him. But all this was to change with the arrival of Vince Lombardi, who saw Hornung as a key figure at halfback in what would become the most feared offense in football for the best part of a decade.

He became the multi-purpose player who would rush, catch passes, return kicks and, occasionally, throw a pass. Cutting the figure of the handsome hero as he strode majestically or veered, scudded and scythed, he would earn a variety of nicknames, all of which condensed to 'The Golden Boy'. He did not win a league rushing title and, in Lombardi's system, he was never likely to be a league-leading receiver. But he certainly had a nose for the end zone and, with the help of an accurate boot, he racked up points at an astonishing rate. He was the NFL leading scorer for three consecutive seasons, beginning in 1959, his best year being

1960 when he set the existing NFL record with 176 points. In both 1960 and 1961 he was voted the NFL's Most Valuable Player. It was an image which gathered a little tarnish in 1963, when he was suspended by Commissioner Rozelle for placing bets on his own team. But with his reinstatement after an absence of one year, the gloss quickly returned.

TOM FEARS (UCLA); End: 6-2, 215; Los Angeles Rams (1948-56)

Career Pass Receiving

Year	No.	Yds.	Avg.	TDs
1948	51	698	13.7	4
1949	77	1,013	13.2	9
1950	84	1,116	13.3	7
1951	32	528	16.5	3
1952	48	600	12.5	6
1953	23	278	12.1	4
1954	36	546	15.2	3
1955	44	569	12.9	2
1956	5	49	9.8	0
Totals	**400**	**5,397**	**13.5**	**38**

Tom Fears entered the NFL fully expecting to be groomed as a defensive back, and he gave a glimpse of his enormous potential in his very first game, when he intercepted a pair of passes and returned one for a touchdown. But keen-eyed new head coach Clark Shaughnessy had seen enough to suggest an offensive role for his rookie and quickly set about the conversion.

Always the innovator, for some time Shaughnessy had been experimenting with a variety of passing systems. When he hit upon what became known as the 'Three End' formation, it quickly was apparent that Fears was a perfect component, lining up ten yards outside the right tackle.

Unusually big for a pure receiver, even forty years on, Fears also was a highly disciplined pattern runner, much in the manner of Raymond Berry and, in more recent times, Steve Largent. Faster than both Berry and Largent, Fears did not possess the elusive moves and speed of his partner, Elroy (Crazylegs) Hirsch, but no one was better at outsmarting opponents to carve out a

Tom Fears evades the grasp of the Bears' George McAfee in 1950.

Gene Upshaw leads his running back through the gap.

GENE UPSHAW (Texas A&I); Guard: 6-5, 255;
Oakland Raiders (1967-81)

downfield opening. He was a clutch performer – the target for the 'must' pass to gain a first down or win a game in the final two minutes.

But as the images are shrouded by the swirling mists of time it is the numbers which remain as the measure of his lasting greatness. In each of his first three seasons he led the league in receiving, amassing 212 receptions, at the time a total which had been exceeded only by the fabled Don Hutson in an NFL career. His 84 receptions in 1950 stood as the NFL record for a decade whilst his total of 18 receptions in one game against Green Bay in that year has never been equalled.

It is arguable which position in pro football is the least noticed, center or guard. A tackle usually is in full view, shoring up the outer reaches of the offensive line and often playing an obvious part in the blocking scheme as he wrestles with a defensive end or outside linebacker. For a brief moment, at least, the center is the focus of attention as he snaps the ball. But the guard is most often hidden away in the crowd.

However, some guards, by their dominance of an opponent at the line of scrimmage or in pass protection, and more conspicuously when pulling into open field to lead a ball-carrier, have a way of proclaiming their own existence. Gene Upshaw was one of the few players who excelled in all three aspects though he expressed a particular delight in pulling to lead a sweep.

The story goes that, in recognising the need for someone to take on Buck Buchanan, the 275-pound defensive right tackle of the Kansas City Chiefs whom the Oakland Raiders faced twice every year, Raiders managing general partner Al Davis decided that he needed the biggest and best guard he could find. Accordingly, Upshaw was the club's first-round pick in the 1967 draft. He repaid the team handsomely over a 15-year career during which he was selected to the Pro Bowl seven times and was voted All-Pro five times. In addition, his value to the Raiders as a team leader was immeasurable. Some time after becoming head coach in 1969, John Madden told the story, 'I named Gene captain in my first year . . . but his teammates have been voting him to that honour ever since'.

Upshaw's unquestioned talents and commitment saw him play 207 consecutive regular-season games before suffering an injury halfway through his final campaign. He has the distinction of being the first exclusive guard from the two-platoon era to be voted to the Pro Football Hall of Fame.

FRAN TARKENTON (Georgia); Quarterback: 6-0, 185; Minnesota Vikings (1961-66 and 1972-78), New York Giants (1967-71)

Career Passing

Year	Att.	Comp.	Pct.	Yds.	Int.	TDs
1961	280	157	56.1	1,997	17	18
1962	329	163	49.5	2,595	25	22
1963	297	170	57.2	2,311	15	15
1964	306	171	55.9	2,506	11	22
1965	329	171	52.0	2,609	11	19
1966	358	192	53.6	2,561	16	17
1967	377	204	54.1	3,088	19	29
1968	337	182	54.0	2,555	12	21
1969	409	220	53.8	2,918	8	23
1970	389	219	56.3	2,777	12	19
1971	386	226	58.5	2,567	21	11
1972	378	215	56.9	2,651	13	18
1973	274	169	61.7	2,113	7	15
1974	351	199	56.7	2,598	12	17
1975	425	273	64.2	2,994	13	25
1976	412	255	61.9	2,961	8	17
1977	258	155	60.1	1,734	14	9
1978	572	345	60.3	3,468	32	25
Totals	**6,467**	**3,686**	**57.0**	**47,003**	**266**	**342**

One thing that certainly can be said of Fran Tarkenton is that, while he was in the game, there never was a dull moment. A rookie for the expansion Minnesota Vikings in 1961, in the very first regular-season game for the franchise, Tarkenton came off the bench to pass for four touchdowns and run for another as the Vikings upset the Chicago Bears 37-13. It was the beginning of what ranks amongst the most exciting individual careers in all of professional sport. 'Exciting' was one word; 'enigmatic' and 'frustrating' were others. His head coach at that time, the tempestuous Norm Van

Fran Tarkenton prepares to unleash one of his 6,467 passes.

Brocklin, might prefer the word 'infuriating' as Tarkenton, often under pressure and forced to leave the pass pocket, would take off on wild and crazy scrambles, buying time while his receivers found an open space.

It was all too much for Van Brocklin, a former quarterback of the Rams and Philadelphia and future Hall-of-Famer. By 1966 he and Tarkenton were not even on speaking terms. In early 1967, the matter was resolved when Van Brocklin resigned and, two months later, Tarkenton was traded to the New York Giants.

The scrambling continued but with the selectivity and wisdom of a player beginning to come to his best. By 1972, when the Vikings traded to bring Tarkenton back, they knew that they were obtaining not only an unorthodox backfield threat but also one of the most prolific passers of all time. By the end of his career, Tarkenton had thrown more passes for more completions, more yards and more touchdowns than any player in history. Entering the 1990 season, all his records still are intact.

In those last seven seasons, he quarterbacked the Vikings to six NFC Central division titles and three Super Bowls.

HOW THE SEASON WORKS

The National Football League consists of twenty-eight teams divided into two **Conferences**, the American Football Conference (AFC) and the National Football Conference (NFC). Each conference has fourteen teams, and is subdivided into two five-team **Divisions** and one four-team **Division**. These are essentially based on sensible geographical considerations but also take into account the traditional rivalries which were in existence when the expanded NFL was restructured in 1970. The teams are listed below in order of their final 1989 division standings since this is of importance in arriving at a team's schedule (fixture list) for 1990.

THE SCHEDULE

When considering a team's schedule, it's best to set aside the four teams who each finished the 1989 season in fifth place in their divisions. Looking at the remaining twenty-four, every team plays twelve games against others from its own conference. Again, excluding the four fifth-placed teams, every team will play four games against teams from the rival conference (known as Interconference games), specifically to allow fans in the cities of one conference the opportunity of seeing the star players and teams of the other conference. The

AMERICAN FOOTBALL CONFERENCE

Eastern Division

		W	L	T
Buffalo	AE-1	9	7	0
Indianapolis	AE-2	8	8	0
Miami	AE-3	8	8	0
New England	AE-4	5	11	0
N.Y. Jets	AE-5	4	12	0

Central Division

		W	L	T
Cleveland	AC-1	9	6	1
Houston	AC-2	9	7	0
Pittsburgh	AC-3	9	7	0
Cincinnati	AC-4	8	8	0

Western Division

		W	L	T
Denver	AW-1	11	5	0
Kansas City	AW-2	8	7	1
L.A. Raiders	AW-3	8	8	0
Seattle	AW-4	7	9	0
San Diego	AW-5	6	10	0

NATIONAL FOOTBALL CONFERENCE

Eastern Division

		W	L	T
N.Y. Giants	NE-1	12	4	0
Philadelphia	NE-2	11	5	0
Washington	NE-3	10	6	0
Phoenix	NE-4	5	11	0
Dallas	NE-5	1	15	0

Central Division

		W	L	T
Minnesota	NC-1	10	6	0
Green Bay	NC-2	10	6	0
Detroit	NC-3	7	9	0
Chicago	NC-4	6	10	0
Tampa Bay	NC-5	5	11	0

Western Division

		W	L	T
San Francisco	NW-1	14	2	0
L.A. Rams	NW-2	11	5	0
New Orleans	NW-3	9	7	0
Atlanta	NW-4	3	13	0

structure of a team's schedule depends on whether it plays in a four-team or a five-team division.

Four-Team Division

A typical schedule, e.g., for the Pittsburgh Steelers, appears below. It is set out, deliberately not in chronological order but to emphasise that the schedule has a quite definite structure.

Pittsburgh Steelers (AFC Central)

Cincinnati Bengals	AFC Central	Home
Cincinnati Bengals	AFC Central	Away
Cleveland Browns	AFC Central	Home
Cleveland Browns	AFC Central	Away
Houston Oilers	AFC Central	Home
Houston Oilers	AFC Central	Away
Miami Dolphins	AFC East	Home
New England Patriots	AFC East	Home
New York Jets	AFC East	Away
Denver Broncos	AFC West	Away
Los Angeles Raiders	AFC West	Away
San Diego Chargers	AFC West	Home
Atlanta Falcons	NFC West	Home
Los Angeles Rams	NFC West	Home
New Orleans Saints	NFC West	Away
San Francisco 49ers	NFC West	Away

The Steelers will always play their division rivals, Cincinnati, Cleveland and Houston, both home and away. The flavour of intra-conference competition is maintained by six games, every year, against teams from outside their division but within their conference. There will always be three games against the AFC East and three against the AFC West. Again, every year, there will be four games against teams from a particular division of the rival conference, based on a three-year cycle. In 1990, they play the NFC West; in 1991, they will play teams from the NFC East and in 1992, the NFC Central. For every NFL team, a complete list of opponents, other than those within a team's own division, is arrived at by applying the following formula. The letters and numbers refer to Conference, Division and final standing in that division. Thus, the Phoenix Cardinals, who are in the National Conference Eastern Division and finished fourth in that division, are identified as NE-4. Equally, the Houston Oilers, who are in the American Conference Central Division and finished second in that division, are labelled AC-2.

AFC EAST-AE

AE-1		AE-2		AE-3		AE-4		AE-5	
H	**A**	**H**	**A**	**H**	**A**	**H**	**A**	**H**	**A**
AW-1	AC-1	AW-1	AC-2	AW-3	AC-1	AW-2	AC-3	AC-1	AC-2
AW-3	AC-2	AW-2	AC-4	AW-4	AC-3	AW-4	AC-4	AC-3	AC-4
NE-2	NE-1	NE-1	NE-2	NE-2	NE-1	NE-1	NE-2	AW-5	AW-5
NE-4	NE-3	NE-3	NE-4	NE-4	NE-3	NE-3	NE-4	NE-5	NC-5

AFC CENTRAL-AC

AC-1		AC-2		AC-3		AC-4	
H	**A**	**H**	**A**	**H**	**A**	**H**	**A**
AE-1	AE-5	AE-1	AW-2	AE-3	AE-5	AE-2	AW-3
AE-3	AW-1	AE-2	AW-4	AE-4	AW-1	AE-4	AW-4
AW-5	AW-2	AE-5	AW-5	AW-5	AW-3	AE-5	AW-5
NW-2	NW-1	NW-1	NW-2	NW-2	NW-1	NW-1	NW-2
NW-4	NW-3	NW-3	NW-4	NW-4	NW-3	NW-3	NW-4

AFC WEST-AW

AW-1		AW-2		AW-3		AW-4		AW-5	
H	**A**	**H**	**A**	**H**	**A**	**H**	**A**	**H**	**A**
AC-1	AE-1	AC-1	AE-2	AC-3	AE-1	AC-2	AE-3	AC-2	AC-1
AC-3	AE-2	AC-2	AE-4	AC-4	AE-3	AC-4	AE-4	AC-4	AC-3
NC-2	NC-1	NC-1	NC-2	NC-2	NC-1	NC-1	NC-2	AE-5	AE-5
NC-4	NC-3	NC-3	NC-4	NC-4	NC-3	NC-3	NC-4	NC-5	NE-5

NFC EAST-NE

NE-1		NE-2		NE-3		NE-4		NE-5	
H	**A**	**H**	**A**	**H**	**A**	**H**	**A**	**H**	**A**
NC-1	NW-1	NC-1	NW-2	NC-4	NC-3	NC-2	NW-3	NC-5	NC-5
NC-3	NW-2	NC-2	NW-4	NW-3	NW-1	NC-4	NW-4	NW-1	NW-2
AE-1	AE-2	AE-2	AE-1	AE-1	AE-2	AE-2	AE-1	NW-3	NW-4
AE-3	AE-4	AE-4	AE-3	AE-3	AE-4	AE-4	AE-3	AW-5	AE-5

NFC CENTRAL-NC

NC-1		NC-2		NC-3		NC-4		NC-5	
H	**A**	**H**	**A**	**H**	**A**	**H**	**A**	**H**	**A**
NW-1	NE-1	NW-2	NE-2	NE-3	NE-1	NW-2	NE-3	NE-5	NE-5
NW-3	NE-2	NW-1	NE-4	NW-4	NW-3	NW-4	NE-4	NW-2	NW-1
AW-1	AW-2	AW-2	AW-1	AW-1	AW-2	AW-2	AW-1	NW-4	NW-3
AW-3	AW-4	AW-4	AW-3	AW-3	AW-4	AW-4	AW-3	AE-5	AW-5

NFC WEST-NW

NW-1		NW-2		NW-3		NW-4	
H	**A**	**H**	**A**	**H**	**A**	**H**	**A**
NC-5	NC-1	NE-1	NC-2	NC-3	NC-1	NE-2	NC-3
NE-1	NC-2	NE-2	NC-4	NC-5	NE-3	NE-4	NC-4
NE-3	NE-5	NE-5	NC-5	NE-4	NE-5	NE-5	NC-5
AC-1	AC-2	AC-2	AC-1	AC-1	AC-2	AC-2	AC-1
AC-3	AC-4	AC-4	AC-3	AC-3	AC-4	AC-4	AC-3

Five-Team Division (Top Four Teams Only)

In the NFC East the schedules for the top four teams have identical structure and include home and away games against the other four teams in the division. Each of the top four teams plays two games against NFC Central teams and two against the NFC West. Also, they play the top four teams in the AFC East as part of their three-year cycle of interconference games. In 1991, they will play teams from the AFC Central and in 1992, the AFC West. Below is the schedule structure for the New York Giants.

New York Giants (NFC East)

Dallas Cowboys	NFC East	Home
Dallas Cowboys	NFC East	Away
Philadelphia Eagles	NFC East	Home
Philadelphia Eagles	NFC East	Away
Phoenix Cardinals	NFC East	Home
Phoenix Cardinals	NFC East	Away
Washington Redskins	NFC East	Home
Washington Redskins	NFC East	Away
Detroit Lions	NFC Central	Home
Minnesota Vikings	NFC Central	Home
Los Angeles Rams	NFC West	Away
San Francisco 49ers	NFC West	Away
Buffalo Bills	AFC East	Home
Indianapolis Colts	AFC East	Away
Miami Dolphins	AFC East	Home
New England Patriots	AFC East	Away

Fifth-Placed Teams

In the AFC, the two fifth-placed teams will each play eight games against teams from their own division and will always play single games against each of the four AFC Central division teams. In the NFC, the two fifth-placed teams each play eight games against teams within their own division and will always play single games against the four NFC West teams. Each of the four fifth-placed teams is guaranteed home and away games against the other fifth-placed team in its own conference, and single games against the two fifth-placed teams from the rival conference. The schedule structures for all four teams are set out as follows:

New York Jets (AE-5)

AFC East		8 games
AFC Central		4 games
San Diego	(AW-5)	Home
San Diego	(AW-5)	Away
Dallas	(NE-5)	Home
Tampa Bay	(NC-5)	Away

San Diego (AW-5)

AFC West		8 games
AFC Central		4 games
New York Jets	(AE-5)	Home
New York Jets	(AE-5)	Away
Dallas	(NE-5)	Away
Tampa Bay	(NC-5)	Home

Dallas (NE-5)

NFC East		8 games
NFC West		4 games
Tampa Bay	(NC-5)	Home
Tampa Bay	(NC-5)	Away
New York Jets	(AE-5)	Away
San Diego	(AW-5)	Home

Tampa Bay (NC-5)

NFC Central		8 games
NFC West		4 games
Dallas	(NE-5)	Home
Dallas	(NE-5)	Away
New York Jets	(AE-5)	Home
San Diego	(AW-5)	Away

THE PLAYOFFS

On completion of the regular season, each conference holds an elimination competition known as the Playoffs. Under a new playoff format introduced for the 1990 season, the teams involved will be the three division winners and three Wild Card teams, namely, those three, other than the division winners, who have the best won-lost-tied records. In 1990, the three Wild Cards, together with the division winner with the poorest record, will contest the first round of the playoffs with the victors joining the two division winners with the better records in the conference semi-finals. Had this system been in operation for the 1989 season, Kansas City (AFC) and Green Bay (NFC) would have advanced to the playoffs, where they would have been joined in the first round by division winners Buffalo (AE-1) and Minnesota (NC-1). Operating on the best-versus-worst principle, the team with the best record will play the team which has the poorest record.

Home-Field Advantage in the Playoffs

The game site is determined on the best-versus-worst principle, with the team which has the better won-lost-tied record always given home-field advantage. Taking the AFC as the example, in the 1989 playoffs the pecking order of teams was as follows:

	W	L	T
Denver†	11	5	0
Cleveland†	9	6	1
Buffalo†	9	7	0
Houston*	9	7	0
Pittsburgh*	9	7	0

† Division Champions
* Wild Card teams

TIE-BREAKING PROCEDURES

Ties are broken by the following list of criteria:

Teams in the same division

A: *Two teams*
1. Head-to-head (best record in games played between the two teams)
2. Best record in games played within the division
3. Best record in games played within the conference
4. Best record in common games
5. Best net points scored in division games (just like goal difference in soccer)
6. Best net points in all games

B: *Three or More Teams* (if two teams remain tied after all other teams are eliminated, the tie-breaking procedure reverts to A:1.)
1. Head-to-head (best record in games played between the teams)
2. Best record in games played within the division
3. Best record in games played within the conference
4. Best record in common games
5. Best net points in division games
6. Best net points in all games

Tie-Breakers for the Wild Card places

(a) If the teams are from the same division, the division tie-breaker is applied.
(b) If the teams are from different divisions, the following procedure is adopted:

C: *Two Teams*
1. Head-to-head (if they have played each other)
2. Best record in games played within the conference
3. Best record in common games (minimum of four)
4. Best average net points in conference games
5. Best net points in all games

D: *Three or More Teams* (If two teams remain tied after all other teams are eliminated, the tie-breaking procedure reverts to A:1, or C:1, whichever is applicable.)
1. Head-to-head sweep (this applies only if one team has either beaten or lost to all the others)
2. Best record in games played within the conference
3. Best record in common games (minimum of four)
4. Best average net points in conference games
5. Best net points in all games

1989 Tie-Breakers

Houston-Pittsburgh (Home-field advantage):
A:1; Houston beat Pittsburgh twice.
Philadelphia-L.A. Rams (Home-field advantage):
C:3; Order: Philadelphia (7-3), Rams (5-4).

THE SUPER BOWL

Though the obvious comparison is with the FA Cup final, the Super Bowl is best seen as the culmination of an end-of-season knockout competition, involving the champions of six mini-leagues together with the Wild Card teams, the latter being considered, perhaps, as potential giant-killers. (Only one team, the Oakland Raiders, has won the Super Bowl Championship starting out as a Wild Card.) Unlike for the FA Cup final, the Super Bowl venue changes from year to year and, since the site is chosen some three years in advance, it is possible for one team to be playing 'at home'. This has never occurred, though both the Los Angeles Rams and the San Francisco 49ers were close to home when they played in Super Bowls XIV and XIX respectively. In selecting the venue, great importance is placed on the likelihood of good weather. Consequently, with the exception of the Pontiac Silverdome (this is a domed stadium), all past Super Bowl stadia have been in the 'sunshine belt', stretching from Florida to California. Super Bowl XXV will be played at Tampa Stadium, Tampa, Florida, while for only the second time the game will go to a cold northern state when Super Bowl XXVI will be held in Hubert H. Humphrey Metrodome, Minneapolis, Minnesota.

THE PRO BOWL

At the end of the season, the best players from each conference fly off to Hawaii to give the fans out there a treat. The teams are selected by a ballot of head coaches and players in each conference. Each team has two equal votes, those being the head coach's and a consensus of the players' selections. Coaches and players may vote only for players in their own conference and may not vote for players from their own teams. In the most recent AFC-NFC Pro Bowl, a Dave Krieg-inspired rally could not overhaul the NFC, which held out for a 27-21 win extending its lead in the series to 12-8.

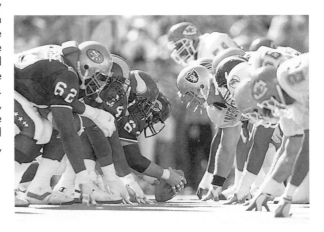

RIGHT: The linemen, wearing their respective team helmets, square off in the 1990 Pro Bowl.

AFC-NFC Pro Bowl Results – NFC leads series 12-8

YEAR	DATE	WINNER	LOSER	SITE	ATTENDANCE
1990	Feb. 4	NFC 27	AFC 21	Honolulu	50,445
1989	Jan. 29	NFC 34	AFC 3	Honolulu	50,113
1988	Feb. 7	AFC 15	NFC 6	Honolulu	50,113
1987	Feb. 1	AFC 10	NFC 6	Honolulu	50,101
1986	Feb. 2	NFC 28	AFC 24	Honolulu	50,101
1985	Jan. 27	AFC 22	NFC 14	Honolulu	50,385
1984	Jan. 29	NFC 45	AFC 3	Honolulu	50,445
1983	Feb. 6	NFC 20	AFC 19	Honolulu	49,883
1982	Jan. 31	AFC 16	NFC 13	Honolulu	50,402
1981	Feb. 1	NFC 21	AFC 7	Honolulu	50,360
1980	Jan. 27	NFC 37	AFC 27	Honolulu	49,800
1979	Jan. 29	NFC 13	AFC 7	Los Angeles	46,281
1978	Jan. 23	NFC 14	AFC 13	Tampa	51,337
1977	Jan. 17	AFC 24	NFC 14	Seattle	64,752
1976	Jan. 26	NFC 23	AFC 20	New Orleans	30,546
1975	Jan. 20	NFC 17	AFC 10	Miami	26,484
1974	Jan. 20	AFC 15	NFC 13	Kansas City	66,918
1973	Jan. 21	AFC 33	NFC 28	Dallas	37,091
1972	Jan. 23	AFC 26	NFC 13	Los Angeles	53,647
1971	Jan. 24	NFC 27	AFC 6	Los Angeles	48,222

BELOW: NFC cornerback Jerry Gray (L.A. Rams) was voted the Pro Bowl MVP.

PRO BOWL ROSTERS

(Original selections – starters in capitals)

OFFENSE	AMERICAN FOOTBALL CONFERENCE		NATIONAL FOOTBALL CONFERENCE	
Wide Receivers	ANDRE REED	Buffalo	JERRY RICE	San Francisco
	WEBSTER SLAUGHTER	Cleveland	STERLING SHARPE	Green Bay
	Anthony Miller	San Diego	Henry Ellard	L.A. Rams
	Brian Blades	Seattle	John Taylor	San Francisco
Tight Ends	RODNEY HOLMAN	Cincinnati	KEITH JACKSON	Philadelphia
	Ferrell Edmunds	Miami	Steve Jordan	Minnesota
Tackles	ANTHONY MUNOZ	Cincinnati	GARY ZIMMERMAN	Minnesota
	CHRIS HINTON	Indianapolis	JACKIE SLATER	L.A. Rams
	Tunch Ilkin	Pittsburgh	Luis Sharpe	Phoenix
Guards	MIKE MUNCHAK	Houston	RANDALL McDANIEL	Minnesota
	BRUCE MATTHEWS	Houston	TOM NEWBERRY	L.A. Rams
	Max Montoya	Cincinnati	Guy McIntyre	San Francisco
Centers	RAY DONALDSON	Indianapolis	JAY HILGENBERG	Chicago
	Kent Hull	Buffalo	Doug Smith	L.A. Rams
Quarterbacks	WARREN MOON	Houston	JOE MONTANA	San Francisco
	Boomer Esiason	Cincinnati	Don Majkowski	Green Bay
Running Backs	CHRISTIAN OKOYE	Kansas City	BARRY SANDERS	Detroit
	JAMES BROOKS	Cincinnati	NEAL ANDERSON	Chicago
	Thurman Thomas	Buffalo	Dalton Hilliard	New Orleans
	Eric Dickerson	Indianapolis	Roger Craig	San Francisco

DEFENSE				
Defensive Ends	BRUCE SMITH	Buffalo	CHRIS DOLEMAN	Minnesota
	LEE WILLIAMS	San Diego	REGGIE WHITE	Philadelphia
	Howie Long	L.A. Raiders	Charles Mann	Washington
Interior Linemen	MICHAEL DEAN PERRY	Cleveland	KEITH MILLARD	Minnesota
	Greg Kragen	Denver	Jerry Ball	Detroit
Outside Linebackers	DERRICK THOMAS	Kansas City	TIM HARRIS	Green Bay
	CLAY MATTHEWS	Cleveland	LAWRENCE TAYLOR	N.Y. Giants
	Leslie O'Neal	San Diego	Kevin Greene	L.A. Rams
			Pat Swilling*	New Orleans
Inside Linebackers	KARL MECKLENBURG	Denver	MIKE SINGLETARY	Chicago
	JOHN OFFERDAHL	Miami	CHRIS SPIELMAN	Detroit
	Shane Conlan	Buffalo	Vaughan Johnson	New Orleans
	Mike Johnson*	Cleveland		
Cornerbacks	ALBERT LEWIS	Kansas City	JERRY GRAY	L.A. Rams
	FRANK MINNIFIELD	Cleveland	CARL LEE	Minnesota
	Kevin Ross	Kansas City	Eric Allen	Philadelphia
Safeties	DAVID FULCHER	Cincinnati	JOEY BROWNER	Minnesota
	ERIK McMILLAN	N.Y. Jets	RONNIE LOTT	San Francisco
	Dennis Smith	Denver	Tim McDonald	Phoenix

SPECIAL TEAMS				
Placekicker	DAVID TREADWELL	Denver	ED MURRAY	Detroit
Punter	REGGIE ROBY	Miami	RICH CAMARILLO	Phoenix
Kick Returner	ROD WOODSON	Pittsburgh	DAVE MEGGETT	N.Y. Giants
Specialist	RUFUS PORTER	Seattle	RON WOLFLEY	Phoenix
Head Coach	BUD CARSON	Cleveland	JOHN ROBINSON	L.A. Rams

* Special selection made by head coach

An All-Pro Team

Anyone can pick his or her own All-Pro team and just about everyone does. Here's my dream team.

Wide Receivers	Jerry Rice	San Francisco
	Sterling Sharpe	Green Bay
Tight End	Rodney Holman	Cincinnati
Tackles	Anthony Munoz	Cincinnati
	Gary Zimmerman	Minnesota
Guards	Mike Munchak	Houston
	Bill Fralic	Atlanta
Center	Jay Hilgenberg	Chicago
Quarterback	Joe Montana	San Francisco
Running Backs	Bo Jackson	L.A. Raiders
	Barry Sanders	Detroit
Defensive Ends	Bruce Smith	Buffalo
	Reggie White	Philadelphia
Defensive Tackles	Keith Millard	Minnesota
	Michael Dean Perry	Cleveland
Outside Linebackers	Lawrence Taylor	N.Y. Giants
	Tim Harris	Green Bay
Inside Linebackers	Mike Singletary	Chicago
	Chris Spielman	Detroit
Safeties	Joey Browner	Minnesota
	Ronnie Lott	San Francisco
Cornerbacks	Albert Lewis	Kansas City
	Jerry Gray	L.A. Rams
Placekicker	Eddie Murray	Detroit
Punter	Sean Landeta	N.Y. Giants
Punt Returner	Deion Sanders	Atlanta
Kickoff Returner	Dennis Gentry	Chicago
Special-team Specialist	Rufus Porter	Seattle
Head Coach	Chuck Noll	Pittsburgh

ABOVE: Anthony Munoz (#78) is the best left tackle of the modern era.

BELOW LEFT: Outside linebacker Lawrence Taylor (#56) has the ability to dominate the course of a game.

BELOW: Dennis Gentry has scored touchdowns on kickoff returns of 88, 91 and 94 yards.

CHAPTER FOUR

ALL-TIME RECORDS

CHAMPIONS 1920-1989

National Football League 1920-1969
(Until 1933 based solely on regular-season play)

1920	Akron Pros
1921	Chicago Staleys
1922	Canton Bulldogs
1923	Canton Bulldogs
1924	Cleveland Bulldogs
1925	Chicago Cardinals
1926	Frankford Yellow Jackets
1927	New York Giants
1928	Providence Steam Roller
1929	Green Bay Packers
1930	Green Bay Packers
1931	Green Bay Packers
1932	Chicago Bears 9 – Portsmouth Spartans 0 (Championship Playoff)

NFL Championship Games 1933-69

1933	Chicago Bears 23 – New York Giants 21
1934	New York Giants 30 – Chicago Bears 13
1935	Detroit Lions 26 – New York Giants 7
1936	Green Bay Packers 21 – Boston Redskins 6
1937	Washington Redskins 28 – Chicago Bears 21
1938	New York Giants 23 – Green Bay Packers 17
1939	Green Bay Packers 27 – New York Giants 0
1940	Chicago Bears 73 – Washington Redskins 0
1941	Chicago Bears 37 – New York Giants 9
1942	Washington Redskins 14 – Chicago Bears 6
1943	Chicago Bears 41 – Washington Redskins 21
1944	Green Bay Packers 14 – New York Giants 7
1945	Cleveland Rams 15 – Washington Redskins 14
1946	Chicago Bears 24 – New York Giants 14
1947	Chicago Cardinals 28 – Philadelphia Eagles 21
1948	Philadelphia Eagles 7 – Chicago Cardinals 0
1949	Philadelphia Eagles 14 – Los Angeles Rams 0
1950	Cleveland Browns 30 – Los Angeles Rams 28
1951	Los Angeles Rams 24 – Cleveland Browns 17
1952	Detroit Lions 17 – Cleveland Browns 7
1953	Detroit Lions 17 – Cleveland Browns 16
1954	Cleveland Browns 56 – Detroit Lions 10
1955	Cleveland Browns 38 – Los Angeles Rams 14
1956	New York Giants 47 – Chicago Bears 7
1957	Detroit Lions 59 – Cleveland Browns 14
1958	Baltimore Colts 23 – New York Giants 17 (OT)
1959	Baltimore Colts 31 – New York Giants 16
1960	Philadelphia Eagles 17 – Green Bay Packers 13
1961	Green Bay Packers 37 – New York Giants 0
1962	Green Bay Packers 16 – New York Giants 7
1963	Chicago Bears 14 – New York Giants 10
1964	Cleveland Browns 27 – Baltimore Colts 0
1965	Green Bay Packers 23 – Cleveland Browns 12
1966	Green Bay Packers 34 – Dallas Cowboys 27
1967	Green Bay Packers 21 – Dallas Cowboys 17
1968	Baltimore Colts 34 – Cleveland Browns 0
1969	Minnesota Vikings 27 – Cleveland Browns 7

AFL Championship Games 1960-1969

1960	Houston Oilers 24 – Los Angeles Chargers 16
1961	Houston Oilers 10 – San Diego Chargers 3
1962	Dallas Texans 20 – Houston Oilers 17 (OT)
1963	San Diego Chargers 51 – Boston Patriots 10
1964	Buffalo Bills 20 – San Diego Chargers 7
1965	Buffalo Bills 23 – San Diego Chargers 0
1966	Kansas City Chiefs 31 – Buffalo Bills 7
1967	Oakland Raiders 40 – Houston Oilers 7
1968	New York Jets 27 – Oakland Raiders 23
1969	Kansas City Chiefs 17 – Oakland Raiders 7

CONFERENCE CHAMPIONSHIP GAMES 1970-1989

NFC

1970	Dallas Cowboys 17 – San Francisco 49ers 10
1971	Dallas Cowboys 14 – San Francisco 49ers 3
1972	Washington Redskins 26 – Dallas Cowboys 3
1973	Minnesota Vikings 27 – Dallas Cowboys 10
1974	Minnesota Vikings 14 – Los Angeles Rams 10
1975	Dallas Cowboys 37 – Los Angeles Rams 7
1976	Minnesota Vikings 24 – Los Angeles Rams 13
1977	Dallas Cowboys 23 – Minnesota Vikings 6
1978	Dallas Cowboys 28 – Los Angeles Rams 0
1979	Los Angeles Rams 9 – Tampa Bay Buccaneers 0
1980	Philadelphia Eagles 20 – Dallas Cowboys 7
1981	San Francisco 49ers 28 – Dallas Cowboys 27
1982	Washington Redskins 31 – Dallas Cowboys 17

1983	Washington Redskins 24 – San Francisco 49ers 21
1984	San Francisco 49ers 23 – Chicago Bears 0
1985	Chicago Bears 24 – Los Angeles Rams 0
1986	New York Giants 17 – Washington Redskins 0
1987	Washington Redskins 17 – Minnesota Vikings 10
1988	San Francisco 49ers 28 – Chicago Bears 3
1989	San Francisco 49ers 30 – Los Angeles Rams 3

AFC

1970	Baltimore Colts 27 – Oakland Raiders 17
1971	Miami Dolphins 21 – Baltimore Colts 0
1972	Miami Dolphins 21 – Pittsburgh Steelers 17
1973	Miami Dolphins 27 – Oakland Raiders 10
1974	Pittsburgh Steelers 24 – Oakland Raiders 13
1975	Pittsburgh Steelers 16 – Oakland Raiders 10
1976	Oakland Raiders 24 – Pittsburgh Steelers 7
1977	Denver Broncos 20 – Oakland Raiders 17
1978	Pittsburgh Steelers 34 – Houston Oilers 5
1979	Pittsburgh Steelers 27 – Houston Oilers 13
1980	Oakland Raiders 34 – San Diego Chargers 27
1981	Cincinnati Bengals 27 – San Diego Chargers 7
1982	Miami Dolphins 14 – New York Jets 0
1983	Los Angeles Raiders 30 – Seattle Seahawks 14
1984	Miami Dolphins 45 – Pittsburgh Steelers 28
1985	New England Patriots 31 – Miami Dolphins 14
1986	Denver Broncos 23 – Cleveland Browns 20 (OT)
1987	Denver Broncos 38 – Cleveland Browns 33
1988	Cincinnati Bengals 21 – Buffalo Bills 10
1989	Denver Broncos 37 – Cleveland Browns 21

Steve Largent retired in possession of all the major NFL pass receiving records.

Super Bowl 1966-1989

Season	SB	Winner		Loser		Stadium	Attendance
1966	I	Green Bay	35	Kansas City	10	Los Angeles Coliseum	61,946
1967	II	Green Bay	33	Oakland	14	Miami Orange Bowl	75,546
1968	III	N.Y. Jets	16	Baltimore	7	Miami Orange Bowl	75,389
1969	IV	Kansas City	23	Minnesota	7	New Orleans Tulane Stadium	80,562
1970	V	Baltimore	16	Dallas	13	Miami Orange Bowl	79,204
1971	VI	Dallas	24	Miami	3	New Orleans Tulane Stadium	81,023
1972	VII	Miami	14	Washington	7	Los Angeles Coliseum	90,182
1973	VIII	Miami	24	Minnesota	7	Houston Rice Stadium	71,882
1974	IX	Pittsburgh	16	Minnesota	6	New Orleans Tulane Stadium	80,997
1975	X	Pittsburgh	21	Dallas	17	Miami Orange Bowl	80,187
1976	XI	Oakland	32	Minnesota	14	Pasadena Rose Bowl	103,438
1977	XII	Dallas	27	Denver	10	New Orleans Superdome	75,583
1978	XIII	Pittsburgh	35	Dallas	31	Miami Orange Bowl	79,484
1979	XIV	Pittsburgh	31	L.A. Rams	19	Pasadena Rose Bowl	103,985
1980	XV	Oakland	27	Philadelphia	10	New Orleans Superdome	76,135
1981	XVI	San Francisco	26	Cincinnati	21	Pontiac Silverdome	81,270
1982	XVII	Washington	27	Miami	17	Pasadena Rose Bowl	103,667
1983	XVIII	L.A. Raiders	38	Washington	9	Tampa Stadium	72,920
1984	XIX	San Francisco	38	Miami	16	Stanford Stadium	84,059
1985	XX	Chicago	46	New England	10	New Orleans Superdome	73,818
1986	XXI	N.Y. Giants	39	Denver	20	Pasadena Rose Bowl	101,063
1987	XXII	Washington	42	Denver	10	San Diego Jack Murphy Stadium	73,302
1988	XXIII	San Francisco	20	Cincinnati	16	Miami Joe Robbie Stadium	75,179
1989	XXIV	San Francisco	55	Denver	10	New Orleans Superdome	72,919

ALL-TIME INDIVIDUAL RECORDS
(Regular Season only — New Records and Records tied are in bold type)

CAREER BEST

SEASONS PLAYED	26	George Blanda
GAMES PLAYED	340	George Blanda
POINTS	2,002	George Blanda (9-TD, 943-EP, 335-FG)
EXTRA POINTS	943	George Blanda
FIELD GOALS	373	Jan Stenerud
TOUCHDOWNS		
Rushing and Pass Receiving	126	Jim Brown (106-R, 20-P)
Rushing	110	Walter Payton
Pass Receiving	**100**	**Steve Largent**
Passes Thrown	342	Fran Tarkenton
By Interception Return	9	Ken Houston
By Punt Return	8	Jack Christiansen
		Rick Upchurch
By Kickoff Return	6	Ollie Matson
		Gale Sayers
		Travis Williams
By Fumble Recovery Return	4	Billy Thompson
YARDAGE		
Rushing	16,726	Walter Payton
Pass Receiving	**13,089**	**Steve Largent**
Passing	47,003	Fran Tarkenton
HOW MANY TIMES		
Pass Receptions	**819**	**Steve Largent**
Passes Completed	3,686	Fran Tarkenton
Interceptions	81	Paul Krause
100-Yard Rushing Games	77	Walter Payton
100-Yard Pass Receiving Games	50	Don Maynard
1,000-Yard Rushing Seasons	10	Walter Payton
1,000-Yard Pass Receiving Seasons	8	Steve Largent
MOST SEASONS LEADING LEAGUE		
Points	5	Don Hutson, Green Bay 1940-44
		Gino Cappelletti, Boston 1961, 1963-66
Extra Points	8	George Blanda, Chicago Bears 1956, Houston 1961-62, Oakland 1967-69, 1972, 1974
Field Goals	5	Lou Groza, Cleveland Browns 1950, 1952-54, 1957
Touchdowns	8	Don Hutson, Green Bay 1935-38, 1941-44
Touchdowns, Rushing	5	Jim Brown, Cleveland Browns 1957-59, 1963, 1965
Touchdowns, Pass Receiving	9	Don Hutson, Green Bay 1935-38, 1940-44
Touchdowns, Passes Thrown	4	Johnny Unitas, Baltimore 1957-60
		Len Dawson, Dallas Texans 1962, Kansas City 1963, 1965-66
Yards, Rushing	8	Jim Brown, Cleveland Browns 1957-61, 1963-65
Yards, Pass Receiving	7	Don Hutson, Green Bay 1936, 1938-39, 1941-44
Yards, Passing	5	Sonny Jurgensen, Philadelphia 1961-62, Washington 1966-67, 1969
Pass Receptions	8	Don Hutson, Green Bay 1936-37, 1939, 1941-45
Passes Completed	5	Sammy Baugh, Washington 1937, 1943, 1945, 1947-48
Pass Interceptions	3	Everson Walls, Dallas 1981-82, 1985

SEASON BEST

POINTS	176	Paul Hornung, Green Bay 1960 (15-TD, 41-EP, 15-FG)
EXTRA POINTS	66	Uwe von Schamann, Miami 1984
FIELD GOALS	35	Ali Haji-Sheikh, N.Y. Giants 1983

TOUCHDOWNS

Rushing and Pass Receiving	24	John Riggins, Washington 1983 (24-R)
Rushing	24	John Riggins, Washington 1983
Pass Receiving	22	Jerry Rice, San Francisco 1987
Passes Thrown	48	Dan Marino, Miami 1984
By Interception Return	4	Ken Houston, Houston 1971
		Jim Kearney, Kansas City 1972
By Punt Return	4	Jack Christiansen, Detroit 1951
		Rick Upchurch, Denver 1976
By Kickoff Return	4	Travis Williams, Green Bay 1967
		Cecil Turner, Chicago 1970
By Fumble Recovery Return	2	By many players

YARDAGE

Rushing	2,105	Eric Dickerson, L.A. Rams 1984
Pass Receiving	1,746	Charley Hennigan, Houston 1961
Passing	5,084	Dan Marino, Miami 1984

HOW MANY TIMES

Pass Receptions	106	Art Monk, Washington 1984
Passes Completed	378	Dan Marino, Miami 1986
Interceptions	14	Dick (Night Train) Lane, L.A. Rams 1952

GAME BEST

POINTS	40	Ernie Nevers (6-TD, 4-EP), Chicago Cardinals v Chicago Bears 1929
EXTRA POINTS	9	Pat Harder, Chicago Cardinals v N.Y. Giants 1948
		Bob Waterfield, L.A. Rams v Baltimore 1950
		Charlie Gogolak, Washington v N.Y. Giants 1966
FIELD GOALS	7	Jim Bakken, St Louis v Pittsburgh 1967
		Rich Karlis, Minnesota v L.A. Rams 1989

TOUCHDOWNS

All methods of scoring	6	Ernie Nevers (6-R), Chicago Cardinals v Chicago Bears 1929
		Dub Jones (4-R, 2-P), Cleveland v Chicago Bears 1951
		Gale Sayers (4-R, 1-P, 1-Ret), Chicago Bears v San Francisco 1965
Rushing	6	Ernie Nevers, Chicago Cardinals v Chicago Bears 1929
Pass Receiving	5	Bob Shaw, Chicago Cardinals v Baltimore 1950
		Kellen Winslow, San Diego v Oakland 1981
Passes Thrown	7	Sid Luckman, Chicago Bears v N.Y. Giants 1943
		Adrian Burk, Philadelphia v Washington 1954
		George Blanda, Houston v N.Y. Titans 1961
		Y.A. Tittle, N.Y. Giants v Washington 1962
		Joe Kapp, Minnesota v Baltimore 1969

YARDAGE

Rushing	275	Walter Payton, Chicago v Minnesota 1977
Pass Receiving	**336**	**Willie (Flipper) Anderson, L.A. Rams v New Orleans 1989**
Passing	554	Norm Van Brocklin, L.A. Rams v N.Y. Yanks 1951

HOW MANY TIMES

Rushing Attempts	45	Jamie Morris, Washington v Cincinnati 1988
Pass Receptions	18	Tom Fears, L.A. Rams v Green Bay 1950
Passes Completed	42	Richard Todd, N.Y. Jets v San Francisco 1980
Interceptions	4	By many players

LONGEST

Touchdown Rushing	99 yds	Tony Dorsett, Dallas v Minnesota 1983
Touchdown Pass Receiving	99 yds	Andy Farkas (from Filchock), Washington v Pittsburgh 1939
		Bobby Mitchell (from Izo), Washington v Cleveland 1963
		Pat Studstill (from Sweetan), Detroit v Baltimore 1966
		Gerry Allen (from Jurgensen), Washington v Chicago 1968
		Cliff Branch (from Plunkett), L.A. Raiders v Washington 1983
		Mike Quick (from Jaworski), Philadelphia v Atlanta 1985
Field Goal	63 yds	Tom Dempsey, New Orleans v Detroit 1970

Punt Return (All TDs)	98 yds	Gil LeFebvre, Cincinnati v Brooklyn 1933
		Charlie West, Minnesota v Washington 1968
		Dennis Morgan, Dallas v St Louis 1974
Kickoff Return (All TDs)	106 yds	Al Carmichael, Green Bay v Chicago Bears 1956
		Noland Smith, Kansas City v Denver 1967
		Roy Green, St Louis v Dallas 1979
Interception Return (TD)	103 yds	Vencie Glenn, San Diego v Denver 1987
Fumble Recovery Return (TD)	104 yds	Jack Tatum, Oakland v Green Bay 1972

TEAM RECORDS

Most Championships	11	Green Bay, 1929-31, 1936, 1939, 1944, 1961-62, 1965-67
	9	Chicago Staleys/Bears, 1921, 1932-33, 1940-41, 1943, 1946, 1963, 1985
	5	N.Y. Giants, 1927, 1934, 1938, 1956, 1986
	4	Baltimore, 1958-59, 1968, 1970
		Cleveland Browns, 1950, 1954-55, 1964
		Detroit, 1935, 1952-53, 1957
		Oakland/L.A. Raiders, 1967, 1976, 1980, 1983
		Pittsburgh, 1974-75, 1978-79
		San Francisco, 1981, 1984, 1988-89
		Washington, 1937, 1942, 1982, 1987
Most Consecutive Games Won (inc. playoffs)	18	Chicago Bears, 1933-34 and 1941-42
		Miami, 1972-73
Most Consecutive Games Won (exc. playoffs)	17	Chicago Bears, 1933-34
Most Consecutive Games Lost	26	Tampa Bay, 1976-77
Most Points in a Season	541	Washington, 1983
Fewest Points in a Season (Since 1932)	37	Cincinnati-St Louis, 1934
Most Points in a Game	72	Washington v N.Y. Giants, 1966
Most Points (Both Teams) in a Game	113	Washington v N.Y. Giants, 1966
Fewest Points (Both Teams) in a Game	0	Many teams; last time N.Y. Giants v Detroit, 1943

ALL-TIME TOP TWENTY
(1989 Active players in capitals)
All-Time Leading Rushers

		Yrs.	Att.	Yards	Ave.	TDs
1.	Walter Payton	13	3,838	16,726	4.4	110
2.	Tony Dorsett	12	2,936	12,739	4.3	77
3.	Jim Brown	9	2,359	12,312	5.2	106
4.	Franco Harris	13	2,949	12,120	4.1	91
5.	John Riggins	14	2,916	11,352	3.9	104
6.	O.J. Simpson	11	2,404	11,236	4.7	61
7.	ERIC DICKERSON	7	2,450	11,226	4.6	82
8.	Earl Campbell	8	2,187	9,407	4.3	74
9.	OTTIS ANDERSON	11	2,274	9,317	4.1	69
10.	Jim Taylor	10	1,941	8,597	4.4	83
11.	Joe Perry	14	1,737	8,378	4.8	53
12.	Larry Csonka	11	1,891	8,081	4.3	64
13.	GERALD RIGGS	8	1,788	7,465	4.2	52
14.	Mike Pruitt	11	1,844	7,378	4.0	51
15.	MARCUS ALLEN	8	1,781	7,275	4.1	63
16.	Leroy Kelly	10	1,727	7,274	4.2	74
17.	George Rogers	7	1,692	7,176	4.2	54
18.	FREEMAN McNEIL	9	1,605	7,146	4.5	30
19.	John Henry Johnson	13	1,571	6,803	4.3	48
20.	Wilbert Montgomery	9	1,540	6,789	4.4	45

All-Time Leading Receivers

		Yrs.	No.	Yards	Ave.	TDs
1.	STEVE LARGENT	14	819	13,089	16.0	100
2.	Charlie Joiner	18	750	12,146	16.2	65
3.	ART MONK	10	662	9,165	13.8	47
4.	Charley Taylor	13	649	9,110	14.0	79
5.	OZZIE NEWSOME	12	639	7,740	12.1	45
6.	Don Maynard	15	633	11,834	18.7	88
7.	Raymond Berry	13	631	9,275	14.7	68
8.	JAMES LOFTON	12	607	11,251	18.5	57
9.	Harold Carmichael	14	590	8,985	15.2	79
10.	Fred Biletnikoff	14	589	8,974	15.2	76
11.	Harold Jackson	15	579	10,372	17.9	76
12.	Lionel Taylor	10	567	7,195	12.7	45
13.	Wes Chandler	11	559	8,966	16.0	56
14.	Lance Alworth	11	542	10,266	18.9	85
15.	Kellen Winslow	9	541	6,741	12.5	45
16.	John Stallworth	14	537	8,723	16.2	63
17.	STANLEY MORGAN	13	534	10,352	19.4	67
18.	J. T. SMITH	12	526	6,749	12.8	33
19.	Bobby Mitchell	11	521	7,954	15.3	65
20.	Nat Moore	13	510	7,546	14.8	74

All-Time Leading Scorers

		Yrs.	TDs	EPs	FGs	Total
1.	George Blanda	26	9	943	335	2,002
2.	Jan Stenerud	19	0	580	373	1,699
3.	Jim Turner	16	1	521	304	1,439
4.	Mark Moseley	16	0	482	300	1,382
5.	Jim Bakken	17	0	534	282	1,380
6.	Fred Cox	15	0	519	282	1,365
7.	Lou Groza	17	1	641	234	1,349
8.	PAT LEAHY	16	0	496	255	1,261
9.	CHRIS BAHR	14	0	490	241	1,213
10.	Gino Cappelletti*	11	42	350	176	1,130
11.	Ray Wersching	15	0	456	222	1,122
12.	Don Cockroft	13	0	432	216	1,080
13.	Garo Yepremian	14	0	444	210	1,074
14.	Bruce Gossett	11	0	374	219	1,031
15.	NICK LOWERY	11	0	338	225	1,013
16.	Sam Baker	15	2	428	179	977
17.	JIM BREECH	11	0	418	184	970
18.	Rafael Septien	10	0	420	180	960
19.	Lou Michaels**	13	1	386	187	955
20.	EDDIE MURRAY	10	0	307	212	943

* Includes four two-point conversions
** Includes a safety recorded in 1965 when Michaels
   played as a defensive end.

Twelve-year veteran J.T. Smith deservedly broke into the all-time top twenty receivers list.

Cleveland quarterback Bernie Kosar jumped straight into fifth place in the all-time passer ratings.

All-Time Passer Ratings

		Yrs.	Att.	Comp.	Yards	TDs	Int.	Rating
1.	JOE MONTANA	11	4,059	2,593	31,054	216	107	94.0
2.	DAN MARINO	7	3,650	2,174	27,853	220	125	89.3
3.	BOOMER ESIASON	6	2,285	1,296	18,350	126	76	87.3
4.	DAVE KRIEG	10	2,843	1,644	20,858	169	116	83.7
5.	BERNIE KOSAR	5	1,940	1,134	13,888	75	47	83.4
	Roger Staubach	11	2,958	1,685	22,700	153	109	83.4
7.	KEN O'BRIEN	8	2,467	1,471	17,589	96	68	83.0
8.	JIM KELLY	4	1,742	1,032	12,901	81	63	82.7
	Neil Lomax	8	3,153	1,817	22,771	136	90	82.7
10.	Len Dawson	19	3,741	2,136	28,711	239	183	82.6
	Sonny Jurgensen	18	4,262	2,433	32,224	255	189	82.6
12.	Ken Anderson	16	4,475	2,654	32,838	197	160	81.9
13.	Danny White	13	2,950	1,761	21,959	155	132	81.7
14.	Bart Starr	16	3,149	1,808	24,718	152	138	80.5
15.	Fran Tarkenton	18	6,467	3,686	47,003	342	266	80.4
16.	TONY EASON	7	1,536	898	10,987	61	50	80.3
17.	Dan Fouts	15	5,604	3,297	43,040	254	242	80.2
18.	JIM McMAHON	8	1,831	1,050	13,335	77	66	79.2
19.	Otto Graham	6	1,565	872	13,499	88	94	78.2
	Bert Jones	10	2,551	1,430	18,190	124	101	78.2
	Johnny Unitas	18	5,186	2,830	40,239	290	253	78.2

Passes Completed	No.
1. Fran Tarkenton	3,686
2. Dan Fouts	3,297
3. Johnny Unitas	2,830
4. Ken Anderson	2,654
5. Jim Hart	2,593
JOE MONTANA	2,593
7. John Brodie	2,469
8. Sonny Jurgenson	2,433
9. JOE FERGUSON	2,367
10. Roman Gabriel	2,366
11. John Hadl	2,363
12. Norm Snead	2,276
13. Ken Stabler	2,270
14. RON JAWORSKI	2,187
15. DAN MARINO	2,174
16. Len Dawson	2,136
17. STEVE DeBERG	2,118
Y.A. Tittle	2,118
19. Craig Morton	2,053
20. Joe Theismann	2,044

Yards Passing	Yards
1. Fran Tarkenton	47,003
2. Dan Fouts	43,040
3. Johnny Unitas	40,239
4. Jim Hart	34,665
5. John Hadl	33,503
6. Ken Anderson	32,838
7. Sonny Jurgensen	32,224
8. John Brodie	31,548
9. JOE MONTANA	31,054
10. Norm Snead	30,797
11. JOE FERGUSON	29,796
12. Roman Gabriel	29,444
13. Len Dawson	28,711
14. Y.A. Tittle	28,339
15. RON JAWORSKI	28,190
16. Terry Bradshaw	27,989
17. Ken Stabler	27,938
18. Craig Morton	27,908
19. DAN MARINO	27,853
20. Joe Namath	27,663

Touchdown Passes	No.
1. Fran Tarkenton	342
2. Johnny Unitas	290
3. Sonny Jurgensen	255
4. Dan Fouts	254
5. John Hadl	244
6. Len Dawson	239
7. George Blanda	236
8. DAN MARINO	220
9. JOE MONTANA	216
10. John Brodie	214
11. Terry Bradshaw	212
Y.A. Tittle	212
13. Jim Hart	209
14. Roman Gabriel	201
15. Ken Anderson	197
16. JOE FERGUSON	196
Bobby Layne	196
Norm Snead	196
19. Ken Stabler	194
20. Bob Griese	192

Index of Retired Players
Listed in the All-Time Statistics

ALLEN Gerry, Baltimore (1966), Washington (1967-69)

ALWORTH Lance, San Diego (1962-70), Dallas (1971-72)

ANDERSON Ken, Cincinnati (1971-86)

BAKER Sam, Washington (1953 and 1956-59), Cleveland (1960-61), Dallas Cowboys (1962-63), Philadelphia (1964-69)

BAKKEN Jim, St Louis (1962-78)

BAUGH Sammy, Washington (1937-52)

BERRY Raymond, Baltimore (1955-67)

BILETNIKOFF Fred, Oakland (1965-78)

BLANDA George, Chicago Bears (1949 and 1950-58), Baltimore (1950), Houston (1960-66), Oakland (1967-75)

BRADSHAW Terry, Pittsburgh (1970-83)

BRANCH Cliff, Oakland/L.A. Raiders (1972-85)

BRODIE John, San Francisco (1957-73)

BROWN Jim, Cleveland (1957-65)

BURK Adrian, Baltimore (1950), Philadelphia (1951-56)

CAMPBELL Earl, Houston (1978-84), New Orleans (1984-85)

CAPPELLETTI Gino, Boston Patriots (1960-70)

CARMICHAEL Al, Green Bay (1953-58), Denver (1960-61)

CARMICHAEL Harold, Philadelphia (1971-83), Dallas (1984)

CHANDLER Wes, New Orleans (1978-81), San Diego (1981-87), San Francisco (1988)

CHRISTIANSEN Jack, Detroit (1951-58)

COCKROFT Don, Cleveland (1968-80)

COX Fred, Minnesota (1963-77)

CSONKA Larry, Miami (1968-74 and 1979), N.Y. Giants (1976-78)

DAWSON Len, Pittsburgh (1957-59), Cleveland (1960-61), Dallas Texans/Kansas City (1962-75)

DEMPSEY Tom, New Orleans (1969-70), Philadelphia (1971-74), L.A. Rams (1975-76), Houston (1977), Buffalo (1978-79)

DORSETT Tony, Dallas (1977-87), Denver (1988)

FARKAS Andy, Washington (1938-44), Detroit (1945)

FEARS Tom, L.A. Rams (1948-56)

FILCHOCK Frank, Pittsburgh (1938), Washington (1938-41 and 1944-45), N.Y. Giants (1946), Baltimore (1950)

FOUTS Dan, San Diego (1973-87)

GABRIEL Roman, L.A. Rams (1962-72), Philadelphia (1973-77)

GOGOLAK Charlie, Washington (1966-68), Boston/New England (1970-72)

GOSSETT Bruce, L.A. Rams (1964-69), San Francisco (1970-74)

GRAHAM Otto, Cleveland Browns (1946-55)

GRIESE Bob, Miami (1967-80)

GROZA Lou, Cleveland Browns (1946-59 and 1961-67)

HADL John, San Diego (1962-72), L.A. Rams (1973-74), Green Bay (1974-75), Houston (1976-77)

HAJI-SHEIKH Ali, N.Y. Giants (1983-85), Atlanta (1986), Washington (1987)

HARDER Pat, Chicago Cardinals (1946-50), Detroit (1951-53)

HARRIS Franco, Pittsburgh (1972-83), Seattle (1984)

HART Jim, St Louis (1966-83), Washington (1984)

HENNIGAN Charley, Houston (1960-66)

HORNUNG Paul, Green Bay (1957-62 and 1964-66)

HOUSTON Ken, Houston (1967-72), Washington (1973-80)

HUTSON Don, Green Bay (1935-45)

IZO George, St Louis (1960), Washington (1961-64), Detroit (1965), Pittsburgh (1966)

JACKSON Harold, L.A. Rams (1968 and 1973-77), Philadelphia (1969-72), New England (1978-81), Minnesota (1982), Seattle (1983)

JOHNSON John Henry, San Francisco (1954-56), Detroit (1957-59), Pittsburgh (1960-65), Houston (1966)

JOINER Charlie, Houston (1969-72), Cincinnati (1972-75), San Diego (1976-86)

JONES Bert, Baltimore (1973-81), L.A. Rams (1982)

JONES Dub, Miami (AAFC) (1946), Brooklyn (AAFC) (1946-48), Cleveland (1948-55)

JURGENSEN Sonny, Philadelphia (1957-63), Washington (1964-74)

KAPP Joe, Minnesota (1967-69), Boston Patriots (1970)

KEARNEY Jim, Detroit (1965-66), Kansas City (1967-75), New Orleans (1976)

KELLY Leroy, Cleveland (1964-73)

KRAUSE Paul, Washington (1964-67), Minnesota (1968-79)

LANE Dick (Night Train), L.A. Rams (1952-53), Chicago Cardinals (1954-59), Detroit (1960-65)

LAYNE Bobby, Chicago Bears (1948), N.Y. Bulldogs (1949), Detroit (1950-58), Pittsburgh (1958-62)

LeFEBVRE Gil, Cincinnati Reds (1933-34), Detroit (1935)

LUCKMAN Sid, Chicago Bears (1939-50)

MATSON Ollie, Chicago Cardinals (1952 and 1954-58), L.A. Rams (1959-62), Detroit (1963), Philadelphia (1964-66)

MAYNARD Don, N.Y. Giants (1958), N.Y. Titans/Jets (1960-72), St Louis (1973)

MICHAELS Lou, L.A. Rams (1958-60), Pittsburgh (1961-63), Baltimore (1964-69), Green Bay (1971)

MITCHELL Bobby, Cleveland (1958-61), Washington (1962-68)

MONTGOMERY Wilbert, Philadelphia (1977-84), Detroit (1985)

MOORE Nat, Miami (1974-86)

MORGAN Dennis, Dallas (1974), Philadelphia (1975)

MORTON Craig, Dallas (1965-74), N.Y. Giants (1974-76), Denver (1977-82)

MOSELEY Mark, Philadelphia (1970), Houston (1971-72), Washington (1974-86), Cleveland (1986)

NAMATH Joe, N.Y. Jets (1965-76), L.A. Rams (1977)

NEVERS Ernie, Duluth Eskimos (1926-27), Chicago Cardinals (1929-31)

PAYTON Walter, Chicago (1975-87)

PERRY Joe, San Francisco (1948-60 and 1963), Baltimore (1961-62)

PLUNKETT Jim, New England (1971-75), San Francisco (1976-77), Oakland/L.A. Raiders (1978-85)

PRUITT Mike, Cleveland (1976-84), Buffalo (1985), Kansas City (1985-86)

RIGGINS John, N.Y. Jets (1971-75), Washington (1976-79 and 1981-85)

ROGERS George, New Orleans (1981-84), Washington (1985-87)

SAYERS Gale, Chicago (1965-71)

SEPTIEN Rafael, L.A. Rams (1977), Dallas (1978-86)

SHAW Bob, Cleveland/L.A. Rams (1945-49), Chicago Cardinals (1950)

SIMPSON O.J., Buffalo (1969-77), San Francisco (1978-79)

SMITH Noland, Kansas City (1967-69), San Francisco (1969)

SNEAD Norm, Washington (1961-63), Philadelphia (1964-70), Minnesota (1971), N.Y. Giants (1972-74 and 1976), San Francisco (1974-75)

STABLER Ken, Oakland (1970-79), Houston (1980-81), New Orleans (1982-84)

STARR Bart, Green Bay (1956-71)

STAUBACH Roger, Dallas (1969-79)

STENERUD Jan, Kansas City (1967-79), Green Bay (1980-83), Minnesota (1984-85)

STUDSTILL Pat, Detroit (1961-62 and 1964-67), L.A. Rams (1968-71), New England (1972)

SWEETAN Karl, Detroit (1966-67), New Orleans (1968), L.A. Rams (1969-70)

TARKENTON Fran, Minnesota (1961-66 and 1972-78), N.Y. Giants (1967-71)

TATUM Jack, Oakland (1971-79), Houston (1980)

TAYLOR Charley, Washington (1964-75 and 1977)

TAYLOR Jim, Green Bay (1958-66), New Orleans (1967)

TAYLOR Lionel, Chicago Bears (1959), Denver (1960-66), Houston (1967-68)

THEISMANN Joe, Washington (1974-85)

THOMPSON Billy, Denver (1969-81)

TITTLE Y.A., Baltimore (1948-50), San Francisco (1951-60), N.Y. Giants (1961-64)

TODD Richard, N.Y. Jets (1976-83), New Orleans (1984-85)

TURNER Cecil, Chicago (1968-73)

TURNER Jim, N.Y. Jets (1964-70), Denver (1971-79)

UNITAS Johnny, Baltimore (1956-72), San Diego (1973)

UPCHURCH Rick, Denver (1975-83)

VAN BROCKLIN Norm, L.A. Rams (1949-57), Philadelphia (1958-60)

von SCHAMANN Uwe, Miami (1979-84)

WATERFIELD Bob, Cleveland/L.A. Rams (1945-52)

WERSCHING Ray, San Diego (1973-76), San Francisco (1977-87)

WEST Charlie, Minnesota (1968-73), Detroit (1974-77), Denver (1978-79)

WHITE Danny, Dallas (1976-88)

WILLIAMS Travis, Green Bay (1967-70), L.A. Rams (1971)

WINSLOW Kellen, San Diego (1979-87)

YEPREMIAN Garo, Detroit (1966-67), Miami (1970-78), New Orleans (1979), Tampa Bay (1980-81)

CHAPTER FIVE

EIGHTEEN TO FOLLOW

Of the players offered in last year's Annual as future stars, Buffalo's Thurman Thomas really came charging through as he led the NFL in total yards from scrimmage with 1,913. Thomas was one of no fewer than seven of our selections to earn a first trip to the AFC-NFC Pro Bowl. The others were Miami's Ferrell Edmunds, San Diego's Anthony Miller, Detroit's Chris Spielman, Green Bay's Tim Harris, Vaughan Johnson of New Orleans and Tim McDonald of Phoenix. This year, the offering is not so much a selection of future stars but, rather, a collection of players who, in some cases, already are prominent and have been chosen for the special kind of excitement they may generate when the ball heads their way.

The Dallas Cowboys enter the 1990 campaign following two years in which they have finished with the poorest record in the entire NFL. As might be expected of a club which pioneered the use of computers in personnel selection, the journey back to competitiveness has been plotted with meticulous care, and the cornerstone of the club's reconstruction was laid when, in the 1989 collegiate draft, quarterback **Troy Aikman** was selected with the first option overall. Aikman, whose calm assuredness and dignity typify this great club, did not enjoy the smoothest of rookie years. Only rarely were the Cowboys able to field their preferred starting wide receivers, and an injury suffered against the Giants on Week Four kept him out for the next five games. But he bounced back against the Cardinals, passing for 379 yards and two touchdowns in a thrilling contest. Gradually, his poise showed through as the urgency in his delivery eased away and his passes began to unfurl. He's now ready to bring the Cowboys back into contention.

Another team which has spent too long out of the race for honours, San Diego, has quietly been gathering for a major push and in this they have been helped by the return of **Leslie O'Neal**, a former defensive end who has fought his way back from a crippling knee

Troy Aikman is poised to rekindle the flame.

Leslie O'Neal has every hope of having his best season in the NFL.

with 683 yards, and with nine rushing touchdowns.

Twice each year the Chargers face the Los Angeles Raiders. Which team would want a double dose of **Mervyn Fernandez**? The 6-3, 200-pound wide receiver first played pro football in the CFL, where his talent was immediately noted by Raiders scouts. Though it was not his intention to leave Canada, the Raiders drafted him in the 1983 tenth round and they could only sit and wait as, year after year, he clocked up highly impressive numbers. Regarded as the top receiver of the 'eighties in Canada, in five seasons with the British Columbia Lions he caught 374 passes for 6,408 yards and 55 touchdowns. In 1987 he joined a Raiders club which, with ample depth at wide receiver, did not have a full-time role for him. But after heading the NFL with 26 yards per reception in 1988 he went from strength to strength, leading the Raiders in 1989 with 57 receptions for 1,069 yards and nine touchdowns. Big and strong, Fernandez has top-class speed,

injury and now plays at right outside linebacker. Way back in the 1986 season, O'Neal, who was the eighth player selected in the first round of that year, had rampaged through the campaign and was leading the AFC with 12.5 sacks, five coming in one game against Dallas, when he was injured. Even though missing the final three games he ended up fifth in the AFC list of sackers and was picked Defensive Rookie of the Year by AP. After an absence of almost two full years, O'Neal came back slowly and, last year, showed signs of returning to his best with 12.5 sacks. It was a total which earned him the first of what could be many selections to the AFC-NFC Pro Bowl.

On offense, the Chargers are still searching for an identity and it is not clear just what part the offense will play, but **Marion Butts** could be a key element. In what will be a stiff competition for playing time as the single running back, he is the man with the credentials. In the opening game of the 1989 campaign, he shocked the Raiders with pair of touchdowns, one of which came on a 50-yard romp and represented the Chargers' longest run from scrimmage since the 1985 season. A seventh-round draft pick who was selected as much for his ability as a special-teamer as his productivity from the fullback position, it was only late in the season that Butts was featured in the offense, and he showed the full range of his abilities against the Chiefs on Week Fifteen, when he rushed for 176 yards on a mammoth 39 carries. He led the team in both rushing,

Mervyn Fernandez makes his receptions with great certainty.

bucket hands and a great surge of acceleration after adjusting to make a difficult catch. He could easily become a major NFL receiver. His teammate, tight end **Mike Dyal**, entered the NFL through the side door, signing as a free agent in May, 1988. After spending the year on injured reserve, his chances of gaining a roster spot hardly improved but, with perseverance, he hung on and, with the departure of former All-Pro Todd Christensen, entering the 1989 season he found himself in the position of being the club's pass receiving tight end. Used only sparingly for most of the season, Dyal gradually was eased into the system and it is interesting that one play, a pass completion of 25 or so yards to which he adds around eight yards after the catch, worked on half-a-dozen occasions. Against Denver on Week Thirteen, he turned a 29-yard reception into a 67-yard touchdown play. A total of 27 receptions in a season is not much upon which to base an argument, but he has obvious value on medium-range plays and, were these to be featured regularly in the Raiders' plans, Dyal could quickly become a recognised star.

Playing in partnership with a legend and identified as his obvious successor is not the easiest way to embark upon a career, but that was the responsibility thrust upon Seattle wide receiver **Brian Blades**, who was drafted in the 1988 second round with a view to taking over from future Hall of Famer Steve Largent. As a rookie, Blades slotted into the system without fuss and logged figures similar to those of Largent except in scoring touchdowns — he had eight against Largent's two. The Seahawks had used their draft option well and this was confirmed in 1989 when, with Largent injured and unavailable for six games, Blades took control with 77 receptions for 1,063 yards and five touchdowns. Remarkably, it is almost as if he has been cast from the same mold as the great man. A disciplined pattern runner with a built-in sense for leaving opponents stranded, he is equally effective operating down the sideline or on crossing patterns. And with just a touch of the showman, he'll make the odd one-handed circus catch. If his 1990 AFC-NFC Pro Bowl selection labels him a star for the present, his undoubted potential tags him as a superstar of the future.

Cincinnati's **David Fulcher** is another who qualifies for that description. Already Fulcher has been selected to two AFC-NFC Pro Bowls but he has yet to earn the widespread acclaim accorded to such perennial all-star performers as San Francisco's Ronnie Lott. Fulcher's great value, the one which separates him from the rest, is the versatility arising out of his size and speed. At 6-3 and 228 pounds, he can play the role of an extra linebacker against the run — he is a crushing tackler — while his explosive burst from an outside position enables the Bengals to use him as a pass rusher. In the more common role of pass defender, his 1989 haul of eight interceptions shows all the stealth and cunning of the pure hunter. More than any other, he is the player around whom the Bengals defense will form in its 1990 bid for honours. When it comes to offense, the Bengals have all the potential firepower any team needs but their success may depend upon both starting wide receivers playing at top form. Last year, following a holdout, Eddie Brown took time to warm up, but **Tim McGee** came blazing through to record his best campaign in four years as a pro. In the AFC, only Pro Bowlers Andre Reed, Webster Slaughter and Anthony Miller caught passes for more yardage than McGee's 1,211 and, amongst the AFC's leading receivers, just the deep specialists, Slaughter and Fernandez, averaged better than McGee's 18.6 yards per reception. McGee had a career day against Detroit on Week Eleven, when he caught 11 passes for an AFC season-best 194 yards and a touchdown.

Tim McGee is about to add another one to the list.

Bubba McDowell (#25) homes in on his target.

In the 1989 draft, the Browns traded up to obtain running back **Eric Metcalf** and they can hardly be disappointed with a young man who made a variety of contributions, including leading the team in rushing, catching a club rookie-record 54 passes, ranking equal-ninth in the NFL with a kickoff return average of 23.2 yards and scoring a team-leading ten touchdowns. Looking beyond statistics, there is general agreement amongst scouts that Metcalf is the most elusive running back in the NFL. Old timers love to say that Walter Payton made some of the greatest three-yard gains in pro football, meaning that he should have been dropped for a loss but, somehow, wriggled out of trouble. Metcalf has that skill, though perhaps more in the manner of Gale Sayers, whose fabled moves come

to mind when describing the young Browns star. In his rookie year, Metcalf's tendency to over-elaborate occasionally took him outside the normal range of protection offered by his offensive line. Only this, it is felt, kept his average per carry to a modest 3.4 yards.

A select few NFL defenders seem to have an instinct for homing in on the ball and the signs are that this elite group has a new member with the arrival of Houston's 1989 third-round draftee, **Bubba McDowell**. Though not the biggest strong safety in pro football, McDowell tackles with every ounce of his 195 pounds and the effect was to cause an Oilers-high four fumbles. In addition to coming second on the team with 88 tackles, McDowell had four interceptions and blocked two punts on special team duty. Oilers new head coach Jack Pardee could hardly disguise his satisfaction at having McDowell when he said, 'It is very unusual for a third-round draft choice to come in and be a dominant player in his first year. I'm just glad we have Bubba on our team.'

Just for a few moments early in Super Bowl XXIV, it appeared that Denver might have a weapon with which, at least, to make life difficult for the 49ers. On Denver's second series, rookie running back **Bobby Humphrey** caught a 27-yard pass and then bounded for gains of ten, six and three yards as he helped the Broncos to two first-downs en route to their field goal response to San Francisco's opening touchdown. After the 49ers had been stopped on the ensuing drive, there was a buzz of excitement at the prospect of Humphrey lighting the fuse. But on first-down from midfield he fumbled under pressure. It is the kind of thing which happens to the very best – a Walter Payton fumble early in Super Bowl XX led to a New England field goal – but, as some post-game analysts would have it, with the resulting loss of possession went the Broncos' one real chance of causing an upset. That memory apart, Humphrey had enjoyed a campaign which was only little short of sensational. Used with caution in the first four games, he stepped up the pace on Week Five and ended the season with the third-best, single-season rushing total, 1,151 yards, in Denver history. A 1989 supplemental draft pick, Humphrey has brought the

kind of consistent sparkle and penetrative power that should keep Denver in the forefront of the competition to represent the AFC in Super Bowl XXV.

Two thumping losses at the start of the season appeared to signal difficult times for the Pittsburgh Steelers, but they fought back to earn a playoff spot with an impressive effort in which **Rod Woodson** played no little part. A superior athlete with an extraordinary range of skills, Woodson made a slow start to his NFL career after a holdout which caused him to miss the first half of his rookie season in 1987. And even though he was voted the team's co-MVP in 1988, there was the residual feeling that he still had not brought all his talents to bear. However, by 1989 he was ready. Starting 14 games at cornerback, he had three interceptions, forced four fumbles and recovered three, and defensed 18 passes. In the wild card showdown with Houston, Woodson both forced and recovered a fumble by Oilers running back Lorenzo White to set up the

Rod Woodson is set to emerge as one of the NFL's major multi-purpose players.

Bobby Humphrey carries many of the Broncos' hopes.

game-winning field goal in overtime. He may even have been more valuable as a kick returner, in which he earned a first trip to the AFC-NFC Pro Bowl after leading the NFL with an average of 27.3 yards on kickoffs. A solid punt returner too, he brings the prospect of a big play every time he touches the ball.

Woodson's teammate, **Merril Hoge**, entered the campaign having led the team in 1988 with 705 yards rushing, but he hadn't turned many heads. And with the arrival of top draftee Tim Worley, the opportunities to show his paces diminished. But this tough competitor accepted the role of workhorse fullback without complaint and, with eight touchdowns, had the satisfaction of leading the club. His moments of glory came in the playoffs, beginning against Houston when he became only the second Pittsburgh player to rush for 100 yards in a postseason game (Franco Harris achieved that feat five times) and scored the late touchdown which took the game into overtime. Against Denver, in a pulsating AFC Championship Game, he rushed for 120 yards, becoming the first Steeler to have consecutive 100-yards-rushing games in the postseason and, for good measure, he caught eight passes for 60 yards. Again, his 49- and 45-yard runs in the postseason were the second- and third-highest in Steelers playoff history. Hoge must now be seen as yet another rising star in the young Pittsburgh squad.

Thirteen players on the Rams' squad were picked for some kind of award in 1989. **Robert Delpino** was not amongst them and yet he played an important role in a team effort which was halted only when it came up against the 49ers juggernaut in the NFC Championship Game. A sometime starter at fullback, Delpino, who was a fifth-round draft pick in 1988, has survived and shows every indication of prospering in a Rams offense which, at times, seems overburdened with talent at running back. One reason may be that he's always ready to answer the call. Mostly he is a blocker for halfback Greg Bell but, when the Rams need the tough yards, Delpino delivers the goods, last year at an average of 4.7 yards on 78 carries. As a receiver he chipped in with 34 catches for a useful 334 yards and on kickoff returns averaged 19.6 over 17 trips. As supporting evidence for a curriculum vitae it is not the most awe-inspiring set of numbers but there is something special about the way Delpino carries himself. He has a style, a promise, always threatening to engage an extra gear, reminiscent of a young Chuck Muncie with all that inherent ability asking to be set free. If Delpino is yet to have his day, wide receiver **Willie (Flipper) Anderson** already may have had enough for a career. As the junior partner of seven-year veteran Henry Ellard, Anderson was not the major target for quarterback Jim Everett, yet, by his sheer brilliance, he has gone some way towards achieving parity. Over 44 receptions he

Robert Delpino has immense latent talent.

averaged an astounding 26 yards. In a breathtaking display approaching historic perfection, against New Orleans, he caught 15 passes for an NFL single-game record 336 yards. Later, his overtime touchdown would settle a gripping divisional playoff encounter with the Giants, and just a little more weight on a Jim Everett pass could so easily have given him his moment of glory against the 49ers in the NFC Championship Game. Would a more experienced receiver have made the adjustment? We may find out in the coming season.

From time to time we are reminded that there is a place in the NFL for small men and, in 1989, Giants rookie **David Meggett** made his own statement on that subject. An NCAA Division I-AA product, Meggett's explosive speed and quicksilver moves were evident in the season opener when he turned his first reception as a pro into a 62-yard touchdown. It was the start of a useful collection which, by the end of the season, amounted to 34 catches at an average of 15.6 yards. Used sparingly as a running back, Meggett underlined his versatility as a dual-purpose kick returner, returning a punt 76 yards for a touchdown on the final weekend and earning a coveted Pro Bowl berth. It could be the first of many.

If consistency and steady improvement are deserving of reward, then New Orleans wide receiver **Eric Martin** is in line for a bonus. In 1985 he caught at least one pass in all but one game. The following year he was the only Saints player to catch a pass in every game, and then, in 1987, he led the team with 44 receptions. 1988 saw him exceed 1,000 yards in an NFL campaign for the first time and in 1989 he repeated, setting single-season, career-best marks with five 100-yards-receiving games and eight touchdowns. With deceptive speed and good moves, Martin has fought his way to the top of his profession in an offense which has not specialised in the passing game. The scouting report on Martin might well conclude, 'Continued progress is anticipated'

That may also be true of Tampa Bay tight end **Ron Hall**, who has improved steadily as a blocker and has become a solid receiver. Nicknamed 'Ironman' by Buccaneers head coach Ray Perkins for his mental and physical toughness, Hall faces a real battle if he is to move ahead of established stars such as Mark Bavaro, Keith Jackson and Steve Jordan, all of whom have caught passes by the bucketful to earn Pro Bowl recognition. For Hall to draw level with the leading group, he'd have to double his receiving tally but, playing in a Tampa Bay offense with two excellent wide receivers attracting multiple coverage, it is just possible that he may be given a little extra space to make his bid. It is one of the more interesting prospects to savour as we enter the 1990 season.

David Meggett makes a deep sidestep on one of his kick returns.

Eric Martin accelerates into his downfield run.

CHAPTER SIX

AMERICAN FOOTBALL CONFERENCE

TEAM RANKINGS

	OFFENSE						DEFENSE					
	Total Yds.	Rushing	Passing	Points For	No. Intercepted	No. Sacked	Total Yds.	Rushing	Passing	Points Against	Interceptions	Sacks
Buffalo	2	2	4	1	7 =	6	6	6	8	8	3	6
Cincinnati	1	1	3	2	1 =	9	9	14	6	3	4 =	10
Cleveland	8	11	6	5	3	4 =	4	3	7	2	1	4
Denver	7	4	11	4	7 =	10	2	1	2	1	4 =	2
Houston	5	6	5	3	4	7	7	2	11	14	4 =	7 =
Indianapolis	12	8	12	9	5	3	11	10	9	7	4 =	3
Kansas City	6	3	9	7	10 =	2	1	4	1	4	11 =	7 =
L.A. Raiders	10	5	13	8	9	11	5	7	4	6	9	9
Miami	3	14	1	6	13	1	13	13	12	11	11 =	5
New England	4	10	2	10	14	4 =	12	8	13	12	10	12 =
N.Y. Jets	9	12	7	13	12	14	14	12	14	13	11 =	14
Pittsburgh	14	9	14	12	1 =	13	10	9	10	9	11 =	14
San Diego	11	7	10	11	6	8	3	5	3	5	2	1
Seattle	13	13	8	14	10 =	12	8	11	5	10	14	11

AFC PASSERS

	Att	Comp	% Comp	Yards	Ave Gain	TD	% TD	Long	Int	% Int	Rating Points
Esiason, Boomer, *Cin.*	455	258	56.7	3525	7.75	28	6.2	t74	11	2.4	92.1
Moon, Warren, *Hou.*	464	280	60.3	3631	7.83	23	5.0	55	14	3.0	88.9
Kelly, Jim, *Buff.*	391	228	58.3	3130	8.01	25	6.4	t78	18	4.6	86.2
Kosar, Bernie, *Clev.*	513	303	59.1	3533	6.89	18	3.5	t97	14	2.7	80.3
Marino, Dan, *Mia.*	550	308	56.0	3997	7.27	24	4.4	t78	22	4.0	76.9
DeBerg, Steve, *K.C.*	324	196	60.5	2529	7.81	11	3.4	50	16	4.9	75.8
Krieg, Dave, *Sea.*	499	286	57.3	3309	6.63	21	4.2	t60	20	4.0	74.8
O'Brien, Ken, *Jets*	477	288	60.4	3346	7.01	12	2.5	57	18	3.8	74.3
Elway, John, *Den.*	416	223	53.6	3051	7.33	18	4.3	69	18	4.3	73.7
McMahon, Jim, *S.D.*	318	176	55.3	2132	6.70	10	3.1	t69	10	3.1	73.5
Brister, Bubby, *Pitt.*	342	187	54.7	2365	6.92	9	2.6	t79	10	2.9	73.1
Trudeau, Jack, *Ind.*	362	190	52.5	2317	6.40	15	4.1	71	13	3.6	71.3
Grogan, Steve, *N.E.*	261	133	51.0	1697	6.50	9	3.4	t55	14	5.4	60.8

Non-qualifiers

	Att	Comp	% Comp	Yards	Ave Gain	TD	% TD	Long	Int	% Int	Rating Points
Reich, Frank, *Buff.*	87	53	60.9	701	8.06	7	8.0	t63	2	2.3	103.7
Wilhelm, Erik, *Cin.*	56	30	53.6	425	7.59	4	7.1	t46	2	3.6	87.3
Beuerlein, Steve, *Raiders*	217	108	49.8	1677	7.73	13	6.0	t67	9	4.1	78.4
Eason, Tony, *N.E.-Jets*	141	79	56.0	1016	7.21	4	2.8	t63	6	4.3	70.5
Wilson, Marc, *N.E.*	150	75	50.0	1006	6.71	3	2.0	t65	5	3.3	64.5
Chandler, Chris, *Ind.*	80	39	48.8	537	6.71	2	2.5	t82	3	3.8	63.4
Schroeder, Jay, *Raiders*	194	91	46.9	1550	7.99	8	4.1	t84	13	6.7	60.3
Tolliver, Billy Joe, *S.D.*	185	89	48.1	1097	5.93	5	2.7	49	8	4.3	57.9
Jaworski, Ron, *K.C.*	61	36	59.0	385	6.31	2	3.3	32	5	8.2	54.3
Flutie, Doug, *N.E.*	91	36	39.6	493	5.42	2	2.2	36	4	4.4	46.6
Stouffer, Kelly, *Sea.*	59	29	49.2	270	4.58	0	0.0	29	3	5.1	40.9
Blackledge, Todd, *Pitt.*	60	22	36.7	282	4.70	1	1.7	30	3	5.0	36.9

t = Touchdown
Leader based on rating points, minimum 224 attempts

AFC RECEIVERS – Most Receptions

	No	Yards	Ave	Long	TD
Reed, Andre, *Buff.*	88	1312	14.9	t78	9
Blades, Brian, *Sea.*	77	1063	13.8	t60	5
Johnson, Vance, *Den.*	76	1095	14.4	69	7
Williams, John L., *Sea.*	76	657	8.6	t51	6
Miller, Anthony, *S.D.*	75	1252	16.7	t69	10
Hill, Drew, *Hou.*	66	938	14.2	50	8
Slaughter, Webster, *Clev.*	65	1236	19.0	t97	6
McGee, Tim, *Cin.*	65	1211	18.6	t74	8
Clayton, Mark, *Mia.*	64	1011	15.8	t78	9
Brooks, Bill, *Ind.*	63	919	14.6	t55	4
Toon, Al, *Jets*	63	693	11.0	t37	6
Jensen, Jim, *Mia.*	61	557	9.1	20	6
Langhorne, Reggie, *Clev.*	60	749	12.5	t62	2
Thomas, Thurman, *Buff.*	60	669	11.2	t74	6
Fernandez, Mervyn, *Raiders*	57	1069	18.8	t75	9
Givins, Ernest, *Hou.*	55	794	14.4	48	3
Sievers, Eric, *N.E.*	54	615	11.4	46	0
Metcalf, Eric, *Clev.*	54	397	7.4	t68	4
Rison, Andre, *Ind.*	52	820	15.8	61	4
Brown, Eddie, *Cin.*	52	814	15.7	46	6
Bentley, Albert, *Ind.*	52	525	10.1	61	3
Lipps, Louis, *Pitt.*	50	944	18.9	t79	5
Holman, Rodney, *Cin.*	50	736	14.7	t73	9
Dykes, Hart Lee, *N.E.*	49	795	16.2	42	5
Duper, Mark, *Mia.*	49	717	14.6	41	1
Jones, Cedric, *N.E.*	48	670	14.0	t65	6
Jeffires, Haywood, *Hou.*	47	619	13.2	t45	2
Townsell, JoJo, *Jets*	45	787	17.5	t63	5
Paige, Stephone, *K.C.*	44	759	17.3	50	2
Duncan, Curtis, *Hou.*	43	613	14.3	55	5
Skansi, Paul, *Sea.*	39	488	12.5	26	5
Nelson, Darrin, *Minn.-S.D.*	38	380	10.0	49	0
Hector, Johnny, *Jets*	38	330	8.7	32	2
Carter, Rodney, *Pitt.*	38	267	7.0	t22	3
Brooks, James, *Cin.*	37	306	8.3	25	2

t = Touchdown

AFC RECEIVERS – Most Yards

	Yards	No	Ave	Long	TD
Reed, Andre, *Buff.*	1312	88	14.9	t78	9
Miller, Anthony, *S.D.*	1252	75	16.7	t69	10
Slaughter, Webster, *Clev.*	1236	65	19.0	t97	6
McGee, Tim, *Cin.*	1211	65	18.6	t74	8
Johnson, Vance, *Den.*	1095	76	14.4	69	7
Fernandez, Mervyn, *Raiders*	1069	57	18.8	t75	9
Blades, Brian, *Sea.*	1063	77	13.8	t60	5
Clayton, Mark, *Mia.*	1011	64	15.8	t78	9
Lipps, Louis, *Pitt.*	944	50	18.9	t79	5
Hill, Drew, *Hou.*	938	66	14.2	50	8
Brooks, Bill, *Ind.*	919	63	14.6	t55	4
Rison, Andre, *Ind.*	820	52	15.8	61	4
Brown, Eddie, *Cin.*	814	52	15.7	46	6
Dykes, Hart Lee, *N.E.*	795	49	16.2	42	5
Givins, Ernest, *Hou.*	794	55	14.4	48	3
Townsell, JoJo, *Jets*	787	45	17.5	t63	5
Paige, Stephone, *K.C.*	759	44	17.3	50	2
Langhorne, Reggie, *Clev.*	749	60	12.5	t62	2
Holman, Rodney, *Cin.*	736	50	14.7	t73	9
Duper, Mark, *Mia.*	717	49	14.6	41	1
Toon, Al, *Jets*	693	63	11.0	t37	6
Gault, Willie, *Raiders*	690	28	24.6	t84	4
Jones, Cedric, *N.E.*	670	48	14.0	t65	6
Thomas, Thurman, *Buff.*	669	60	11.2	t74	6
Williams, John L., *Sea.*	657	76	8.6	t51	6
Jeffires, Haywood, *Hou.*	619	47	13.2	t45	2
Sievers, Eric, *N.E.*	615	54	11.4	46	0
Duncan, Curtis, *Hou.*	613	43	14.3	55	5
Jensen, Jim, *Mia.*	557	61	9.1	20	6
Fryar, Irving, *N.E.*	537	29	18.5	52	3
Bentley, Albert, *Ind.*	525	52	10.1	61	3
Banks, Fred, *Mia.*	520	30	17.3	61	1
Dyal, Mike, *Raiders*	499	27	18.5	t67	2
Skansi, Paul, *Sea.*	488	39	12.5	26	5
Morgan, Stanley, *N.E.*	486	28	17.4	t55	3
Mandley, Pete, *K.C.*	476	35	13.6	44	1

t = Touchdown

Andre Reed led the AFC in both receptions and receiving yards.

AFC RUSHERS

	Att	Yards	Ave	Long	TD
Okoye, Christian, *K.C.*	370	1480	4.0	59	12
Dickerson, Eric, *Ind.*	314	1311	4.2	t21	7
Thomas, Thurman, *Buff.*	298	1244	4.2	38	6
Brooks, James, *Cin.*	221	1239	5.6	t65	7
Humphrey, Bobby, *Den.*	294	1151	3.9	40	7
Jackson, Bo, *Raiders*	173	950	5.5	t92	4
Stephens, John, *N.E.*	244	833	3.4	t35	7
Worley, Tim, *Pitt.*	195	770	3.9	38	5
Hector, Johnny, *Jets*	177	702	4.0	24	3
Butts, Marion, *S.D.*	170	683	4.0	t50	9
Smith, Sammie, *Mia.*	200	659	3.3	25	6
Metcalf, Eric, *Clev.*	187	633	3.4	t43	6
Warner, Curt, *Sea.*	194	631	3.3	34	3
Hoge, Merril, *Pitt.*	186	621	3.3	31	8
Perryman, Bob, *N.E.*	150	562	3.7	18	2
Kinnebrew, Larry, *Buff.*	131	533	4.1	25	6
Highsmith, Alonzo, *Hou.*	128	531	4.1	25	4
Spencer, Tim, *S.D.*	134	521	3.9	15	3
Williams, John L., *Sea.*	146	499	3.4	21	1
Smith, Steve, *Raiders*	117	471	4.0	21	1
Pinkett, Allen, *Hou.*	94	449	4.8	60	1
Vick, Roger, *Jets*	112	434	3.9	t39	5
Ball, Eric, *Cin.*	98	391	4.0	27	3
McNeil, Freeman, *Jets*	80	352	4.4	t19	2
Winder, Sammy, *Den.*	110	351	3.2	16	2
White, Lorenzo, *Hou.*	104	349	3.4	33	5
Nelson, Darrin, *Minn.-S.D.*	67	321	4.8	28	0
Rozier, Mike, *Hou.*	88	301	3.4	17	2
Bentley, Albert, *Ind.*	75	299	4.0	22	1
Allen, Marcus, *Raiders*	69	293	4.2	15	2
Jennings, Stanford, *Cin.*	83	293	3.5	17	2
Manoa, Tim, *Clev.*	87	289	3.3	22	3
Esiason, Boomer, *Cin.*	47	278	5.9	24	0
Moon, Warren, *Hou.*	70	268	3.8	19	4
Elway, John, *Den.*	48	244	5.1	31	3
Stradford, Troy, *Mia.*	66	240	3.6	13	1
Saxon, James, *K.C.*	58	233	4.0	19	3
Heard, Herman, *K.C.*	63	216	3.4	28	0
Logan, Marc, *Mia.*	57	201	3.5	14	0
Lipps, Louis, *Pitt.*	13	180	13.8	t58	1
Redden, Barry, *Clev.*	40	180	4.5	t38	1
Mueller, Vance, *Raiders*	48	161	3.4	19	2
Jones, Keith, *Clev.*	43	160	3.7	15	1
Krieg, Dave, *Sea.*	40	160	4.0	18	0
Davis, Kenneth, *Buff.*	29	149	5.1	21	1
Alexander, Jeff, *Den.*	45	146	3.2	11	2
Pelluer, Steve, *K.C.*	17	143	8.4	27	2
McMahon, Jim, *S.D.*	29	141	4.9	15	0
Bernstine, Rod, *S.D.*	15	137	9.1	t32	1
Kelly, Jim, *Buff.*	29	137	4.7	19	2
Williams, Warren, *Pitt.*	37	131	3.5	13	1
Mack, Kevin, *Clev.*	37	130	3.5	12	1
McNair, Todd, *K.C.*	23	121	5.3	25	0
Taylor, Craig, *Cin.*	30	111	3.7	16	3
Bratton, Melvin, *Den.*	30	108	3.6	9	1

t = Touchdown

AFC SCORING – Kickers

	XP	XPA	FG	FGA	PTS
Treadwell, David, *Den.*	39	40	27	33	120
Norwood, Scott, *Buff.*	46	47	23	30	115
Zendejas, Tony, *Hou.*	40	40	25	37	115
Lowery, Nick, *K.C.*	34	35	24	33	106
Jaeger, Jeff, *Raiders*	34	34	23	34	103
Stoyanovich, Pete, *Mia.*	38	39	19	26	95
Biasucci, Dean, *Ind.*	31	32	21	27	94
Anderson, Gary, *Pitt.*	28	28	21	30	91
Bahr, Matt, *Clev.*	40	40	16	24	88
Bahr, Chris, *S.D.*	29	30	17	25	80
Breech, Jim, *Cin.*	37	38	12	14	73
Johnson, Norm, *Sea.*	27	27	15	25	72
Leahy, Pat, *Jets*	29	30	14	21	71
Staurovsky, Jason, *N.E.*	14	14	14	17	56

RIGHT: Kansas City's Christian Okoye won his first NFL rushing title.

OPPOSITE: Buffalo's Thurman Thomas led the entire NFL with 1,913 yards from scrimmage.

92

AFC SCORING – Touchdowns

	TD	TDR	TDP	TDM	PTS
Okoye, Christian, *K.C.*	12	12	0	0	72
Thomas, Thurman, *Buff.*	12	6	6	0	72
Miller, Anthony, *S.D.*	11	0	10	1	66
Metcalf, Eric, *Clev.*	10	6	4	0	60
Brooks, James, *Cin.*	9	7	2	0	54
Butts, Marion, *S.D.*	9	9	0	0	54
Clayton, Mark, *Mia.*	9	0	9	0	54
Fernandez, Mervyn, *Raiders*	9	0	9	0	54
Holman, Rodney, *Cin.*	9	0	9	0	54
Reed, Andre, *Buff.*	9	0	9	0	54
Dickerson, Eric, *Ind.*	8	7	1	0	48
Hill, Drew, *Hou.*	8	0	8	0	48
Hoge, Merril, *Pitt.*	8	8	0	0	48
Humphrey, Bobby, *Den.*	8	7	1	0	48
McGee, Tim, *Cin.*	8	0	8	0	48
Johnson, Vance, *Den.*	7	0	7	0	42
Stephens, John, *N.E.*	7	7	0	0	42
Vick, Roger, *Jets*	7	5	2	0	42
Williams, John L., *Sea.*	7	1	6	0	42

AFC KICKOFF RETURNERS

	No	Yards	Ave	Long	TD
Woodson, Rod, *Pitt.*	36	982	27.3	†84	1
Logan, Marc, *Mia.*	24	613	25.5	†97	1
Miller, Anthony, *S.D.*	21	533	25.4	†91	1
Martin, Sammy, *N.E.*	24	584	24.3	38	0
Jefferson, James, *Sea.*	22	511	23.2	†97	1
Metcalf, Eric, *Clev.*	31	718	23.2	49	0
Jennings, Stanford, *Cin.*	26	525	20.2	33	0
Bell, Ken, *Den.*	30	602	20.1	33	0
Adams, Stefon, *Raiders*	22	425	19.3	37	0
Townsell, JoJo, *Jets*	34	653	19.2	69	0
Tucker, Erroll, *Buff.-N.E.*	23	436	19.0	37	0
Copeland, Danny, *K.C.*	26	466	17.9	36	0
Johnson, Kenny, *Hou.*	21	372	17.7	39	0
Holland, Jamie, *S.D.*	29	510	17.6	34	0
Humphery, Bobby, *Jets*	24	414	17.3	52	0

t=Touchdown
Leader based on average return, minimum 20 returns

AFC PUNTERS

	No	Yards	Long	Ave	Total Punts	TB	Blk	Opp Ret	Ret Yds	In 20	Net Ave
Montgomery, Greg, *Hou.*	56	2422	63	43.3	58	7	2	24	191	15	36.1
Stark, Rohn, *Ind.*	79	3392	64	42.9	80	10	1	51	558	14	32.9
Roby, Reggie, *Mia.*	58	2458	58	42.4	59	6	1	26	256	18	35.3
Newsome, Harry, *Pitt.*	82	3368	57	41.1	83	9	1	45	361	15	34.1
Gossett, Jeff, *Raiders*	67	2711	60	40.5	67	7	0	41	301	12	33.9
Horan, Mike, *Den.*	77	3111	63	40.4	77	5	0	28	370	24	34.3
Goodburn, Kelly, *K.C.*	67	2688	54	40.1	67	5	0	40	325	25	33.8
Ilesic, Hank, *S.D.*	76	3049	64	40.1	76	7	0	39	408	11	32.9
Johnson, Lee, *Cin.*	61	2446	62	40.1	63	11	2	33	323	14	30.2
Rodriguez, Ruben, *Sea.*	75	2995	59	39.9	76	8	1	41	334	17	32.9
Kidd, John, *Buff.*	65	2564	60	39.4	67	9	2	25	227	15	32.2
Prokop, Joe, *Jets*	87	3426	76	39.4	87	4	0	34	257	29	35.5
Wagner, Bryan, *Clev.*	97	3817	60	39.4	97	6	0	49	418	32	33.8
Feagles, Jeff, *N.E.*	63	2392	64	38.0	64	2	1	38	346	13	31.3

Leader based on gross average, minimum 40 punts

AFC SACKERS

	No
Williams, Lee, *S.D.*	14.0
Smith, Bruce, *Buff.*	13.0
O'Neal, Leslie, *S.D.*	12.5
Fletcher, Simon, *Den.*	12.0
Porter, Rufus, *Sea.*	10.5
Townsend, Greg, *Raiders*	10.5
Cross, Jeff, *Mia.*	10.0
Grossman, Burt, *S.D.*	10.0
Hand, Jon, *Ind.*	10.0
Thomas, Derrick, *K.C.*	10.0
Holmes, Ron, *Den.*	9.0
Childress, Ray, *Hou.*	8.5
Johnson, Ezra, *Ind.*	8.5
Bickett, Duane, *Ind.*	8.0
Nash, Joe, *Sea.*	8.0
Williams, Brent, *N.E.*	8.0
Baker, Al, *Clev.*	7.5
Green, Hugh, *Mia.*	7.5
Mecklenburg, Karl, *Den.*	7.5
Byrd, Dennis, *Jets*	7.0
Jeter, Gary, *N.E.*	7.0
Lloyd, Greg, *Pitt.*	7.0
Perry, Michael Dean, *Clev.*	7.0
Thompson, Donnell, *Ind.*	7.0
Fuller, William, *Hou.*	6.5
Griffin, Leonard, *K.C.*	6.5
Hairston, Carl, *Clev.*	6.5
Smith, Neil, *K.C.*	6.5
Willis, Keith, *Pitt.*	6.5
Buck, Jason, *Cin.*	6.0
Jones, Sean, *Hou.*	6.0
Talley, Darryl, *Buff.*	6.0
Bennett, Cornelius, *Buff.*	5.5
Carreker, Alphonso, *Den.*	5.5
Davis, Scott, *Raiders*	5.5
Long, Howie, *Raiders*	5.0
Sochia, Brian, *Mia.*	5.0
Johnson, Tim, *Pitt.*	4.5
Lageman, Jeff, *Jets*	4.5
McGrew, Larry, *N.E.*	4.5
Skow, Jim, *Cin.*	4.5
Banks, Robert, *Clev.*	4.0
Blaylock, Anthony, *Clev.*	4.0
Brown, Vincent, *N.E.*	4.0
Martin, Chris, *K.C.*	4.0
Matthews, Clay, *Clev.*	4.0
Meads, Johnny, *Hou.*	4.0
Nichols, Gerald, *Jets*	4.0
Seals, Leon, *Buff.*	4.0
Bryant, Jeff, *Sea.*	3.5
Golic, Bob, *Raiders*	3.5
Williams, Reggie, *Cin.*	3.5
Wise, Mike, *Raiders*	3.5

AFC PUNT RETURNERS

	No	FC	Yards	Ave	Long	TD
Verdin, Clarence, *Ind.*	23	5	296	12.9	t49	1
Schwedes, Scott, *Mia.*	18	3	210	11.7	t70	1
McNeil, Gerald, *Clev.*	49	15	496	10.1	49	0
Hollis, David, *Sea.*	18	7	164	9.1	21	0
Townsell, JoJo, *Jets*	33	12	299	9.1	30	0
Sutton, Mickey, *G.B.-Buff.*	31	10	273	8.8	26	0
Tucker, Erroll, *Buff.-N.E.*	19	4	165	8.7	25	0
Martin, Sammy, *N.E.*	19	2	164	8.6	28	0
Adams, Stefon, *Raiders*	19	5	156	8.2	15	0
Mandley, Pete, *K.C.*	19	2	151	7.9	19	0
Woodson, Rod, *Pitt.*	29	2	207	7.1	20	0
Worthen, Naz, *K.C.*	19	5	133	7.0	17	0
Bell, Ken, *Den.*	21	3	143	6.8	24	0
Johnson, Kenny, *Hou.*	19	21	122	6.4	19	0

t = Touchdown
Leader based on average return, minimum 18 returns

AFC INTERCEPTORS

	No	Yards	Ave	Long	TD
Wright, Felix, *Clev.*	9	91	10.1	t27	1
Fulcher, David, *Cin.*	8	87	10.9	22	0
Taylor, Keith, *Ind.*	7	225	32.1	t80	1
Byrd, Gill, *S.D.*	7	38	5.4	22	0
McMillan, Erik, *Jets*	6	180	30.0	t92	1
Braxton, Tyrone, *Den.*	6	103	17.2	t34	1
Kelso, Mark, *Buff.*	6	101	16.8	43	0
Prior, Mike, *Ind.*	6	88	14.7	t58	1
Anderson, Eddie, *Raiders*	5	233	46.6	t87	2
Hasty, James, *Jets*	5	62	12.4	t34	1
Brown, Steve, *Hou.*	5	54	10.8	41	0
Hurst, Maurice, *N.E.*	5	31	6.2	t16	1
Robinson, Eugene, *Sea.*	5	24	4.8	20	0
Odomes, Nate, *Buff.*	5	20	4.0	13	0
Lyles, Robert, *Hou.*	4	66	16.5	48	0
McDowell, Bubba, *Hou.*	4	65	16.3	21	0
Woodruff, Dwayne, *Pitt.*	4	57	14.3	35	0
Glenn, Vencie, *S.D.*	4	52	13.0	31	0
Seale, Sam, *S.D.*	4	47	11.8	25	0
Lewis, Albert, *K.C.*	4	37	9.3	22	0
Oliver, Louis, *Mia.*	4	32	8.0	23	0
Dishman, Cris, *Hou.*	4	31	7.8	31	0
Ross, Kevin, *K.C.*	4	29	7.3	23	0
Thomas, Eric, *Cin.*	4	18	4.5	t18	1
Everett, Thomas, *Pitt.*	3	68	22.7	32	0
Gash, Thane, *Clev.*	3	65	21.7	t36	2
Henderson, Wymon, *Den.*	3	58	19.3	25	0
Lloyd, Greg, *Pitt.*	3	49	16.3	31	0
Dixon, Rickey, *Cin.*	3	47	15.7	28	0
Washington, Lionel, *Raiders*	3	46	15.3	t32	1
Johnson, Mike, *Clev.*	3	43	14.3	23	0
Woodson, Rod, *Pitt.*	3	39	13.0	39	0
Atwater, Steve, *Den.*	3	34	11.3	30	0
Eaton, Tracey, *Hou.*	3	33	11.0	20	0
Minnifield, Frank, *Clev.*	3	29	9.7	25	0
Little, David, *Pitt.*	3	23	7.7	13	0
McDaniel, Terry, *Raiders*	3	21	7.0	20	0
Harper, Mark, *Clev.*	3	8	2.7	8	0
Bennett, Roy, *S.D.*	3	4	1.3	4	0
McNeal, Don, *Mia.*	3	-6	-2.0	0	0

t = Touchdown

LEFT: AFC sack leader Lee Williams has become a consistent force for San Diego.

RIGHT: Felix Wright led the NFL with nine interceptions.

BUFFALO BILLS

Address One Bills Drive, Orchard Park,
New York 14127.
Stadium Rich Stadium, Orchard Park.
Capacity 80,290 *Playing Surface* AstroTurf.
Team Colours Royal Blue, Scarlet Red, and White.
Head Coach Marv Levy – 5th year; 10th NFL.
Championships Division 1980,'88,'89; AFL 1964,'65.
History AFL 1960-69, AFC 1970-

Offense

Good teamwork, the odd flash of attacking brilliance and solid defense may be enough to give Buffalo a third straight division title. Comforting solidity comes from the offensive line which has Will Wolford and Howard Ballard at tackle, Jim Ritcher and Joe Devlin at guard and Pro Bowler Kent Hull at center. This group played together unchanged for the entire campaign and built the platform for a balanced offense which ranked fifth in the NFL. The unit should continue in the same vein, with Leonard Burton and John Davis the veteran backups and a pair of 300-pounders, Glenn Parker and Brent Griffith, coming in the draft. When the line makes a hole, running back Thurman Thomas is through like a rocket. In both rushing and pass receiving, 1989 was the year that Thomas stepped onto the edge of superstardom as he led the entire NFL in yards from scrimmage and did it with style. Much of the time, fullback Larry Kinnebrew was blocking for Thomas but, in his own right, he had quite a year with 533 yards at an average of 4.1 and six touchdowns. It is a starting duo which should not be altered but, for the future, the Bills drafted Carwell Gardner, who has been described as a 'bigger, faster and stronger version of (Houston's) Alonzo Highsmith', and Eddie Fuller. Last year brought the answer to a major question, namely, 'What happens if quarterback Jim Kelly is hurt?' The response came on Weeks Six to Eight, when backup Frank Reich stood in for the injured Kelly and the Bills won all three games. However, had anyone questioned Kelly's right to start, that answer, too, was supplied

when he unleashed a withering hail of passes which almost brought the Bills an heroic victory over Cleveland in the divisional playoffs. In wide receiver Andre Reed, the Bills may have the best in their history. Without attracting much attention outside Buffalo, Reed has gathered in most of the Bills' receiving records and, last year, won the AFC individual title. Less extravagantly, with 140 career receptions for the club, Pete Metzelaars has become the most prolific tight end in team history. The speedy Don Beebe will challenge veteran James Lofton for the right to start in partnership with Reed.

Defense

Defensively, the Bills were not the overpowering force which propelled the team to the 1988 division title but in 1989 injuries may have been a factor – the absence of Pro Bowl outside linebacker Cornelius Bennett coincided with three late-season losses. With everyone healthy, Buffalo has a linebacking quartet to compare with that of the NFC's Giants. Bennett and right outside linebacker Darryl Talley are the birds of prey while on the insides, Shane Conlan and Ray Bentley tackle with fury. Responding to the injuries, Scott Radecic showed that he could play either of the inside and outside roles with confident authority. On the three-man defensive line, tremendous pressure comes from the great All-Pro right defensive end, Bruce Smith, who has proved to be too much for even the very best offensive tackles to handle. At the left defensive end position, 13th-year veteran Art Still, a former Pro Bowler, is used mostly against the run and gives way to Leon Seals on passing downs. Seals helped himself to four quarterback sacks and may have a greater part to play as Still approaches retirement. There could be a problem at nose tackle, a position left vacant by the departure of 11-year starter and former Pro Bowler Fred Smerlas, who has signed for the 49ers as a Plan-B free agent. However, the promise of backup Jeff Wright, who had three sacks playing on relief duty last year, may have been one of the reasons that Buffalo chose not to protect Smerlas. For the defensive secondary, following the premature retirement of injured cornerback Derrick Burroughs, the Bills drafted James Williams in the first round. Williams might be expected to step in ahead of backups Mickey Sutton and Chris Hale and challenge left cornerback Kirby Jackson. Nate Odomes, who came second on the team with five interceptions and forced three fumbles, is secure on the right corner. At free safety, Mark Kelso is coming off another fine year in which he led the club with six interceptions, raising his total over the last three years to 19. Strong safety Leonard Smith, a 1983 first-round pick of the Cardinals, had a couple of interceptions but his great value comes as a punishing tackler.

1990 SCHEDULE OF GAMES

September
9	INDIANAPOLIS	4:00
16	at Miami	1:00
24	at New York Jets (Mon.)	9:00
30	DENVER	1:00

October
7	LOS ANGELES RAIDERS (Sun. night)	7:30
14	*Open date*	
21	NEW YORK JETS	1:00
28	at New England	1:00

November
4	at Cleveland	1:00
11	PHOENIX	1:00
18	NEW ENGLAND	1:00
26	at Houston (Mon.)	8:00

December
2	PHILADELPHIA	1:00
9	at Indianapolis	1:00
15	at New York Giants (Sat.)	12:30
23	MIAMI	1:00
30	at Washington	1:00

1990 DRAFT

Round	Name	Pos.	Ht.	Wt.	College
1.	Williams, James	CB	5-9	172	Fresno State
2.	Gardner, Carwell	RB	6-1	232	Louisville
3.	Parker, Glenn	T	6-5	301	Arizona
4.	Fuller, Eddie	RB	5-9	199	Louisiana State
6.	Nies, John	P	6-1	199	Arizona
7.	Griffith, Brent	G	6-5	300	Minnesota-Duluth
7.	Collins, Brent	LB	6-1	238	Carson-Newman
7.	DeRiggi, Fred	NT	6-1	268	Syracuse
8.	Patton, Marvcus	LB	6-1	216	UCLA
9.	Hines, Clarkston	WR	5-11	163	Duke
10.	Lodish, Mike	DT	6-2	270	UCLA
11.	Edwards, Al	WR	5-6	159	Northwestern St., La.

VETERAN ROSTER

No.	Name	Pos.	Ht.	Wt.	NFL Year	College
54	Bailey, Carlton	LB	6-2	237	3	North Carolina
75	Ballard, Howard	T	6-6	315	3	Alabama A&M
82	Beebe, Don	WR	5-11	177	2	Chadron State, Neb.
55	Bennett, Cornelius	LB	6-2	235	4	Alabama
50	Bentley, Ray	LB	6-2	235	5	Central Michigan
61	Burton, Leonard	T	6-3	277	5	South Carolina
90	Cofield, Timmy	LB	6-4	242	5	Elizabeth City State
58	Conlan, Shane	LB	6-3	235	4	Penn State
79	Davis, John	T	6-4	310	5	Georgia Tech
23	Davis, Kenneth	RB	5-10	209	5	Texas Christian
70	Devlin, Joe	G-T	6-5	280	14	Iowa
	Doctor, Tom	LB	6-0	240	1	Canisius
45	Drane, Dwight	S	6-2	205	5	Oklahoma
85	Franklin, Darryl	WR	5-11	185	1	Washington
59	Frerotte, Mitch	T-G	6-3	285	2	Penn State
7	Gilbert, Gale	QB	6-3	210	3	California
22	Hagy, John	S	5-11	190	3	Texas
26	Hale, Chris	CB	5-7	161	2	Southern California
67	Hull, Kent	C	6-5	275	5	Mississippi State
47	Jackson, Kirby	CB	5-10	180	4	Mississippi State
12	Kelly, Jim	QB	6-3	215	5	Miami
38	Kelso, Mark	S	5-11	185	5	William & Mary
28	Kinnebrew, Larry	RB	6-2	256	7	Tennessee State
86	Kolesar, John	WR	5-10	187	1	Michigan
63	Lingner, Adam	C	6-4	268	8	Illinois
80	Lofton, James	WR	6-3	190	13	Stanford
84	McKeller, Keith	TE	6-4	245	3	Jacksonville State
88	Metzelaars, Pete	TE	6-7	250	9	Wabash
21	Mims, Carl	DB	5-10	180	1	Sam Houston State
57	Monger, Matt	LB	6-1	240	5	Oklahoma State
39	Mueller, Jamie	RB	6-1	230	4	Benedictine College
11	Norwood, Scott	K	6-0	207	6	James Madison
37	Odomes, Nate	CB	5-10	188	4	Wisconsin
94	Pike, Mark	DE	6-4	272	4	Georgia Tech
97	Radecic, Scott	LB	6-3	236	7	Penn State
83	Reed, Andre	WR	6-1	190	6	Kutztown State
14	Reich, Frank	QB	6-4	210	6	Maryland
40	Riddick, Robb	RB	6-0	195	8	Millersville State
51	Ritcher, Jim	G	6-3	273	11	North Carolina State
87	Rolle, Butch	TE	6-4	245	5	Michigan State
96	Seals, Leon	DE	6-5	267	4	Jackson State
78	Smith, Bruce	DE	6-4	280	6	Virginia Tech
30	Smith, Don	RB	5-11	200	3	Mississippi State
46	Smith, Leonard	S	5-11	202	8	McNeese State
72	Still, Art	DE	6-7	265	13	Kentucky
20	Sutton, Mickey	CB-KR	5-9	172	5	Montana
56	Talley, Darryl	LB	6-4	235	8	West Virginia
89	Tasker, Steve	WR-KR	5-9	185	6	Northwestern
34	Thomas, Thurman	RB	5-10	198	3	Oklahoma State
3	Tuten, Rick	P	6-2	220	2	Florida State
69	Wolford, Will	T	6-5	290	5	Vanderbilt
91	Wright, Jeff	NT	6-2	270	3	Central Missouri State

Special Teams

Following the departure of Plan-B free agent punter John Kidd, there will be a battle involving Rick Tuten, who swung the boot seven times to modest effect with Philadelphia, and draftee John Nies. Scott Norwood is cool, accurate and has greater range than most place-kickers in the NFL. With the departure of Ronnie Harmon as a Plan-B free agent, Beebe probably will return most of the kickoffs with Sutton continuing as one of the better punt returners in the AFC.

Linebacker Cornelius Bennett lends breathtaking speed to the Bills' defense.

INDIANAPOLIS COLTS

Address P.O. Box 535000, Indianapolis,
  Indiana 46253.
Stadium Hoosier Dome, Indianapolis.
  Capacity 60,127 *Playing Surface* AstroTurf.
Team Colours Royal Blue and White.
Head Coach Ron Meyer – 5th year; 8th NFL.
Championships Division 1970,'75,'76,'77,'87;
  Conference 1970; NFL 1958,'59,'68;
  Super Bowl 1970.
History NFL 1953-69, AFC 1970-
  (Until 1984, they were known as the Baltimore
  Colts. A team of the same name played in the
  AAFC, from 1947 to 1949, and in the NFL in 1950,
  at the end of which they went out of business.)

Offense

From being at one point primed to make a major challenge for the division title, the Colts are in the midst of a reshuffle and it could be two or three seasons before the pieces fall into place. In a trade which will not be completed until next year's draft, when Atlanta will have the Colts' first-round option, Indianapolis sent All-Pro tackle Chris Hinton, All-NFL Rookie wide receiver Andre Rison and a fifth-round option to Atlanta in exchange for the Falcons' first- and fourth-round draft options. With the first-rounder Indianapolis made quarterback Jeff George the 1990 overall first selection and the fourth-round option brought wide receiver Stacey Simmons. It was in the scouting combine workouts that George looked sensational and sparked the trading activity. But many observers feel that he has to develop quickly into another Dan Marino to equalise the terms of the deal. It leaves the Colts with three potential starters and it could be that one of the two veterans, Chris Chandler and Jack Trudeau, could be traded in exchange for help in positions of need. And those could be on the offensive line, where the loss of Hinton quickly followed the departure of Plan-B free agent Ben Utt, who started all 16 games at right guard in

1989. The remedial treatment may emerge from a group which includes Brian Baldinger, Zefross Moss and Pat Tomberlin. It would help if either of the draftees, Bill Schultz and Pat Cunningham, could come through. Thankfully, the remaining starters, Randy Dixon, Kevin Call and Pro Bowl center Ray Donaldson, are high-class players. Another difficulty arises with the strong suggestion that superstar running back Eric Dickerson might retire. With him the Colts are likely to run all over any opponent but, without him, Albert Bentley will be given the chance to prove what many scouts feel, namely, that he can rush for 1,000 yards in a season. At wide receiver, Bill Brooks has all the experience and speed any starter would need, while Clarence Verdin could take full advantage of his opportunities for greater playing time. A steady blocking tight end, Pat Beach, completes the package.

Defense

The Colts are coming off a modest campaign in which they ranked 22nd in the NFL, a position which, after a survey of their personnel, is a little surprising. Defensive left end Donnell Thompson is noted for his ability to apply pressure and generally close down on opponents. Defensive right end Jon Hand really has come through, last year leading the team with ten sacks and generally making himself unwelcome in the opposing backfield. Nose tackle Harvey Armstrong is making progress but, rarely, is double-teamed. Backup Mitchell Benson, a 1989 third-round draftee, could push Armstrong but the club may miss Ezra Johnson, the great veteran who contributed 8.5 sacks but has been signed by Houston as a Plan-B free agent. The real strength of this defense lies at linebacker, where there is an overabundance of genuine starters. Currently with that status are former Pro Bowl outside linebackers Chip Banks and Duane Bickett, with Fredd Young and Jeff Herrod on the insides. Young has been to four Pro Bowls, both as a special-teamer and a linebacker. Another former starter, outside linebacker O'Brien Alston, is returning from injured reserve and young Quintus McDonald showed considerable promise in his rookie season. In order, Herrod and Young led the team in tackles with 154 and 122. Bickett had eight sacks and 11 quarterback pressures with Banks crowding the passer nine times and making two interceptions. Perhaps because three members of the starting secondary were middle-round draftees and one was a free agent, entering the campaign, it was not regarded with much awe. But it has made quiet progress and has emerged as a competent group. The starters are strong safety Michael Ball and free safety Mike Prior, with Eugene Daniel and John Baylor on the corners. Last year Prior, who was a 1987 free-agent signing, had six interceptions while another free-agent signing (1988), nickel back Keith Taylor, led the club with seven interceptions which he returned for 225 yards, including an 80-yard touchdown. Former starting cornerback Chris Goode has been joined by draftees Alan Grant and Harvey Wilson in reserve. Grant is considered to be raw but he does have fine instincts and adjusts quickly to the ball.

VETERAN ROSTER NFL

No.	Name	Pos.	Ht.	Wt.	Year	College
97	Alston, O'Brien	LB	6-6	241	3	Maryland
79	Armstrong, Harvey	NT	6-3	282	8	Southern Methodist
62	Baldinger, Brian	T-G	6-4	272	8	Duke
31	Ball, Michael	S	6-0	217	3	Southern
51	Banks, Chip	LB	6-4	245	8	Southern California
36	Baylor, John	CB	6-0	203	2	Southern Mississippi
81	Beach, Pat	TE	6-4	252	8	Washington State
95	Benson, Mitchell	NT	6-3	302	2	Texas Christian
20	Bentley, Albert	RB	5-11	214	6	Miami
4	Biasucci, Dean	K	6-0	189	6	Western Carolina
50	Bickett, Duane	LB	6-5	251	6	Southern California
80	Brooks, Bill	WR	6-0	185	5	Boston University
71	Call, Kevin	T	6-7	308	7	Colorado State
17	Chandler, Chris	QB	6-4	218	3	Washington
91	Clancy, Sam	DE	6-7	284	7	Pittsburgh
38	Daniel, Eugene	CB	5-11	188	7	Louisiana State
29	Dickerson, Eric	RB	6-3	224	8	Southern Methodist
69	Dixon, Randy	G	6-3	302	4	Pittsburgh
53	Donaldson, Ray	C	6-3	292	11	Georgia
67	Eisenhooth, Stan	C	6-5	290	3	Towson State
37	Goode, Chris	CB	6-0	195	4	Alabama
78	Hand, Jon	DE	6-7	301	5	Alabama
54	Herrod, Jeff	LB	6-0	246	3	Mississippi
45	Hunter, Ivy Joe	RB	6-0	237	2	Kentucky
63	Knight, Steve	T-G	6-4	326	2	Tennessee
59	Larson, Kurt	LB	6-4	236	2	Michigan State
96	McDonald, Quintus	LB	6-3	240	2	Penn State
73	Moss, Zefross	T	6-6	315	2	Alabama State
39	Prior, Mike	S	6-0	210	5	Illinois State
86	Pruitt, James	WR	6-3	201	5	Cal State-Fullerton
3	Stark, Rohn	P	6-3	203	9	Florida State
27	Taylor, Keith	DB	5-11	206	3	Illinois
99	Thompson, Donnell	DE	6-4	280	10	North Carolina
68	Tomberlin, Pat	G	6-2	312	1	Florida State
10	Trudeau, Jack	QB	6-3	219	5	Illinois
83	Verdin, Clarence	WR-KR	5-8	170	5	S.W. Louisiana
56	Young, Fredd	LB	6-1	235	7	New Mexico State

1990 SCHEDULE OF GAMES		
September		
9	at Buffalo	4:00
16	NEW ENGLAND	12:00
23	at Houston	12:00
30	at Philadelphia	1:00
October		
7	KANSAS CITY	12:00
14	Open date	
21	DENVER	12:00
28	MIAMI	1:00
November		
5	NEW YORK GIANTS (Mon.)	9:00
11	at New England	1:00
18	NEW YORK JETS	4:00
25	at Cincinnati	1:00
December		
2	at Phoenix	2:00
9	BUFFALO	1:00
16	at New York Jets	1:00
22	WASHINGTON (Sat. night)	8:00
30	at Miami	1:00

Special Teams

Taking care of the Colts' kicking game, both placekicker Dean Biasucci and punter Rohn Stark are former Pro Bowlers. Remarkably, Biasucci has been successful with 51 of his last 55 field goals from inside 45 yards, and it is a measure of Stark's power that his 1989 punting average of 42.9 yards was the second-lowest of his career. Returning punts, Verdin topped the AFC and ranked second in the NFL with an average of 12.9 yards. The club is hoping that he can increase his yield on kickoff returns.

1990 DRAFT

Round	Name	Pos.	Ht.	Wt.	College
1.	George, Jeff	QB	6-4	221	Illinois
2.	Johnson, Anthony	RB	6-0	216	Notre Dame
4.	Simmons, Stacey	WR	5-9	183	Florida
4.	Schultz, Bill	G	6-4	289	Southern California
4.	Grant, Alan	CB	5-9	188	Stanford
4.	Cunningham, Pat	T	6-6	275	Texas A&M
6.	Walker, Tony	LB	6-2	230	Southeast Missouri
7.	Singletary, James	LB	6-2	230	East Carolina
8.	Clark, Ken	RB	5-9	203	Nebraska
8.	Wilson, Harvey	S	6-1	190	Southern
9.	Huffman, Darvell	WR	5-7	156	Boston University
11.	Smith, Carnel	DE	6-1	265	Pittsburgh
12.	Benhart, Gene	QB	6-4	212	Western Illinois
12.	Brown, Dean	G	6-2	295	Notre Dame

Inside linebacker Fredd Young should be approaching his best.

99

MIAMI DOLPHINS

Address Joe Robbie Stadium, 2269 N.W. 199th Street, Miami, Florida 33056.
Stadium Joe Robbie Stadium, Miami. *Capacity* 73,000 *Playing Surface* Grass (PAT).
Team Colours Aqua, Coral, and White.
Head Coach Don Shula – 21st year; 28th NFL.
Championships Division 1971, '72, '73, '74, '79, '81, '83, '84, '85; Conference 1971, '72, '73, '82, '84; Super Bowl 1972, '73.
History AFL 1966-69, AFC 1970-

Offense

The combination of several Plan-B signings and a draft which could satisfy immediate needs suggests that 1990 could be the dawn of a new era for the Dolphins. Beginning with the offensive line, right tackle Ronnie Lee has been lost to Plan-B free agency, but Mark Dennis is capable of moving into Lee's starting spot to join a group which has Harry Galbreath and Roy Foster as the guards, Jeff Uhlenhake at center and Jeff Dellenbach at left tackle. Dennis, then, would be the only change in one of the NFL's best pass-protection lines, but there is the prospect of an immediate impact from the draft which brought Richmond Webb, a tremendously powerful drive blocker, and the massive guard, Keith Sims, in the first two rounds. Any kind of pass protection could set the stage for quarterback Dan Marino to unleash a passing game which, not long ago, was the scourge of the league. At wide receiver, Mark Clayton and Mark Duper still can present a nightmare for opposing defensive coordinators and, with Fred Banks, Andre Brown, Scott Schwedes and the veteran Jim Jensen hovering in the background, there are no problems with depth. The setup will be complete if tight end Ferrell Edmunds can bring his wide-ranging talents into focus. Even in a modest 1989 campaign, Edmunds did enough to earn a place in the Pro Bowl. It is not clear how the Dolphins will dovetail their rushing and passing games but, in Sammie Smith at running back, they have a player with the size, speed and moves to give Marino, who is hurtling towards all the NFL career

records, much more than just an option. Smith started slowly in his 1989 rookie season, averaging only 3.3 yards per carry. But with just a little more elbow room which might come from a beefed-up offensive line and the blocking help of the fullback, Smith has the potential to win games on his own. Such are the Dolphins' expectations of Tony Paige, the former Jets and Detroit starting fullback who was a Plan-B free-agent signing, that he was pencilled in to start long before training camp. He could be the key to springing Smith or his backup, Troy Stradford.

Defense

The Dolphins' defense was shoved around a little in 1989 but there are hopes for improvement and, certainly at linebacker, they are much deeper with the signing of Plan-B free agents Cliff Odom and Mike Reichenbach. Odom, an inside linebacker who spent the 1989 season languishing as a reserve for the Colts, will now be in competition with another former Colts starter, Barry Krauss, who joined the Dolphins under similar circumstances and enjoyed a new lease of life. Krauss, who is projected to start on the inside with current Pro Bowler John Offerdahl, led the Dolphins with 119 tackles. Reichenbach, a six-year starter with the Eagles, is a natural backup for Offerdahl. Right outside linebacker Hugh Green, a former Pro Bowler, is another who was rejuvenated as he had a career, single-season best 7.5 sacks. Green should be coming under increased pressure from the towering Eric Kumerow, a 1988 first-round draftee who has taken time to find a role with the club after being tried at both outside linebacker and defensive end. Alternatively, Kumerow may pressure E. J. Junior to start on the left side, but here he would be in competition with another good reserve, Rick Graf. The defensive line of T. J. Turner, Brian Sochia and Jeff Cross will be better for having played together for almost the entire season. Cross, who registered a team-leading ten sacks, was a revelation. However, it has to be a disappointment that former first-round pick John Bosa has not yet lived up to his potential. The defensive secondary has been under pressure for some years but there is gathering strength at safety where the former University of Florida pairing of Jarvis Williams and Louis Oliver promises greatness. Oliver, who confirmed the Dolphins' estimate of his collegiate form, was the team leader with four interceptions. Paul Lankford should continue to start at cornerback, extending a sequence which began back in 1985 except for when he was injured. But there will be a change on the other corner, where former 49ers starter and Pro Bowler Tim McKyer, for whom Miami traded, should step into the place vacated by William Judson, who has departed as a Plan-B free agent.

1990 SCHEDULE OF GAMES

September
9	at New England	4:00
16	BUFFALO	1:00
23	at New York Giants	1:00
30	at Pittsburgh	1:00

October
7	NEW YORK JETS	1:00
14	*Open date*	
18	NEW ENGLAND (Thurs. night)	8:00
25	at Indianapolis	1:00

November
4	PHOENIX	1:00
11	at New York Jets	1:00
19	LOS ANGELES RAIDERS (Mon.)	9:00
25	at Cleveland	1:00

December
2	at Washington	1:00
9	PHILADELPHIA (Sun. night)	8:00
16	SEATTLE	1:00
23	at Buffalo	1:00
30	INDIANAPOLIS	1:00

Special Teams

Just a little improvement by placekicker Pete Stoyanovich on field goals in the range 40-46 yards could give Miami an outstanding special teams output. Punter Reggie Roby regularly features amongst the conference leaders and is the current Pro Bowler. Schwedes averaged 11.7 yards on 18 punt returns compared with the AFC-leading average of 12.9, and Marc Logan came third in the NFL with his kickoff return average, which was boosted to 25.5 by a 97-yard touchdown.

1990 DRAFT

Round	Name	Pos.	Ht.	Wt.	College
1.	Webb, Richmond	T	6-6	291	Texas A&M
2.	Sims, Keith	G	6-2	310	Iowa State
3.	Oglesby, Alfred	DT	6-3	271	Houston
4.	Mitchell, Scott	QB	6-6	231	Utah
5.	Holt, Leroy	RB	5-10	236	Southern California
6.	Vanhorse, Sean	CB	5-9	178	Howard
8.	Woods, Thomas	WR	5-10	174	Tennessee
9.	Ross, Phil	TE	6-3	230	Oregon State
12.	Harden, Bobby	S	6-0	192	Miami

VETERAN ROSTER

					NFL	
No.	Name	Pos.	Ht.	Wt.	Year	College
86	Banks, Fred	WR	5-10	180	5	Liberty
51	Batiste, Dana	LB	6-0	238	1	Texas A&M
97	Bosa, John	DE	6-4	270	4	Boston College
82	Brown, Andre	WR	6-3	210	2	Miami
37	Brown, J.B.	CB	6-0	192	2	Maryland
83	Clayton, Mark	WR	5-9	184	8	Louisville
91	Cross, Jeff	DE	6-4	270	3	Missouri
65	Dellenbach, Jeff	T-C	6-5	282	6	Wisconsin
74	Dennis, Mark	T	6-6	290	4	Illinois
85	Duper, Mark	WR	5-9	190	9	Northwestern St., La.
80	Edmunds, Ferrell	TE	6-6	252	3	Maryland
	Elder, Donnie	CB-KR	5-9	175	5	Memphis State
61	Foster, Roy	G	6-4	277	9	Southern California
62	Galbreath, Harry	G	6-1	275	3	Tennessee
35	Glenn, Kerry	CB	5-9	175	4	Minnesota
99	Graf, Rick	LB	6-5	249	4	Wisconsin
41	Grant, African	S	6-0	200	1	Illinois
55	Green, Hugh	LB	6-2	228	10	Pittsburgh
92	Griggs, David	LB	6-3	239	2	Virginia
	Harvey, Stacy	LB	6-4	245	2	Arizona State
21	Higgs, Mark	RB-KR	5-7	188	3	Kentucky
29	Hobley, Liffort	S	6-0	202	5	Louisiana State
11	Jensen, Jim	WR-RB	6-4	224	10	Boston University
54	Junior, E.J.	LB	6-3	242	10	Alabama
88	Kinchen, Brian	TE	6-2	232	3	Louisiana State
58	Krauss, Barry	LB	6-3	260	12	Alabama
90	Kumerow, Eric	LB-DE	6-7	268	3	Ohio State
44	Lankford, Paul	CB	6-1	190	9	Penn State
20	Logan, Marc	RB	5-11	220	4	Kentucky
13	Marino, Dan	QB	6-4	224	8	Pittsburgh
89	Martin, Tony	WR	6-0	174	1	Mesa, Colorado
	McKyer, Tim	CB	6-0	174	5	Texas-Arlington
27	Moore, Stevon	CB	5-11	205	1	Mississippi
93	Odom, Cliff	LB	6-2	251	10	Texas-Arlington
56	Offerdahl, John	LB	6-3	240	5	Western Michigan
25	Oliver, Louis	S	6-2	226	2	Florida
49	Paige, Tony	RB	5-10	235	7	Virginia Tech
52	Reichenbach, Mike	LB	6-2	235	7	E. Stroudsburg State
4	Roby, Reggie	P	6-2	246	8	Iowa
81	Schwedes, Scott	WR-PR	6-0	182	4	Syracuse
9	Secules, Scott	QB	6-3	219	3	Virginia
33	Smith, Sammie	RB	6-2	226	2	Florida State
70	Sochia, Brian	NT	6-3	278	8	N.W. Oklahoma State
18	Stoudt, Cliff	QB	6-4	218	12	Youngstown State
10	Stoyanovich, Pete	K	5-10	180	2	Indiana
23	Stradford, Troy	RB	5-9	192	4	Boston College
24	Thomas, Rodney	CB	5-10	190	3	Brigham Young
95	Turner, T.J.	DE	6-4	280	5	Houston
63	Uhlenhake, Jeff	C	6-3	282	2	Ohio State
26	Williams, Jarvis	S	5-11	198	3	Florida
	Wilson, Karl	DE	6-4	275	4	Louisiana State

Free safety Louis Oliver fitted in smoothly.

NEW ENGLAND PATRIOTS

Address Sullivan Stadium, Route 1, Foxboro, Mass. 02035.
Stadium Sullivan Stadium, Foxboro.
   Capacity 60,794 *Playing Surface* SuperTurf.
Team Colours Red, White, and Blue.
Head Coach Rod Rust – 1st year.
Championships Division 1978,'86; Conference 1985.
History AFL 1960-69, AFC 1970-
   (Until 1971, they were known as the Boston Patriots.)

Offense

New England enters the 1990s with uncertainty at quarterback lingering as a problem. The air was cleared a little by the departure of Tony Eason to the New York Jets and the subsequent release of Doug Flutie, but it is unlikely that draftee Tommy Hodson can step in immediately ahead of veterans Marc Wilson and Steve Grogan. In reality, the situation isn't that bad, for Wilson does have his good patches and Grogan seems to be able to go on for ever. It would be no surprise to see Grogan launch the campaign. There may be a difficulty at center, where the departures of Plan-B free agents Mike Baab, Mike Morris and Curtis Wilson have left veterans Gerry Feehery and Bob White holding the fort. This apart, the offensive line will be helped by the return of guard Ron Wooten, who has started and at the very least will provide sound backup behind Sean Farrell and Paul Fairchild. Danny Villa and Bruce Armstrong are stalwarts at tackle, ahead of David Viaene, who gained experience in four starts. It was a disappointment that second-year running back John Stephens did not reproduce his power and sparkle following a rookie year when he came second in the AFC, albeit almost 500 yards behind Eric Dickerson. His loss of form meant that the Patriots needed to throw more often and opponents took advantage. Former Redskin Jamie Morris could add effervescence but Stephens has to improve, and in this quest he'll have solid block-ing from fullback Robert Perryman, backed up by Mosi Tatupu and George Adams. For those occasions when the Patriots are allowed to pass out of choice rather than necessity, the selection is mouthwatering. Twice in the recent past they have used first-round options to pick potential superstar wide receivers in Irving Fryar and Hart Lee Dykes, who are the current starters ahead of Cedric Jones. However, it may be the 1989 third round which produces the best of all. The draftee, Greg McMurtry, has a deceptive stride, outstanding catching ability and, importantly, great poise. In addition, tight end Eric Sievers, who sometimes lines up wide, has blossomed. Sadly, we may have seen the last of Stanley Morgan, who has been released.

Defense

It was one of the major talking points of the 1989 season that the Patriots suffered so many injuries to defensive starters. The most critical was at outside linebacker, with All-Pro Andre Tippett missing the entire year because of a shoulder injury. He should be ready to resume at left outside linebacker in a unit which has been given a significant boost by the arrival of first-round draftee Chris Singleton. Bigger than most outside linebackers, Singleton can dominate games and is set to start immediately in the place vacated by departed Plan-B free agent Lawrence McGrew. On the insides, the holes are plugged by two no-nonsense pros, Ed Reynolds and Johnny Rembert. Vincent Brown and Bruce Scholtz hover in reserve. The defensive line did not escape injuries, in particular the one which kept defensive end Garin Veris out for the entire season. Defensive right end Brent Williams was a tower of strength, leading the team in sacks for the second year in a row. Nose tackle Tim Goad built on the platform established in his rookie year and is now the unchal-lenged starter. With the arrival of first-round draftee Ray Agnew, the combinations for the three-man line begin to look very attractive. Defensive left end Ken Sims, who also has had his share of injuries, probably will start but will be replaced by either Agnew or Veris on passing downs. Injury problems continued in the defensive secondary, which missed cornerback Ronnie Lippett for the entire campaign. Subsequently, three-time Pro Bowl cornerback Raymond Clayborn and backup Howard Feggins were lost as Plan-B free agents. However, former starting cornerback Ernest Gibson has returned and Lippett is projected to be back. In addition, rookie Maurice Hurst was a revela-tion, leading the team with five interceptions, one of which he returned for a touchdown to beat Buffalo. There are no problems at safety where Roland James and Fred Marion have formed a fine partnership since the 1984 season. Draftee Junior Robinson could make a name for himself as a nickel back.

1990 SCHEDULE OF GAMES

September
9	MIAMI	4:00
16	at Indianapolis	12:00
23	at Cincinnati	1:00
30	NEW YORK JETS	4:00

October
7	SEATTLE	1:00
14	*Open date*	
18	at Miami (Thurs. night)	8:00
28	BUFFALO	1:00

November
4	at Philadelphia	1:00
11	INDIANAPOLIS	1:00
18	at Buffalo	1:00
25	at Phoenix	2:00

December
2	KANSAS CITY	1:00
9	at Pittsburgh	1:00
15	WASHINGTON (Sat.)	4:00
23	at New York Jets	1:00
30	NEW YORK GIANTS	1:00

Special Teams

Jason Staurovsky replaced Greg Davis and did quite well, failing on only three of 17 field goal attempts and landing a 50-yarder. But the search is on for a punter to fill the spot made vacant by the release of Jeff Feagles. Kickoff returner Sammy Martin lay sixth in the NFL with an average of 24.3 yards when his season ended with an injury on Week Ten. He should be back. And any one of Martin, Fryar, Hurst and Erroll Tucker can return punts at a moment's notice.

Rookie cornerback Maurice Hurst led the Patriots with five interceptions.

1990 DRAFT

Round	Name	Pos.	Ht.	Wt.	College
1.	Singleton, Chris	LB	6-2	244	Arizona
1.	Agnew, Ray	DE	6-3	281	North Carolina State
3.	Hodson, Tommy	QB	6-2	189	Louisiana State
3.	McMurtry, Greg	WR	6-2	204	Michigan
5.	Robinson, Junior	DB	5-9	181	East Carolina
5.	Melander, Jon	T	6-6	276	Minnesota
5.	Gray, James	RB	5-10	197	Texas Tech
9.	Bouwens, Shawn	G	6-4	279	Nebraska Wesleyan
10.	Landry, Anthony	RB	5-9	194	Stephen F. Austin
11.	Smith, Sean	DE	6-7	270	Georgia Tech
12.	Donelson, Ventson	CB	5-10	178	Michigan State
12.	Rose, Blaine	G	6-5	265	Maryland

VETERAN ROSTER   NFL

No.	Name	Pos.	Ht.	Wt.	Year	College
33	Adams, George	RB	6-1	225	6	Kentucky
39	Allen, Marvin	RB	5-10	208	3	Tulane
78	Armstrong, Bruce	T	6-4	284	4	Louisville
28	Bowman, Jim	S	6-2	215	6	Central Michigan
59	Brown, Vincent	LB	6-2	245	3	Mississippi Valley St.
22	Coleman, Eric	CB	6-0	190	2	Wyoming
46	Cook, Marv	TE	6-4	234	2	Iowa
87	Dawson, Lin	TE	6-3	240	9	North Carolina State
67	Douglas, David	G-C	6-4	280	5	Tennessee
88	Dykes, Hart Lee	WR	6-4	218	2	Oklahoma State
66	Fairchild, Paul	G	6-4	270	7	Kansas
62	Farrell, Sean	G	6-3	260	9	Penn State
63	Feehery, Gerry	C	6-2	270	7	Syracuse
80	Fryar, Irving	WR-PR	6-0	200	7	Nebraska
74	Gambol, Chris	T	6-6	303	3	Iowa
91	Gannon, Chris	DE	6-6	265	2	S.W. Louisiana
43	Gibson, Ernest	CB	5-10	176	7	Furman
72	Goad, Tim	NT	6-3	280	3	North Carolina
14	Grogan, Steve	QB	6-4	210	16	Kansas State
58	Harvey, Richard	LB	6-2	227	1	Tulane
37	Hurst, Maurice	CB	5-10	185	2	Southern
38	James, Roland	S	6-2	191	11	Tennessee
50	Jarostchuk, Ilia	LB	6-3	236	4	New Hampshire
99	Jeter, Gary	DE	6-4	260	14	Southern California
68	Johnson, Damian	G	6-5	290	5	Kansas State
83	Jones, Cedric	WR	6-1	184	9	Duke
93	Jordan, Tim	LB	6-3	226	4	Wisconsin
42	Lippett, Ronnie	CB	5-11	180	7	Miami
91	Lowry, Orlando	LB	6-4	236	7	Ohio State
31	Marion, Fred	S	6-2	191	9	Miami
82	Martin, Sammy	WR-KR	5-11	175	3	Louisiana State
23	McSwain, Rod	CB	6-1	198	7	Clemson
24	Morris, Jamie	RB	5-7	188	3	Michigan
81	Mowatt, Zeke	TE	6-3	240	7	Florida State
34	Perryman, Robert	RB	6-1	233	4	Michigan
52	Rembert, Johnny	LB	6-3	234	8	Clemson
95	Reynolds, Ed	LB	6-5	242	8	Virginia
51	Scholtz, Bruce	LB	6-6	244	9	Texas
85	Sievers, Eric	TE	6-4	238	10	Maryland
77	Sims, Kenneth	DE	6-5	271	8	Texas
4	Staurovsky, Jason	K	5-9	170	4	Tulsa
44	Stephens, John	RB	6-1	215	3	Northwestern St., La.
30	Tatupu, Mosi	RB	6-0	227	13	Southern California
49	Taylor, Kitrick	WR	5-11	190	3	Washington State
45	Timpson, Michael	WR	5-10	175	1	Penn State
56	Tippett, Andre	LB	6-3	241	8	Iowa
21	Tucker, Erroll	CB-KR	5-8	170	3	Utah
60	Veris, Garin	DE	6-4	255	5	Stanford
70	Viaene, Dave	T	6-5	300	2	Minnesota-Duluth
73	Villa, Danny	T	6-5	305	4	Arizona State
65	White, Bob	C	6-5	273	4	Rhode Island
96	Williams, Brent	DE	6-4	275	5	Toledo
54	Williams, Ed	LB	6-4	244	5	Texas
15	Wilson, Marc	QB	6-5	205	10	Brigham Young
35	Wonsley, George	RB	5-10	219	7	Mississippi State
61	Wooten, Ron	G	6-4	273	8	North Carolina
25	Zackery, Tony	S	6-2	195	1	Washington

NEW YORK JETS

Address 598 Madison Avenue, New York,
N.Y. 10022.
Stadium Giants Stadium, East Rutherford.
Capacity 76,891 *Playing Surface* AstroTurf.
Team Colours Kelly Green and White.
Head Coach Bruce Coslet – 1st year.
Championships AFL 1968; Super Bowl 1968.
History AFL 1960-69, AFC 1970-
(Until 1963, they were known as the New York
Titans.)

Offense

'A breath of fresh air' was the phrase used by Jets owner Leon Hess and president Steve Gutman to indicate what they felt their club needed. And they found it by hiring new Vice President and General Manager Dick Steinberg. Then Steinberg introduced his own brand of air conditioning by appointing new head coach Bruce Coslet, not protecting several veterans, picking up a few good ones from other teams and, in the draft, coming out with two offensive players, running back Blair Thomas and wide receiver Reggie Rembert, both of whom fall into the 'most exciting available' category. His bid for 1990 begins with a starting offensive line stocked with a mixture of youth and veteran experience. Jim Sweeney is the anchor at center, Jeff Criswell has settled in as the starting left tackle and Mike Haight is beginning to play up to expectations at left guard. Right guard Dan Alexander has departed but Dave Cadigan, who has had injury problems, is set to fill that slot and Reggie McElroy should be back from injury to take over from Curt Singer at right tackle. Ken O'Brien will have his finger on the trigger at quarterback but he does have occasional lapses, and whereas in the past Pat Ryan used to step in for a spell, behind O'Brien will be Tony Eason, whom Steinberg first drafted when he was with the Patriots. Trevor Matich, who is another former Steinberg protege, will be the reserve at center. At running back, the Jets have experienced class in Freeman McNeil and Johnny Hector but the club will want to introduce the devastating

moves and pace of draftee Thomas as quickly as possible. It may be that Hector could be used in rotation with starting fullback Roger Vick, who is a powerful blocker and is a rushing threat in his own right. In 1989, JoJo Townsell gradually established himself as a starting wide receiver and took his responsibilities seriously when the big star, Al Toon, was injured. But Townsell may have to allow access to Rembert, who really does represent the state of the art when it comes to size, grace and flowing moves. At tight end, Keith Neubert has become an effective substitute for starter Mickey Shuler and may be ready to take over.

Defense

When it comes to defense the Jets aren't that hot and the unit did not receive special attention in the draft. The highest selection, defensive back Tony Stargell, came for an area which had lost 1989 starter Bobby Humphery and, clearly, the club intends maintaining this as a strong section. Stargell, who can play either at safety or cornerback, may move in for Humphery on the left corner but there is the possibility that Terry Williams, who was a 1988 second-round pick but has spent much of his short career on injured reserve, could challenge. In 1989, right cornerback James Hasty and free safety Erik McMillan started all year with success, while George Radachowsky started 13 games after an injury to Rich Miano. McMillan led the team with six interceptions, one of which he returned 92 yards for a touchdown, and included in Hasty's five steals was a 34-yard touchdown return. McMillan, a real ball-hawker, also returned fumbles 45 and 74 yards for touchdowns. Unusually, the Jets didn't have many injuries at linebacker and it enabled the smooth introduction of first-round draftee outside linebacker Jeff Lageman. The rookie did quite well, coming second on the team with 4.5 sacks. With 162 tackles, for the fourth time in six years inside linebacker Kyle Clifton led the team, followed by his inside partner, Troy Benson, who had 113. Alex Gordon started all year at left outside linebacker. The worry in this area lies in the absence of depth behind the one class reserve, Joe Mott. The defensive line, too, saw the introduction of a rookie, Ron Stallworth, who started nine games alongside nose tackle Scott Mersereau and defensive left end Paul Frase. If the Jets are looking for signs of a developing pass rush – they had a poor 28 sacks in total – it may come from defensive end Dennis Byrd, who didn't start but was used as the pass rusher in the nickel package and, in leading the team with seven sacks, fell only one short of the team's rookie record set by the great Joe Klecko in 1977. Indeed, more than half of the sack total came from rookies, with Stallworth (2) and Marvin Washington (1.5) topping up those by Byrd and Lageman.

1990 SCHEDULE OF GAMES

September
9	at Cincinnati	4:00
16	CLEVELAND	1:00
24	BUFFALO (Mon.)	9:00
30	at New England	4:00

October
7	at Miami	1:00
14	SAN DIEGO	1:00
21	at Buffalo	1:00
28	at Houston	12:00

November
4	DALLAS	1:00
11	MIAMI	1:00
18	at Indianapolis	4:00
25	PITTSBURGH	4:00

December
2	at San Diego	1:00
9	*Open date*	
16	INDIANAPOLIS	1:00
23	NEW ENGLAND	1:00
30	at Tampa Bay	4:00

Special Teams

The Jets like punter Joe Prokop. His average was modest but this may arise from his accuracy in planting 29 of his efforts inside the opposing 20-yard line. Placekicker Pat Leahy is coming off a so-so campaign but for the Jets not to have Leahy in the lineup is unthinkable. Townsell is a good punt returner, with a better chance than most of cutting loose for a long gain. He was not as effective returning kickoffs, though that may be as much a statement about the special-teams blockers as it is of Townsell's ability.

JoJo Townsell will battle with rookie Reggie Rembert to start.

1990 DRAFT

Round	Name	Pos.	Ht.	Wt.	College
1.	Thomas, Blair	RB	5-10	190	Penn State
2.	Rembert, Reggie	WR	6-4	195	West Virginia
3.	Stargell, Tony	DB	5-11	179	Tennessee State
4.	Taylor, Troy	QB	6-3	201	California
5.	Savage, Tony	DT	6-2	306	Washington State
5.	McWright, Robert	CB	5-8	179	Texas Christian
6.	Mathis, Terance	WR	5-11	167	New Mexico
7.	White, Dwayne	G	6-1	316	Alcorn State
7.	Proctor, Basil	LB	6-3	234	West Virginia
8.	Duffy, Roger	C	6-2	281	Penn State
9.	Dawkins, Dale	WR	6-0	185	Miami
10.	Quast, Brad	LB	6-0	241	Iowa
11.	Kelson, Derrick	CB	5-11	184	Purdue
12.	Davis, Darrell	LB	6-1	256	Texas Christian

VETERAN ROSTER

No.	Name	Pos.	Ht.	Wt.	NFL Year	College
19	Antrum, Glenn	WR	5-11	175	1	Connecticut
30	Baxter, Brad	RB	6-1	231	1	Alabama State
54	Benson, Troy	LB	6-2	235	5	Pittsburgh
42	Booty, John	DB	6-0	179	3	Texas Christian
80	Boyer, Mark	TE	6-4	252	6	Southern California
29	Brown, A.B.	RB	5-9	212	2	West Virginia
87	Burkett, Chris	WR	6-4	210	6	Jackson State
90	Byrd, Dennis	DE	6-5	270	2	Tulsa
66	Cadigan, Dave	G-T	6-4	280	3	Southern California
59	Clifton, Kyle	LB	6-4	236	7	Texas Christian
61	Criswell, Jeff	T	6-7	290	4	Graceland
49	Curtis, Travis	S	5-10	180	4	West Virginia
84	Dressel, Chris	TE	6-4	245	6	Stanford
11	Eason, Tony	QB	6-4	212	8	Illinois
44	Egu, Patrick	RB	5-11	205	2	Nevada-Reno
91	Frase, Paul	DE-DT	6-5	267	3	Syracuse
55	Gordon, Alex	LB	6-5	246	4	Cincinnati
79	Haight, Mike	G-T	6-4	281	5	Iowa
40	Hasty, James	CB	6-0	197	3	Washington State
34	Hector, Johnny	RB	5-11	202	8	Texas A&M
28	Howard, Carl	CB-S	6-2	190	7	Rutgers
85	Kelly, Pat	TE	6-6	252	3	Syracuse
57	Kohlbrand, Joe	LB	6-4	242	6	Miami
56	Lageman, Jeff	LB	6-5	250	2	Virginia
5	Leahy, Pat	K	6-0	196	17	St Louis
93	Lyons, Marty	DE	6-5	269	12	Alabama
64	Matich, Trevor	C	6-4	270	6	Brigham Young
68	McElroy, Reggie	T	6-6	276	8	West Texas State
22	McMillan, Erik	S	6-2	197	3	Missouri
92	McNeil, Emanuel	NT	6-3	285	4	Tennessee-Martin
24	McNeil, Freeman	RB	5-11	212	10	UCLA
94	Mersereau, Scott	DT-DE	6-3	280	4	Southern Connecticut
36	Miano, Rich	S	6-0	200	5	Hawaii
72	Miller, Brett	T	6-7	300	8	Iowa
51	Mott, Joe	LB	6-4	253	2	Iowa
86	Neubert, Keith	TE	6-6	248	2	Nebraska
77	Nichols, Gerald	DT-DE	6-2	267	4	Florida State
7	O'Brien, Ken	QB	6-4	206	8	California-Davis
70	Oliver, Jeff	T	6-4	292	1	Boston College
26	Parker, Anthony	CB	5-10	181	1	Arizona State
6	Prokop, Joe	P	6-2	224	5	Cal Poly-Pomona
25	Radachowsky, G.	S	5-11	195	6	Boston College
71	Rehder, Tom	G-T	6-7	280	3	Notre Dame
82	Shuler, Mickey	TE	6-3	231	13	Penn State
74	Singer, Curt	T	6-5	279	4	Tennessee
96	Stallworth, Ron	DE	6-5	262	2	Auburn
53	Sweeney, Jim	C	6-4	270	7	Pittsburgh
88	Toon, Al	WR	6-4	205	6	Wisconsin
83	Townsell, JoJo	WR-KR	5-9	180	6	UCLA
43	Vick, Roger	RB	6-3	235	4	Texas A&M
97	Washington, Marv.	DE	6-6	260	2	Idaho
33	Williams, Terry	CB	5-11	204	3	Bethune-Cookman
76	Withycombe, Mike	T	6-5	300	3	Fresno State
63	Zawatson, Dave	T	6-5	274	2	California

CINCINNATI BENGALS

Address 200 Riverfront Stadium, Cincinnati, Ohio 45202.
Stadium Riverfront Stadium, Cincinnati. *Capacity* 59,755 *Playing Surface* AstroTurf-8.
Team Colours Black, Orange, and White.
Head Coach Sam Wyche – 7th year.
Championships Division 1970,'73,'81,'88; Conference 1981,'88.
History AFL 1968-69, AFC 1970-

Offense

Cincinnati may have the most potent attack in the AFC and the one major change to last year's starting lineup, in reaction to the loss of Plan-B free agent right guard Max Montoya, is not anticipated as causing a problem. A solution might be to shift Bruce Kozerski from center to right guard allowing Paul Jetton, who has played at center, to make that position his own. More simply, Brian Blados could take a step forward. The rest of the line will be unchanged with Bruce Reimers at left guard, Joe Walter fully recovered from a knee injury at right tackle and future Hall-of-Famer Anthony Munoz at left tackle. Only if injuries strike will the Bengals be in a spot of bother, for there is very little veteran experience in reserve. By contrast, there is overwhelming talent at running back in James Brooks ahead of Stanford Jennings and the mercurial Paul Palmer, the latter who could be sensational if he settled down. At fullback, Ickey Woods – he of shuffling fame – should return and move ahead of Eric Ball. Woods was incredible as a rookie but missed virtually all of last year with an injury. There is yet more big-play potential in draftee Harold Green, who has the size of a fullback and moves of a halfback. When it comes to putting the ball in the air, Cincinnati has an outstanding trio in wide receivers Eddie Brown and Tim McGee, and tight end Rodney Holman. Brown is coming off a modest year compared with his tremendous 1988 campaign but McGee took up the slack, turning in his best year as a pro with a club-leading 65 catches for 1,211 yards and eight touchdowns. Holman, too, has just enjoyed his best campaign and gained a second Pro Bowl selection. Lighting the fuse at quarterback, Boomer Esiason is regarded as the AFC's best passer (as measured by his passer rating), a status he confirmed by leading the conference for the second year in a row. His backup, second-year pro Erik Wilhelm, was highly impressive with his limited opportunities. It minimises the problems of adjusting to different quarterbacks that both are left-handed passers.

Defense

Cincinnati's defense does attract criticism from time to time but the group which enters the 1990 campaign is very little different from the one which almost protected a slender lead against San Francisco in Super Bowl XXIII. One change will be at right outside linebacker, where the loss of inspirational leader Reggie Williams has been countered by the expenditure of the club's first-round option on James Francis. The big rookie could step in for Williams immediately and, if lacking in experience, he will bring an all-action presence, tackling, sacking and even dropping into pass coverage. Lower in the draft came Craig Ogletree, who has a sideline-to-sideline capability that Cincinnati might put to good use. Last year, the main problem was defense against the run, and while draftee inside linebacker Bernard Clark is not likely to displace either of starters Carl Zander and Joe Kelly, together with Ed Brady and Leo Barker, he does bring added depth. Kevin Walker, a 1988 third-round draftee, is a reserve at outside linebacker to starter Leon White. At nose tackle, Tim Krumrie is now restored to full health after playing through his recovery period last year. A two-time Pro Bowler, he is the leader of the defense. Defensive right end Jason Buck led the club with six sacks and shows steady improvement. In the absence of Jim Skow, Skip McClendon did well enough but the return of Skow at defensive left end will strengthen the pass rush. McClendon reverts to reserve status together with David Grant, who can play both at end and nose tackle, Mike Hammerstein and the promising Natu Tuatagaloa. The defensive secondary has become respected throughout the league but there may have to be adjustments following an offseason injury to starting right cornerback Eric Thomas. One option would be to move potential superstar Rickey Dixon from free safety allowing Solomon Wilcots to move up. On the other hand, Wilcots has played at cornerback in the past and it may make more sense not to break up the partnership of Dixon and David Fulcher, who led the club in interceptions and tackles, and is regarded as the premier strong safety in the AFC. Left cornerback Lewis Billups does not look out-of-place in this exalted company.

An injury may keep cornerback Eric Thomas out all year.

1990 DRAFT

Round	Name	Pos.	Ht.	Wt.	College
1.	Francis, James	LB	6-4	243	Baylor
2.	Green, Harold	RB	6-1	216	South Carolina
3.	Clark, Bernard	LB	6-1	250	Miami
4.	Brennan, Mike	T	6-5	270	Notre Dame
5.	James, Lynn	WR	6-0	191	Arizona State
6.	Odegard, Don	S	5-11	177	Nevada-Las Vegas
7.	Ogletree, Craig	LB	6-1	231	Auburn
8.	Wellsandt, Doug	TE	6-3	245	Washington State
9.	Price, Mitchell	DB	5-9	181	Tulane
10.	Crigler, Eric	T	6-7	290	Murray State
11.	O'Connor, Tim	T	6-5	285	Virginia
12.	Riley, Andre	WR	5-9	174	Washington

VETERAN ROSTER

No.	Name	Pos.	Ht.	Wt.	NFL Year	College
42	Ball, Eric	RB	6-2	211	2	UCLA
35	Barber, Chris	S	6-0	190	3	North Carolina A&T
86	Barber, Mike	WR	5-10	172	2	Marshall
53	Barker, Leo	LB	6-2	227	7	New Mexico State
24	Billups, Lewis	CB	5-11	179	5	North Alabama
74	Blados, Brian	T-G	6-5	286	7	North Carolina
55	Brady, Ed	LB	6-2	235	7	Illinois
3	Breech, Jim	K	5-6	161	12	California
21	Brooks, James	RB	5-10	182	10	Auburn
81	Brown, Eddie	WR	6-0	185	6	Miami
99	Buck, Jason	DE	6-5	258	4	Brigham Young
27	Bussey, Barney	S	6-0	205	5	South Carolina
34	Carey, Richard	CB	5-8	171	2	Idaho
29	Dixon, Rickey	S	5-11	196	3	Oklahoma
7	Esiason, Boomer	QB	6-5	215	7	Maryland
33	Fulcher, David	S	6-3	228	5	Arizona State
48	Garrett, John	WR	5-11	180	2	Princeton
98	Grant, David	NT	6-4	300	3	West Virginia
71	Hammerstein, Mike	DE	6-4	270	4	Michigan
40	Holifield, John	RB	6-0	202	4	West Virginia
82	Holman, Rodney	TE	6-3	238	9	Tulane
36	Jennings, Stanford	RB-KR	6-1	205	7	Furman
68	Jetton, Paul	C	6-4	288	2	Texas
11	Johnson, Lee	P	6-2	198	6	Brigham Young
77	Jones, Scott	T	6-5	290	2	Washington
84	Kattus, Eric	TE	6-5	235	5	Michigan
58	Kelly, Joe	LB	6-2	234	5	Washington
64	Kozerski, Bruce	C	6-4	275	7	Holy Cross
69	Krumrie, Tim	NT	6-2	268	8	Wisconsin
88	Martin, Mike	WR-PR	5-10	181	8	Illinois
72	McClendon, Skip	DE	6-7	280	4	Arizona State
85	McGee, Tim	WR	5-10	179	5	Tennessee
73	Moyer, Ken	T	6-6	292	2	Toledo
78	Munoz, Anthony	T	6-6	284	11	Southern California
26	Palmer, Paul	RB	5-9	181	4	Temple
75	Reimers, Bruce	G	6-7	294	7	Iowa State
87	Riggs, Jim	TE	6-5	245	4	Clemson
50	Skow, Jim	DE	6-3	243	5	Nebraska
83	Smith, Kendal	WR	5-9	189	2	Utah State
20	Taylor, Craig	RB	5-11	224	2	West Virginia
22	Thomas, Eric	CB	5-11	181	4	Tulane
96	Tuatagaloa, Natu	DE	6-4	265	2	California
59	Walker, Kevin	LB	6-3	233	2	Maryland
63	Walter, Joe	T	6-6	290	6	Texas Tech
79	Wells, Dana	NT	6-0	272	2	Arizona
51	White, Leon	LB	6-3	237	5	Brigham Young
41	Wilcots, Solomon	S	5-11	190	4	Colorado
12	Wilhelm, Erik	QB	6-3	210	2	Oregon State
30	Woods, Ickey	RB	6-2	232	2	Nevada-Las Vegas
91	Zander, Carl	LB	6-2	235	6	Tennessee

1990 SCHEDULE OF GAMES

September
9	NEW YORK JETS	4:00
16	at San Diego	1:00
23	NEW ENGLAND	1:00

October
1	at Seattle (Mon.)	6:00
7	at Los Angeles Rams	1:00
14	HOUSTON	1:00
22	at Cleveland (Mon.)	9:00
28	at Atlanta (Sun. night)	8:00

November
4	NEW ORLEANS	1:00
11	*Open date*	
18	PITTSBURGH (Sun. night)	8:00
25	INDIANAPOLIS	1:00

December
2	at Pittsburgh	1:00
9	SAN FRANCISCO	1:00
16	at Los Angeles Raiders	1:00
23	at Houston	12:00
30	CLEVELAND	1:00

Special Teams

Placekicker Jim Breech is vastly experienced and is accurate over the medium range but he does not have a powerful leg. And it is the ability to boom a long kickoff which amplifies the value of Lee Johnson, who is a respectable punter in his own right. Wide receivers Mike Martin and Kendal Smith shared the punt returns in 1989. Returning kickoffs is a role which Stanford Jennings should retain. His portfolio includes touchdowns on returns of 98 and 93 yards, the latter coming in Super Bowl XXIII.

CLEVELAND BROWNS

Address Tower B, Cleveland Stadium, Cleveland, Ohio 44114.
Stadium Cleveland Stadium, Cleveland. *Capacity* 80,098 *Playing Surface* Grass.
Team Colours Seal Brown, Orange, and White.
Head Coach Bud Carson – 2nd year.
Championships Division 1971,'80,'85,'86,'87,'89; AAFC 1946,'47,'48,'49; NFL 1950,'54,'55,'64.
History AAFC 1946-49, NFL 1950-69, AFC 1970-

Offense

The Cleveland Browns begin their defense of the division title with the major headache of replacing three veteran starters for the offensive line. Cody Risien has retired and the probability is that both Dan Fike and Ted Banker are not expected back until October at the earliest. Fortunately, former starting center Mike Baab has been re-signed as a Plan-B free agent, and it means that the incumbent, Gregg Rakoczy, could shift to left guard with Tony Jones staying on at right guard. Further good news comes with the return of Rickey Bolden, who could resume in his favoured position of left tackle with Paul Farren, who stood in when Bolden was injured, taking over at right tackle. It is an arrangement which could hold the fort but there'll be plenty of eyes and ears primed to detect the approach of cavalry. Elsewhere, the Browns expect to be first class, beginning at fullback where the power and experience of Kevin Mack will be blended with the elusive speed of last year's exciting rookie halfback, Eric Metcalf. Tim Manoa is a polished performer and, while he is now seen as a reserve to Mack, it would be surprising were his powerful blocking not worked into the system. In addition, the Browns can call on the dual-purpose talents of Barry Redden which means that draftee Leroy Hoard can be brought along at a sensible pace. In addition to the value of Metcalf as a receiver, out of this collection of backs should emerge a genuine rushing threat which, unlike last year when the Browns aver-

aged only 3.6 yards per carry, can help to set up the passing game. Quarterback Bernie Kosar is now a seasoned veteran of great victories and battle-hardening losses. In Webster Slaughter and Reggie Langhorne he has two wide receivers who present a deep threat, though Langhorne catches a greater proportion of medium-range passes. Backup Brian Brennan has the softest hands of all and he puts them to use on the occasional circus reception. The full impact of second-round draftee Lawyer Tillman was deferred for a season by his holdout, but his class is undeniable. Reassuringly, the great veteran tight end, Ozzie Newsome, will be back for one more campaign.

Defense

Head coach Bud Carson likes the 4-3 system but it was surprising when he installed it in a Browns defense which appeared to be short of defensive linemen. The soundness of this decision was apparent at the end of the season when the defense had set a team record with 45 sacks as its contribution to an overall effort which ranked seventh in the NFL. A series of master strokes, including the conversion of defensive end Carl Hairston to defensive left tackle, the re-enthusing of veteran left end Al Baker and the judgement in starting former Oilers Plan-B free agent Robert Banks at right end, and the fullest use of second-year tackle Michael Dean Perry, produced a four-man unit which stood up well. Draftees Anthony Pleasant and Rob Burnett join Andrew Stewart and the fast-improving Tom Gibson in reserve. Any one of several combinations at linebacker would do but the starting lineup should have David Grayson and Pro Bowler Clay Matthews on either side of Mike Johnson. When Grayson was forced to miss the final five games with a neck injury, Van Waiters came in and performed well. Former first-round pick Clifford Charlton can not break into the starting lineup and further class comes with the signing of Lawrence McGrew, who started at outside linebacker for New England. For critical moments such as fourth-and-short and goal-line stands, Eddie Johnson comes into plug the middle. At the heart of the secondary, Felix Wright and Thane Gash rule supreme. A preseason switch saw Wright move from free safety to the strong spot and he responded with an NFL-high nine interceptions. Gash, who swapped places with Wright, led the team in tackles and scored two touchdowns from his three interceptions. As a result of Plan-B movements, in losing Hanford Dixon but signing former New England Pro Bowler Raymond Clayborn, the Browns may have strengthened the cornerback position. Clayborn was felt to be coming to the end of his career but his experience should be worth the step or two that he may have lost. On the other corner, current Pro Bowler Frank Minnifield is challenged only as a last resort.

1990 SCHEDULE OF GAMES

September

9 PITTSBURGH	4:00
16 at New York Jets	1:00
23 SAN DIEGO	1:00
30 at Kansas City	3:00

October

8 at Denver (Mon.)	7:00
14 at New Orleans	12:00
22 CINCINNATI (Mon.)	9:00
28 at San Francisco	1:00

November

4 BUFFALO	1:00
11 *Open date*	
18 HOUSTON	1:00
25 MIAMI	1:00

December

2 LOS ANGELES RAMS	1:00
9 at Houston	12:00
16 ATLANTA	1:00
23 at Pittsburgh	1:00
30 at Cincinnati	1:00

1990 DRAFT

Round	Name	Pos.	Ht.	Wt.	College
2.	Hoard, Leroy	RB	5-11	222	Michigan
3.	Pleasant, Anthony	DE	6-4	240	Tennessee State
4.	Barnett, Harlon	S	5-11	199	Michigan State
5.	Burnett, Rob	DE	6-3	271	Syracuse
6.	Hilliard, Randy	CB	5-10	160	Northwestern St., La.
7.	Galbraith, Scott	TE	6-2	257	Southern California
8.	Jones, Jock	LB	6-3	224	Virginia Tech
9.	Rowell, Eugene	WR	6-1	185	Southern Mississippi
10.	Wallace, Michael	CB	6-1	183	Jackson State
11.	Gordon, Clemente	QB	6-3	222	Grambling
12.	Simien, Kerry	WR	5-9	181	Texas A&I

VETERAN ROSTER

No.	Name	Pos.	Ht.	Wt.	NFL Year	College
61	Baab, Mike	C	6-4	270	9	Texas
9	Bahr, Matt	K	5-10	175	12	Penn State
60	Baker, Al	DE	6-6	280	13	Colorado State
68	Banker, Ted	G	6-3	290	7	Southeast Missouri
97	Banks, Robert	DE	6-5	255	4	Notre Dame
64	Baugh, Tom	C	6-4	290	5	Southern Illinois
24	Blaylock, Tony	CB	5-10	190	3	Winston-Salem State
77	Bolden, Rickey	T	6-4	280	6	Southern Methodist
36	Braggs, Stephen	S	5-9	180	4	Texas
86	Brennan, Brian	WR	5-10	185	7	Boston College
58	Charlton, Clifford	LB	6-3	245	3	Florida
26	Clayborn, Raymond	CB	6-1	186	14	Texas
74	Farren, Paul	T-G	6-6	270	8	Boston University
69	Fike, Dan	G	6-7	285	6	Florida
30	Gash, Thane	S	5-11	200	3	East Tennessee State
71	Gibson, Tom	DE	6-7	250	2	Northern Arizona
79	Graybill, Mike	T	6-7	275	2	Boston University
56	Grayson, David	LB	6-2	235	4	Fresno State
78	Hairston, Carl	DT	6-2	275	15	Maryland-E. Shore
23	Harper, Mark	CB	5-9	185	5	Alcorn State
51	Johnson, Eddie	LB	6-1	225	10	Louisville
59	Johnson, Mike	LB	6-1	225	5	Virginia Tech
95	Jones, Marlon	DE	6-4	260	3	Central State, Ohio
66	Jones, Tony	T	6-5	285	3	Western Carolina
19	Kosar, Bernie	QB	6-5	210	6	Miami
40	Kramer, Kyle	S	6-3	190	2	Bowling Green
88	Langhorne, Reggie	WR	6-2	200	6	Elizabeth City State
34	Mack, Kevin	RB	6-0	230	6	Clemson
42	Manoa, Tim	RB	6-1	240	4	Penn State
57	Matthews, Clay	LB	6-2	245	13	Southern California
53	McGrew, Lawrence	LB	6-5	233	10	Southern California
21	Metcalf, Eric	RB	5-10	185	2	Texas
31	Minnifield, Frank	CB	5-9	180	7	Louisville
82	Newsome, Ozzie	TE	6-2	225	13	Alabama
33	Oliphant, Mike	RB	5-9	170	3	Puget Sound
10	Pagel, Mike	QB	6-2	211	9	Arizona State
92	Perry, Michael Dean	DT	6-0	280	3	Clemson
75	Pike, Chris	DL	6-8	290	2	Tulsa
73	Rakoczy, Gregg	C	6-6	290	4	Miami
35	Redden, Barry	RB	5-10	219	9	Richmond
72	Robbins, Kevin	T	6-4	286	2	Michigan State
52	Rose, Ken	LB	6-1	216	4	Nevada-Las Vegas
70	Simons, Kevin	T-G	6-3	315	2	Tennessee
99	Sims, Darryl	DE	6-5	275	5	Wisconsin
84	Slaughter, Webster	WR	6-0	170	5	San Diego State
96	Stewart, Andrew	DE	6-5	265	2	Cincinnati
65	Tamm, Ralph	G	6-3	285	1	West Chester State
85	Tillman, Lawyer	WR	6-5	230	2	Auburn
15	Wagner, Bryan	P	6-2	200	4	Cal State-Northridge
50	Waiters, Van	LB	6-4	245	3	Indiana
91	Weston, Rhondy	DE	6-5	274	2	Florida
22	Wright, Felix	S	6-2	195	6	Drake

Special Teams

The Browns are happy with the combination of place-kicker Matt Bahr and punter Bryan Wagner, even though their figures are nothing out of the ordinary. It is recognised that the winds in Cleveland Stadium are severe on placekickers while Wagner's good hang-time compensates fully for his lack of distance. Metcalf sends a buzz through the crowd every time he prepares to return kickoffs but punt returner Gerald (Ice Cube) McNeil has been lost to Plan-B free agency, leaving a vacancy.

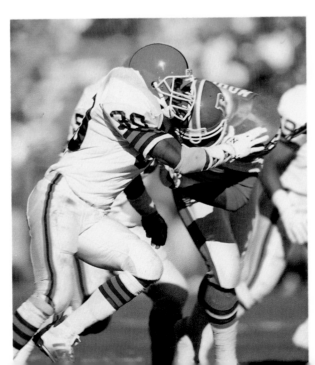

Free safety Thane Gash led the Browns with 134 tackles.

HOUSTON OILERS

Address 6910 Fannin Street, Houston, Texas 77030.
Stadium Astrodome, Houston.
   Capacity 61,000 *Playing Surface* AstroTurf-8.
Team Colours Columbia Blue, Scarlet, and White.
Head Coach Jack Pardee – 1st year; 7th NFL.
Championships AFL 1960,'61.
History AFL 1960-69, AFC 1970-

Offense

In the last three years the Oilers have reached the playoffs each time but they seem to have left their finishing touch at home. A change may be for the better. Under new head coach Jack Pardee they will make much greater use of the passing offense. The system will use four wide receivers and they are likely to be last year's starters, Ernest Givins and Drew Hill, together with Haywood Jeffires and Curtis Duncan. But there will be competition from backup Kenny Jackson and Plan-B signing Gerald (Ice Cube) McNeil in particular. The new approach will be welcome to quarterback Warren Moon, who was unhappy with the strictures imposed by what he saw as the orthodoxy of the game plan under former head coach Jerry Glanville. It will be a complicated system, making great physical and mental demands, but Moon, a disciplined athlete who stays in good condition throughout the offseason, relishes the challenge. Cody Carlson has done well on emergency duty in the past and is the unchallenged reserve to Moon. The new arrangement dispenses with the formal position of tight end and uses one running back. For this role Alonzo Highsmith is perfect. A powerful runner, Highsmith also is a fine receiver and throws a block of earth-shattering proportions. But he is just one of four top-class backs, some of whom have a particular speciality. Mike Rozier shoulders his way for the tough yards while Allen Pinkett cuts and slashes for his gains. Lorenzo White is the more orthodox practitioner who, in another system, might easily be a 1,000-yard rusher.

In recent seasons, Houston has reaped the benefits of what was a careful and patient construction of an offensive line which is the envy of many clubs around the NFL. At tackle, Dean Steinkuhler is coming off his best year in the pros and if Bruce Davis lost a little of his snap because of knee and weight problems, Don Maggs came through well. Davis is not certain to displace Maggs and the promising David Williams will also make a bid to start. Bruce Matthews and Mike Munchak probably form the league's best pairing at guard, while Jay Pennison has shown himself to be one of the better centers.

Defense

1990 could be the year that Houston becomes the AFC's dominating defensive power. A gap created by the Plan-B departure of free safety Jeff Donaldson was quickly filled by the signing of Giants Plan-B free agent Terry Kinard, whose experience at the highest level will be of immense value playing in partnership with Bubba McDowell. An outstanding young strong safety who is destined for stardom, he came second on the team with 88 tackles, had four interceptions and forced four fumbles. McDowell also was prominent on special-team duty, blocking two punts. At cornerback, Steve Brown, who led the club with five interceptions, is unchallenged but it is recognised that Patrick Allen was beaten a little too often on long passes last year. The Oilers feel that a shift away from bump-and-run defense will help him, but he will need to confirm his starting status in camp, where he'll have to fight off Richard Johnson. Up front there will be a change to the 4-3 defense and this, it is hoped, will make much better use of the existing personnel. Going into camp, it is still not clear just how the Oilers are going to apply their best defensive lineman, Ray Childress, who can play at both tackle and end. And in this the development of draftees Jeff Alm and Willis Peguese will be a factor. Assuming that they do not come through to start, Childress, who is a former All-Pro, will probably move to tackle in partnership with Doug Smith, though the latter still has not recovered fully from a gunshot wound. William Fuller is regarded as the best pass rusher and is likely to start at defensive end. The feeling is that Sean Jones could be the other end if, as expected, he returns to his best in the 4-3 system. But the picture is not clear and either of Richard Byrd and Ezra Johnson could be a factor. John Grimsley, the club's leading tackler, should start at middle linebacker, flanked by Robert Lyles and Johnny Meads. But top draftee Lamar Lathon will press all three for playing time. Former starting inside linebacker Al Smith becomes the senior backup for the middle spot.

1990 SCHEDULE OF GAMES

September
9	at Atlanta	4:00
16	at Pittsburgh (Sun. night)	8:00
23	INDIANAPOLIS	12:00
30	at San Diego	1:00

October
7	SAN FRANCISCO	12:00
14	at Cincinnati	1:00
21	NEW ORLEANS	12:00
28	NEW YORK JETS	12:00

November
4	at Los Angeles Rams	1:00
11	*Open date*	
18	at Cleveland	1:00
26	BUFFALO (Mon.)	8:00

December
2	at Seattle	1:00
9	CLEVELAND	12:00
16	at Kansas City	12:00
23	CINCINNATI	12:00
30	PITTSBURGH (Sun. night)	7:00

1990 DRAFT

Round	Name	Pos.	Ht.	Wt.	College
1.	Lathon, Lamar	LB	6-3	240	Houston
2.	Alm, Jeff	DT	6-5	260	Notre Dame
3.	Peguese, Willis	DE	6-3	262	Miami
4.	Still, Eric	G	6-2	277	Tennessee
5.	Newbill, Richard	LB	6-1	240	Miami
6.	Jones, Tony	WR	5-6	144	Texas
7.	Murray, Andy	RB	6-1	241	Kentucky
8.	Tucker, Brett	S	5-10	193	Northern Illinois
9.	Coleman, Pat	WR	5-6	173	Mississippi
10.	Thomas, Dee	CB	5-9	170	Nicholls State
11.	Banes, Joey	T	6-6	272	Houston
12.	Slack, Reggie	QB	6-1	217	Auburn

VETERAN ROSTER

No.	Name	Pos.	Ht.	Wt.	NFL Year	College
29	Allen, Patrick	CB	5-10	182	7	Utah State
31	Arnold, David	CB	6-3	208	2	Michigan
33	Bell, Billy	CB	5-10	170	2	Lamar
24	Brown, Steve	CB	5-11	187	8	Oregon
71	Byrd, Richard	NT	6-4	273	6	Southern Mississippi
14	Carlson, Cody	QB	6-3	194	4	Baylor
79	Childress, Ray	DE	6-6	276	6	Texas A&M
77	Davis, Bruce	T	6-6	315	12	UCLA
28	Dishman, Cris	CB	6-0	178	3	Purdue
80	Duncan, Curtis	WR	5-11	184	4	Northwestern
51	Fairs, Eric	LB	6-3	238	5	Memphis State
88	Ford, Bernard	WR	5-10	171	2	Central Florida
95	Fuller, William	DE	6-3	269	5	North Carolina
97	Garalczyk, Mark	NT	6-6	275	3	Western Michigan
81	Givins, Ernest	WR	5-9	172	5	Louisville
59	Grimsley, John	LB	6-2	238	7	Kentucky
83	Harris, Leonard	WR-KR	5-8	162	5	Texas Tech
87	Harry, Carl	WR-KR	5-9	168	1	Utah
32	Highsmith, Alonzo	RB	6-1	234	4	Miami
85	Hill, Drew	WR	5-9	174	11	Georgia Tech
86	Jackson, Kenny	WR	6-0	183	7	Penn State
84	Jeffires, Haywood	WR	6-2	201	3	North Carolina State
90	Johnson, Ezra	DE	6-4	252	14	Morris Brown
23	Johnson, Richard	CB	6-1	190	6	Wisconsin
96	Jones, Sean	DE	6-7	273	7	Northeastern
27	Kinard, Terry	S	6-1	200	8	Clemson
21	Knight, Leander	DB	6-0	196	2	Montclair State
56	Kozak, Scott	LB	6-3	226	2	Oregon
93	Lyles, Robert	LB	6-1	230	7	Texas Christian
78	Maggs, Don	T	6-5	285	4	Tulane
74	Matthews, Bruce	G	6-5	286	8	Southern California
25	McDowell, Bubba	S	6-1	195	2	Miami
89	McNeil, Gerald	WR-PR	5-7	142	5	Baylor
91	Meads, Johnny	LB	6-2	232	7	Nicholls State
94	Montgomery, Glenn	NT	6-0	274	2	Houston
9	Montgomery, Greg	P	6-4	217	3	Michigan State
1	Moon, Warren	QB	6-3	210	7	Washington
63	Munchak, Mike	G	6-3	284	9	Penn State
52	Pennison, Jay	C	6-1	282	5	Nicholls State
20	Pinkett, Allen	RB	5-9	192	5	Notre Dame
66	Robison, Tommy	G	6-4	290	3	Texas A&M
30	Rozier, Mike	RB	5-10	213	6	Nebraska
53	Seale, Eugene	LB	5-10	250	4	Lamar
54	Smith, Al	LB	6-1	240	4	Utah State
99	Smith, Doug	NT	6-6	286	6	Auburn
70	Steinkuhler, Dean	T	6-3	287	7	Nebraska
44	White, Lorenzo	RB	5-11	218	3	Michigan State
73	Williams, David	T	6-5	292	2	Florida
7	Zendejas, Tony	K	5-8	165	6	Nevada-Reno

Special Teams

Tony Zendejas had a modest campaign, failing on several medium-range field goals but, for his previous record and composure, he will be retained. Punter Greg Montgomery, who led the AFC with a gross average of 43.3 yards, is always likely to bounce one off the underside of the Astrodome. There is much excitement at the prospect of the 'Ice Cube' returning punts and he may help out on kickoff returns, a role in which only Leonard Harris had much success last year.

Running back Allen Pinkett cuts and slashes for his yards.

PITTSBURGH STEELERS

Address Three Rivers Stadium, 300 Stadium Circle, Pittsburgh, Pennsylvania 15212.
Stadium Three Rivers Stadium, Pittsburgh.
Capacity 59,000 *Playing Surface* AstroTurf.
Team Colours Black and Gold.
Head Coach Chuck Noll – 22nd year.
Championships Division 1972, '74, '75, '76, '77, '78, '79, '83, '84; Conference 1974,'75,'78,'79; Super Bowl 1974,'75,'78,'79.
History NFL 1933-69, AFC 1970-
(Until 1940, they were known as the Pittsburgh Pirates.)

Offense

After struggling for the first ten weeks, the Steelers mounted a charge which faltered only late in the divisional playoff game when they were overtaken by the eventual AFC Champion Denver Broncos. One factor in the resurgence was stability on the offensive line, for which there had been six different combinations of personnel in the first seven games before remaining unchanged the rest of the way. The same group, with John Jackson and Tunch Ilkin at tackle, John Rienstra and Terry Long in the guard positions and Dermontti Dawson at center, will launch the Steelers into the campaign. Their style of play depends on speed and the coordination to set up the trap-blocking systems which have become the Steelers' trademark. 1989 first-round pick Tom Ricketts is the reserve at tackle with Brian Blankenship backing up at guard. Craig Wolfley has been lost to Plan-B free agency but the club seems not to be concerned and did not replace him in the draft. One reason may be the selection of Eric Green, who represents the latest in the club's long-time search for the tight end to suit their system. A massive fellow, he is an explosive blocker and, as a senior, he caught 62 passes for 905 yards and ten touchdowns. He may be the final piece in a passing offense which is controlled by a quarterback, Bubby Brister, who bristles with confidence. Draftee Neil O'Donnell has a fine opportunity to become the senior reserve. Louis Lipps is the premier wide receiver. He might expect to average 18 or so yards on his way to approaching 1,000 over the campaign, but it would help if 1989 third-rounder Derek Hill could improve his yield. Behind the starters, there is a distinct drop in recognised productivity with Dwight Stone representing the best of the veterans. Things could open up for the passing game if running back Tim Worley could establish the frequency of his hammer blows. After a slow start to his rookie year, by the end he was looking the part. Even more obviously, Merril Hoge became an exciting factor and could become an equal partner in the Steelers' first great backfield combination since Franco Harris and Rocky Bleier.

Defense

The Steelers used only two options in the top half of the draft for defensive players and these, Kenny Davidson and Craig Veasey, were for the line. This may be in part a recognition that former first-round pick Aaron Jones has made only a modest impact thus far. The starting That trio has Keith Willis and Tim Johnson at defensive end with Gerald Williams at nose tackle. Collectively, they were responsible for 14 sacks. The leading sacker was outside linebacker Greg Lloyd, who has proved to be a true discovery coming as he did from tiny Fort Valley State. In the left outside linebacker spot, Bryan Hinkle knows his way around after starting since the beginning of the 1984 season, the year that current left inside linebacker David Little established himself as a starter. Little led the team with 104 tackles with Lloyd (92) in second place. At right inside linebacker, Hardy Nickerson started the first eight games before going on injured reserve but his replacement, Jerry Olsavsky, stepped in to play with a verve which belied his origins as a 1989 tenth-round draftee. Nickerson is set to regain his starting spot with Olsavsky, Jerrol Williams and A. J. Jenkins as the reserves. In truth, the front seven do not represent the best in Steelers history but the defensive secondary is making its bid for a place in the lore of this great club. Between them, cornerbacks Dwayne Woodruff and Rod Woodson, strong safety Carnell Lake and free safety Thomas Everett missed only three starts. In his eleventh year, Woodruff still applies great timing and almost the speed that once made him the fastest player on the squad. That honour now belongs to Woodson, a former track athlete and multi-purpose football player who improves with every outing. Last year he led the club with four forced fumbles and recovered three fumbles. Lake, a crushing tackler who recovered a team-high five fumbles, played perhaps above the level expected even of a second-round pick out of UCLA while Everett now goes to work with disciplined authority.

1990 SCHEDULE OF GAMES

September
9	at Cleveland	4:00
16	HOUSTON (Sun. night)	8:00
23	at Los Angeles Raiders	1:00
30	MIAMI	1:00

October
7	SAN DIEGO	1:00
14	at Denver	2:00
21	at San Francisco	1:00
29	LOS ANGELES RAMS (Mon.)	9:00

November
4	ATLANTA	1:00
11	Open date	
18	at Cincinnati (Sun. night)	8:00
25	at New York Jets	4:00

December
2	CINCINNATI	1:00
9	NEW ENGLAND	1:00
16	at New Orleans	12:00
23	CLEVELAND	1:00
30	at Houston (Sun. night)	7:00

1990 DRAFT

Round	Name	Pos.	Ht.	Wt.	College
1.	Green, Eric	TE	6-4	274	Liberty
2.	Davidson, Kenny	DE	6-5	274	Louisiana State
3.	O'Donnell, Neil	QB	6-2	217	Maryland
3.	Veasey, Craig	DT	6-1	270	Houston
4.	Calloway, Chris	WR	5-10	180	Michigan
5.	Foster, Barry	RB	5-10	222	Arkansas
6.	Heard, Ronald	WR	5-10	177	Bowling Green
7.	Grayson, Dan	LB	6-1	238	Washington State
8.	Dunbar, Karl	DT	6-4	280	Louisiana State
9.	Jones, Gary	S	6-1	203	Texas A&M
10.	Miles, Eddie	LB	6-1	240	Minnesota
11.	Strzelczyk, Justin	T	6-5	273	Maine
12.	Bell, Richard	RB	6-0	196	Nebraska

VETERAN ROSTER

No.	Name	Pos.	Ht.	Wt.	NFL Year	College
1	Anderson, Gary	K	5-11	180	9	Syracuse
14	Blackledge, Todd	QB	6-3	230	8	Penn State
60	Blankenship, Brian	G-C	6-1	275	4	Nebraska
6	Brister, Bubby	QB	6-3	210	5	Northeast Louisiana
24	Carter, Rodney	RB	6-0	210	4	Purdue
63	Dawson, Dermontti	C	6-2	275	3	Kentucky
27	Everett, Thomas	S	5-9	184	4	Baylor
68	Freeman, Lorenzo	NT	6-5	298	4	Pittsburgh
22	Griffin, Larry	S	6-0	200	5	North Carolina
	Griggs, Billy	TE	6-3	234		Virginia
35	Hall, Delton	CB	6-1	207	4	Clemson
82	Hill, Derek	WR	6-1	193	2	Arizona
53	Hinkle, Bryan	LB	6-2	225	9	Oregon
33	Hoge, Merril	RB	6-2	230	4	Idaho State
	Holmes, Darryl	S	6-2	190	4	Fort Valley State
62	Ilkin, Tunch	T	6-3	266	11	Indiana State
65	Jackson, John	T	6-6	288	3	Eastern Kentucky
99	Jenkins, A.J.	LB-DE	6-2	237	2	Cal State-Fullerton
44	Johnson, David	CB	6-0	185	2	Kentucky
78	Johnson, Tim	DE-DT	6-3	269	4	Penn State
97	Jones, Aaron	DE	6-5	257	3	Eastern Kentucky
37	Lake, Carnell	S	6-1	205	2	UCLA
51	Lanza, Chuck	C	6-2	260	3	Notre Dame
83	Lipps, Louis	WR	5-10	190	7	Southern Mississippi
50	Little, David	LB	6-1	233	10	Florida
95	Lloyd, Greg	LB	6-2	222	3	Fort Valley State
74	Long, Terry	G	5-11	275	7	East Carolina
84	Mularkey, Mike	TE	6-4	237	8	Florida
54	Nickerson, Hardy	LB	6-2	231	4	California
92	Olsavsky, Jerry	LB	6-1	222	2	Pittsburgh
85	O'Shea, Terry	TE	6-4	236	2	California (Pa.)
71	Ricketts, Tom	G-T	6-5	298	2	Pittsburgh
79	Rienstra, John	G	6-5	264	5	Temple
80	Stock, Mark	WR	5-11	177	2	Virginia Military
20	Stone, Dwight	WR-KR	6-0	190	4	Middle Tennessee St.
90	Stowe, Tyronne	LB	6-1	236	4	Rutgers
11	Strom, Rick	QB	6-2	210	2	Georgia Tech
87	Thompson, Weegie	WR	6-6	215	7	Florida State
23	Tyrrell, Tim	RB	6-2	215	7	Northern Illinois
43	Wallace, Ray	RB	6-0	233	4	Purdue
98	Williams, Gerald	NT	6-3	279	5	Auburn
91	Williams, Jerrol	LB	6-5	242	2	Purdue
42	Williams, Warren	RB	6-0	204	3	Miami
93	Willis, Keith	DE	6-1	263	8	Northeastern
49	Woodruff, Dwayne	CB	6-0	195	11	Louisville
26	Woodson, Rod	CB-KR	6-0	196	4	Purdue
38	Worley, Tim	RB	6-2	228	2	Georgia
9	Wright, Randy	QB	6-2	203	6	Wisconsin

Special Teams

Placekicker Gary Anderson, a two-time Pro Bowler, missed a few kickable field goals in 1989 but there is no question of his being replaced. However, the Steelers paid the price for not protecting punter Harry Newsome, who departed as a Plan-B free agent. Currently, the club does not have a punter. On both kickoff and punt returns, Woodson represents one of the most dangerous threats in the NFL, and the extent of his versatility was recognised by selection to his first Pro Bowl.

Tim Worley's consistency is the key to the Steelers' offense.

DENVER BRONCOS

Address 5700 Logan Street, Denver,
  Colorado 80216.
Stadium Denver Mile High Stadium.
  Capacity 76,273 *Playing Surface* Grass (PAT).
Team Colours Orange, Royal Blue, and White.
Head Coach Dan Reeves – 10th year.
Championships Division 1977,'78,'84,'86,'87,'89;
  Conference 1977, '86,'87,'89.
History AFL 1960-69, AFC 1970-

Offense

The Broncos satisfy every condition for having a first-class offense and it is easy to assert that this group promises to be the best of the three units which contested the Super Bowl in the 1980s. It will be little different from last year's AFC Champion squad but one of its key members, running back Bobby Humphrey, has every hope of improving even on a remarkable rookie performance when, with 1,151 yards rushing, he had the third-best single-season total in Denver history. Lining up alongside Humphrey, another rookie, fullback Melvin Bratton, did enough to suggest that the partnership could take Denver well into the 1990s. Bratton, who was seen as a potential first-round draftee before suffering a serious knee injury in postseason play as a 1987 senior, has confirmed his class and starts ahead of Jeff Alexander. Behind Humphrey there's lots of experienced reserve strength in Sammy Winder, Steve Sewell and Plan-B free agent Lorenzo Hampton. At quarterback, John Elway has been overshadowed by several good passers emerging around the league, and three Super Bowl losses have not helped his image. But, without being disrespectful to the remaining members of the squad, using the brilliant coaching of Dan Reeves, Elway has been the single most important reason for the team's success. Rather than being disheartened by defeat, Elway's resolve is all the more firm. His backup, Gary Kubiak, is one of the better reserves in the AFC and he, too, has shown that he can unleash the full array of Denver's receivers. The main target is wide receiver Vance Johnson, who is steadily approaching several club career records. However,

Johnson's partner, Mark Jackson, was a little below par and he will be under pressure from backups Ricky Nattiel and Michael Young. Tight ends Clarence Kay and Orson Mobley should have little difficulty holding off any competition in camp. The Broncos have an offensive line which is a dimension bigger than those of former years. They will line up with Gerald Perry and Ken Lanier at tackle, Jim Juriga and Doug Widell at guard and Keith Kartz at center. All five are genuine NFL starting quality, but, with the departure of Plan-B free agent Mike Ruether, the club does appear to be only starter-deep.

Defense

1989 saw a return to the days when Denver defenses gave up yards only grudgingly as they ranked second in the AFC behind Kansas City. In part the improvement was a result of two exceptionally good Plan-B signings in defensive ends Ron Holmes and Alphonso Carreker, each of whom is a former first-round draftee. Carreker started at defensive left end all year while Holmes gradually established himself when an injury to Andre Townsend opened the door. Townsend remains as a third genuine starter. Greg Kragen is a solid anchor at nose tackle and was truly dominant in a purple patch when Denver ran off four straight wins to clinch the division title. There may be a problem if Kragen is injured since the backup, Brad Henke, is inexperienced and it might require Townsend, who has played the nose tackle position, to fill in. After going through a modest period at linebacker, the Broncos are almost back to the kind of dominance they like. Outside linebacker Simon Fletcher has achieved the level of acclaim afforded to his partner on the inside, Karl Mecklenburg. Fletcher and Mecklenburg, who maintain a heavy pass rush from the right side, led the linebackers with 12 and 7.5 sacks respectively. Michael Brooks grew in stature over a season in which he ironed out the lingering creases of an injury which delayed his impact in the NFL. At left inside linebacker, Rick Dennison has re-established himself over the last two years as a starter following a period when he had to be content as a backup. For his experience he is of great value. The reserves include Marc Munford and Scott Curtis but it was a sound decision to acquire Plan-B free agents Ty Allert and Rod Stephens and, subsequently, Jeroy Robinson in the fourth round of the draft. The defensive secondary is an area of emerging strength with yet more talent arriving in the shape of draftee safety Alton Montgomery. However, he is not expected to displace either of Steve Atwater and Pro Bowler Dennis Smith, and it may be that the club will try him at cornerback, where the current starters are Tyrone Braxton and Wymon Henderson. Otherwise, he should be the successor to Smith.

Tyrone Braxton led the Broncos with six interceptions.

1990 DRAFT

Round	Name	Pos.	Ht.	Wt.	College
2.	Montgomery, Alton	S	6-0	198	Houston
4.	Robinson, Jeroy	LB	6-1	238	Texas A&M
5.	Davidson, Jeff	G	6-4	306	Ohio State
5.	Lang, Le-Lo	CB	5-10	184	Washington
6.	Haliburton, Ronnie	TE	6-4	230	Louisiana State
7.	Sharpe, Shannon	WR	6-1	221	Savannah State
8.	Leggett, Brad	C	6-4	274	Southern California
9.	Ellis, Todd	QB	6-1	203	South Carolina
10.	Szymanski, James	DE	6-5	272	Michigan State
10.	Thompson, Anthony	LB	6-1	230	East Carolina

VETERAN ROSTER

No.	Name	Pos.	Ht.	Wt.	NFL Year	College
40	Alexander, Jeff	RB	6-0	232	2	Southern
57	Allert, Ty	LB	6-2	238	5	Texas
27	Atwater, Steve	S	6-3	217	2	Arkansas
35	Bell, Ken	RB-WR	5-10	190	5	Boston College
54	Bishop, Keith	G	6-3	290	10	Baylor
32	Bratton, Melvin	RB	6-1	225	2	Miami
34	Braxton, Tyrone	CB	5-11	185	4	North Dakota State
56	Brooks, Michael	LB	6-1	235	4	Louisiana State
92	Carreker, Alphonso	DE	6-6	272	7	Florida State
29	Carrington, Darren	CB	6-1	189	2	Northern Arizona
25	Corrington, Kip	S	6-0	175	2	Texas A&M
58	Curtis, Scott	LB	6-1	230	3	New Hampshire
55	Dennison, Rick	LB	6-3	220	9	Colorado State
7	Elway, John	QB	6-3	215	8	Stanford
73	Fletcher, Simon	LB	6-6	240	6	Houston
20	Hampton, Lorenzo	RB	5-11	210	6	Florida
36	Haynes, Mark	CB	5-11	195	11	Colorado
24	Henderson, Wymon	CB	5-10	186	4	Nevada-Las Vegas
68	Henke, Brad	DE-NT	6-3	275	2	Arizona
90	Holmes, Ron	DE	6-4	265	6	Washington
2	Horan, Ron	P	5-11	190	6	Cal State-Long Beach
26	Humphrey, Bobby	RB	6-1	201	2	Alabama
80	Jackson, Mark	WR	5-10	180	5	Purdue
81	Johnson, Jason	WR-KR	5-11	180	3	Illinois State
82	Johnson, Vance	WR	5-11	185	6	Arizona
66	Juriga, Jim	G	6-6	275	3	Illinois
72	Kartz, Keith	C	6-4	270	4	California
88	Kay, Clarence	TE	6-2	237	7	Georgia
71	Kragen, Greg	NT	6-3	265	6	Utah State
8	Kubiak, Gary	QB	6-0	192	8	Texas A&M
76	Lanier, Ken	T	6-3	290	10	Florida State
98	Little, David	TE	6-2	230	7	Middle Tennessee St.
59	Lucas, Tim	LB	6-3	230	4	California
96	McCullough, Jake	DE	6-5	270	2	Clemson
77	Mecklenburg, Karl	LB	6-3	240	8	Minnesota
89	Mobley, Orson	TE	6-5	259	5	Salem College
97	Mraz, Mark	DE	6-4	260	3	Utah State
51	Munford, Marc	LB	6-2	231	4	Nebraska
84	Nattiel, Ricky	WR	5-9	180	4	Florida
60	Perry, Gerald	T	6-6	305	3	Southern
91	Powers, Warren	DE	6-6	287	2	Maryland
74	Provence, Andrew	DE	6-3	270	6	South Carolina
48	Robbins, Randy	S	6-2	189	7	Arizona
30	Sewell, Steve	RB-WR	6-3	210	6	Oklahoma
49	Smith, Dennis	S	6-3	200	10	Southern California
28	Smith, Elliot	CB	6-2	192	1	Alcorn State
65	Smith, Monte	G	6-5	270	2	North Dakota
50	Stephens, Rod	LB	6-1	237	2	Georgia Tech
61	Townsend, Andre	DE-NT	6-3	265	7	Mississippi
9	Treadwell, David	K	6-1	175	2	Clemson
86	Verhulst, Chris	TE	6-3	240	3	Chico State
70	White, Robb	DE	6-4	270	3	South Dakota
67	Widell, Doug	G	6-4	287	2	Boston College
23	Winder, Sammy	RB	5-11	203	9	Southern Mississippi
83	Young, Michael	WR	6-1	183	6	UCLA

1990 SCHEDULE OF GAMES

September

9	at Los Angeles Raiders	1:00
17	KANSAS CITY (Mon.)	7:00
23	SEATTLE	2:00
30	at Buffalo	1:00

October

8	CLEVELAND (Mon.)	7:00
14	PITTSBURGH	2:00
21	at Indianapolis	12:00
28	*Open date*	

November

4	at Minnesota (Sun. night)	7:00
11	at San Diego	1:00
18	CHICAGO	2:00
22	at Detroit (Thanksgiving)	12:30

December

2	LOS ANGELES RAIDERS	2:00
9	at Kansas City	3:00
16	SAN DIEGO	2:00
23	at Seattle (Sun. night)	5:00
30	GREEN BAY	2:00

Special Teams

The soundness of the Broncos' decision to replace Rich Karlis by David Treadwell was confirmed when Treadwell was voted to the Pro Bowl in his first NFL year. A former Pro Bowl punter, Mike Horan, handles the winds and snows of the Rocky Mountains well enough. There is plenty of talent for returning both kickoffs and punts. Nattiel could be given an extended try on punt returns while reserve cornerback Darren Carrington appears to have a flair for returning kickoffs. Ken Bell is the bread-and-butter guy.

KANSAS CITY CHIEFS

Address One Arrowhead Drive, Kansas City, Missouri 64129.

Stadium Arrowhead Stadium, Kansas City. *Capacity* 78,067 *Playing Surface* AstroTurf-8.

Team Colours Red, Gold, and White.

Head Coach Marty Schottenheimer – 2nd year; 7th NFL.

Championships Division 1971; AFL 1962,'66,'69; Super Bowl 1969.

History AFL 1960-69, AFC 1970-
(Until 1963, they were known as the Dallas Texans.)

Offense

Head coach Marty Schottenheimer has taken great strides in bringing the Chiefs back into contention and there is every prospect that he can continue. At quarterback he has his pick of veteran experience in Steve DeBerg, widely talented former Dallas starter Steve Pelluer, whose loping stride and surprising speed can also help the rushing game, and the young Mike Elkins, whose day as the starter can not be long off. The cynical observer may detect a quarterback controversy – and all the problems it brings – but, even swapping and changing would not be too much of a problem for DeBerg and Pelluer. For the offensive backfield, Kansas City has the heavyweight power-back, Christian Okoye, who steam-hammered his way to the 1989 NFL rushing title. He forms the basis of the entire offensive effort but it has to be a source of concern that, should he be injured, the emphasis would need to change in order to allow halfback Herman Heard to function at his best. He has carried the load in the past but he is not likely to be as effective as Okoye. James Saxon and Todd McNair are the senior backups. In recent years the Chiefs' pass receiving corps has slipped a little. Only wide receiver Stephone Paige now offers a dangerous threat. His starting partner, Pete Mandley, is a steady pro while it is fair to say that reserve Emile Harry has

not accepted his opportunities of starting in the past. Fred Jones came in the fourth round of the draft but it may be next year before the really big-name player is sought. There is not likely to be a big yield from the tight end position, where Jonathan Hayes is used more for his value as a blocker than as a receiver. The offensive line, a key area, is taking shape. The starting group should have John Alt and Irv Eatman at tackle, Rich Baldinger and David Lutz in the guard positions and, probably, former All-Pro Mike Webster at center. As Webster approaches the end of his illustrious career, it made sense to acquire draftee Tim Grunhard, who joins backups Mark Cannon and Gene Chilton and Plan-B free agents Frank Winters and Mike Morris.

Defense

The simple message is that the AFC's top defense in 1989 will be even better in 1990. In recognition of the depth of talent available for the defensive line, the club may use four-man fronts more often. Leonard Griffin and Neil Smith will continue at defensive end but an expansion of the line would allow the use of both Bill Maas and Dan Saleaumua, the latter who could make a strong case for being the starting nose tackle in the three-man line after taking his chances well when Maas suffered a broken arm. Former starter Mike Bell is solid insurance with Greg Meisner in reserve for the middle. If the defensive line will be tough, the linebackers could be truly awesome. Again, it will depend upon strategy but the four-man lineup would have last year's first-round sensation, Derrick Thomas, and Chris Martin on the outsides, while the immensely talented first-round draftee, Percy Snow, has arrived to team up with wild-man Dino Hackett on the inside. Conceivably, Thomas, Hackett and Snow could form a three-man set in the 4-3 system, though, of course, only Thomas is a formal outside specialist. It is a pity that Walker Lee Ashley, a hard-nosed competitor who started all last year, will have to settle for being a backup. And there is further depth for the inside positions in last year's pleasant surprise, Rob McGovern, while Louis Cooper is a reserve for the outside. The secondary had been the strength of the defense for at least the last half of the 1980s, and it still is the case that the main characters in that historical greatness could start in 1990. All four of cornerbacks Kevin Ross and Albert Lewis, together with safeties Deron Cherry and Lloyd Burruss, are either current or former Pro Bowlers. There is no question of the cornerbacks being challenged but at safety, as the starters age, there could be more time-sharing. Thus, Kevin Porter could divide the cake with Burruss at strong safety as happened last season. And with free safety Cherry coming off surgery, he could blend with Plan-B free-agent signing Jeff Donaldson, who started last year for Houston.

1990 SCHEDULE OF GAMES

September

9	MINNESOTA	12:00
17	at Denver (Mon.)	7:00
23	at Green Bay	12:00
30	CLEVELAND	3:00

October

7	at Indianapolis	12:00
14	DETROIT	12:00
21	at Seattle	1:00
28	Open date	

November

4	LOS ANGELES RAIDERS	12:00
11	SEATTLE	12:00
18	SAN DIEGO	12:00
25	at Los Angeles Raiders	1:00

December

2	at New England	1:00
9	DENVER	3:00
16	HOUSTON	12:00
23	at San Diego	1:00
29	at Chicago (Sat.)	11:30

Special Teams

Placekicker Nick Lowery slipped from his usual high standards in 1989 but it would be surprising were Plan-B signing Bjorn Nittmo to unseat him. Punter Kelly Goodburn is safe enough. With no touchdowns on kick returns and a longest punt return of just 21 yards, Kansas City could use a general sharpening up of its special-teams effort. Perhaps reserve wide receiver Naz Worthen, who shared the 1989 punt returns with Mandley, could play a greater part on kickoff returns.

Starting defensive end Neil Smith has made steady progress.

1990 DRAFT

Round	Name	Pos.	Ht.	Wt.	College
1.	Snow, Percy	LB	6-2	244	Michigan State
2.	Grunhard, Tim	C	6-2	291	Notre Dame
4.	Jones, Fred	WR	5-8	175	Grambling
5.	Graham, Derrick	T	6-4	312	Appalachian State
5.	Hackemack, Ken	T	6-9	300	Texas
6.	Sims, Tom	DT	6-2	270	Pittsburgh
7.	Szott, Dave	G	6-3	274	Penn State
9.	Owens, Michael	RB	5-11	218	Syracuse
10.	Hudson, Craig	TE	6-2	237	Wisconsin
11.	Thompson, Ernest	RB	6-2	226	Georgia Southern
12.	Jeffery, Tony	WR	5-10	170	San Jose State

VETERAN ROSTER

No.	Name	Pos.	Ht.	Wt.	NFL Year	College
76	Alt, John	T	6-7	300	7	Iowa
54	Ashley, Walker Lee	LB	6-0	231	7	Penn State
77	Baldinger, Rich	G-T	6-4	292	7	Wake Forest
99	Bell, Mike	DE	6-4	262	10	Colorado State
34	Burruss, Lloyd	S	6-0	205	10	Maryland
70	Cannon, Mark	C	6-3	258	7	Texas-Arlington
20	Cherry, Deron	S	5-11	203	10	Rutgers
62	Chilton, Gene	C-G	6-3	286	4	Texas
55	Cooper, Louis	LB	6-2	238	6	Western Carolina
25	Copeland, Danny	S-KR	6-2	210	2	Eastern Kentucky
17	DeBerg, Steve	QB	6-3	214	14	San Jose State
42	Donaldson, Jeff	S	6-0	190	7	Colorado
75	Eatman, Irv	T	6-7	298	5	UCLA
10	Elkins, Mike	QB	6-3	225	2	Wake Forest
22	Gamble, Kenny	RB	5-10	197	2	Colgate
2	Goodburn, Kelly	P	6-2	201	4	Emporia State
49	Griffin, James	S	6-2	203	8	Middle Tennessee St.
98	Griffin, Leonard	DE	6-4	270	5	Grambling
56	Hackett, Dino	LB	6-3	228	5	Appalachian State
26	Harmon, Kevin	RB	6-0	190	3	Iowa
73	Harris, Michael	C-G	6-4	306	2	Grambling
86	Harry, Emile	WR	5-11	178	4	Stanford
85	Hayes, Jonathan	TE	6-5	254	6	Iowa
44	Heard, Herman	RB	5-10	194	7	Southern Colorado
7	Jaworski, Ron	QB	6-1	205	16	Youngstown State
	Jones, Rod	TE	6-4	245	3	Washington
29	Lewis, Albert	CB	6-2	198	8	Grambling
8	Lowery, Nick	K	6-4	189	11	Dartmouth
72	Lutz, David	G-T	6-6	303	8	Georgia Tech
63	Maas, Bill	NT	6-5	268	7	Pittsburgh
89	Mandley, Pete	WR-PR	5-10	195	7	Northern Arizona
57	Martin, Chris	LB	6-2	234	8	Auburn
50	McGovern, Rob	LB	6-2	223	2	Holy Cross
48	McNair, Todd	RB	6-1	185	2	Temple
69	Meisner, Greg	NT	6-3	271	10	Pittsburgh
68	Morris, Mike	C-G	6-5	275	3	Northeast Missouri St.
9	Nittmo, Bjorn	K	5-11	185	2	Appalachian State
35	Okoye, Christian	RB	6-1	260	4	Azusa Pacific
83	Paige, Stephone	WR	6-2	185	8	Fresno State
24	Pearson, Jayice	CB	5-11	185	5	Washington
11	Pelluer, Steve	QB	6-4	212	7	Washington
45	Petry, Stan	CB	5-11	175	2	Texas Christian
27	Porter, Kevin	S	5-10	219	3	Auburn
87	Roberts, Alfredo	TE	6-3	246	3	Miami
31	Ross, Kevin	CB	5-9	182	7	Temple
97	Saleaumua, Dan	NT	6-0	289	4	Arizona State
21	Saxon, James	RB	5-11	215	3	San Jose State
91	Shorts, Peter	DE	6-8	278	1	Illinois State
90	Smith, Neil	DE	6-4	271	3	Nebraska
52	Snipes, Angelo	LB	6-0	227	4	West Georgia
58	Thomas, Derrick	LB	6-3	234	2	Alabama
81	Thomas, Robb	WR	5-11	171	2	Oregon State
94	Ward, David	LB	6-2	232	3	Southern Arkansas
19	Ware, Timmie	WR	5-10	170	4	Southern California
46	Washington, Chas.	DB	6-1	205	2	Cameron, Oklahoma
53	Webster, Mike	C	6-2	260	17	Wisconsin
65	Winters, Frank	C	6-3	280	4	Western Illinois
71	Woods, Rob	T	6-6	280	1	Arizona
84	Worthen, Naz	WR	5-8	177	2	North Carolina State

LOS ANGELES RAIDERS

Address 332 Center Street, El Segundo,
    California 90245.
Stadium Los Angeles Memorial Coliseum.
    Capacity 92,488 *Playing Surface* Grass.
Team Colours Silver and Black.
Head Coach Gene Upshaw – 2nd year.
Championships Division 1970, '72, '73, '74, '75, '76,
    '83, '85; Conference 1976,'80,'83; AFL 1967;
    Super Bowl 1976,'80,'83.
History AFL 1960-69, AFC 1970-
    (Until 1982, they were known as the Oakland
    Raiders.)

Offense

The Raiders are coming off another disappointing campaign but it is not in the nature of the 'Silver and Black' to dwell on the past and they can enter the 1990 season with more than a little optimism. First, the offensive line should be improved by the signing of Plan-B free agent Max Montoya, who will take over from John Gesek at left guard. Montoya's presence should help left tackle Rory Graves and allow Gesek a little more time to learn the ropes. There is just a chance that former Chargers starter James FitzPatrick could be whipped into shape to challenge Graves. Certainly, FitzPatrick has the talent. There are no doubts over the quality from center out to the right with Don Mosebar, Steve Wisniewski and Bruce Wilkerson having settled down as a powerful trio. Behind the offensive line, however, there still remain doubts over who will start at quarterback. Jay Schroeder, for whom the Raiders spent heavily in a trade with Washington, has not turned out to be the immediate answer but the lingering feeling is that, at any moment, he can suddenly blossom. Steve Beuerlein doesn't have Schroeder's arm strength but, in true Raiders spirit, he is convinced that he can do the job. Lining up to catch the passes is perhaps the fastest, most glamorous set of wide receivers in football. Mervyn Fernandez is a big, powerful, rangy

athlete and the elegant Willie Gault is an equally terrifying deep threat. With former first-round pick Tim Brown back to full fitness, Mike Alexander offering great promise and another serious long-ball receiver, Jamie Holland, arriving in a trade, the talent approaches mob proportions. Add to this the potential of exciting tight end Mike Dyal and the full set of choices emerges. At running back, the starting pair should be the great Marcus Allen and fullback Steve Smith. But Vance Mueller, a slashing runner, is on standby duty and, of course, October should see the return of the most feared running back in the NFL, Bo Jackson.

Defense

The Raiders' defense did have a patchwork appearance at times last year, but clever use of personnel and smart trading enabled the unit to stand up under pressure and the reinforcements have now begun to arrive. It was a little surprising when defensive end Anthony Smith was drafted in the first round, but he was regarded as one of the best pass rushers in college football and, even in a group of defensive ends which includes Greg Townsend, Howie Long, Scott Davis and Mike Wise, Smith might have an early role to play. Nose tackle Bob Golic proved to be a fine Plan-B acquisition and he may have surprised many west coast fans with his lateral speed. He is backed up by former starter Bill Pickel. Townsend's role entering the 1990 season is not clear and will depend, amongst other things, on the frequency with which the defense shifts into the 4-3 alignment. Towards the end of last season, he spent more time on the front line but, even with the drafting of Aaron Wallace, who is expected to start right away, Townsend still might be used as an outside linebacker. Wherever he plays, he might be expected to retain his team leadership in sacks. A move to the 4-3 lineup would help solve a shortage at inside linebacker. Currently, three 1989 veterans, Jerry Robinson, Tom Benson and Ricky Hunley, are vying for playing time but Riki Ellison, a 1990 signing from San Francisco, could win the job. The secondary has undergone change and it may be that the great veterans, Mike Haynes and Vann McElroy, have to settle for backup spots. Terry McDaniel will continue to start at left cornerback with Lionel Washington the probable starter on the right. However, the prospects for change are interesting with the drafting of Torin Dorn and the club's intention to attempt the conversion of former Rams wide receiver Ron Brown to play cornerback. For years, Mike Harden was a problem for the Raiders whenever they played Denver and now that he has switched clubs he uses the vast range of his experience as the Raiders' strong safety. Free safety Eddie Anderson has turned out to be a really good signing.

Multi-purpose star Tim Brown is back to full fitness after missing almost all of last season.

Special Teams

Punter Jeff Gossett swung his boot to reasonable effect. He could use a little distance on his gross average but his hang-time is good. However, it must be of some concern to Jeff Jaeger that he failed on ten of his field goal attempts inside the 49-yard range. There are openings for handling both kickoff and punt returns but a fully fit Tim Brown should resume all return duties, helped out by Vance Mueller and Ron Brown, the latter who has scored four touchdowns on kickoff returns.

VETERAN ROSTER

No.	Name	Pos.	Ht.	Wt.	NFL Year	College
44	Adams, Stefon	S	5-10	190	5	East Carolina
80	Alexander, Mike	WR	6-3	195	2	Penn State
32	Allen, Marcus	RB	6-2	210	9	Southern California
33	Anderson, Eddie	S	6-1	200	5	Fort Valley State
54	Benson, Tom	LB	6-2	240	7	Oklahoma
7	Beuerlein, Steve	QB	6-2	210	3	Notre Dame
24	Brown, Ron	CB-KR	5-11	186	7	Arizona State
81	Brown, Tim	WR-KR	6-1	195	2	Notre Dame
59	Burton, Ron	LB	6-1	245	4	North Carolina
99	Campbell, Joe	LB	6-3	242	3	New Mexico State
29	Carter, Russell	S	6-2	200	7	Southern Methodist
70	Davis, Scott	DE	6-7	275	3	Illinois
84	Dyal, Mike	TE	6-2	240	2	Texas A&I
50	Ellison, Riki	LB	6-4	230	7	Southern California
86	Fernandez, Mervyn	WR	6-3	200	4	San Jose State
73	FitzPatrick, James	T	6-7	310	5	Southern California
83	Gault, Willie	WR	6-1	175	8	Tennessee
63	Gesek, John	G	6-5	280	4	Cal State-Sacramento
79	Golic, Bob	NT	6-2	275	11	Notre Dame
6	Gossett, Jeff	P	6-2	195	9	Eastern Illinois
85	Graddy, Sam	WR	5-10	165	3	Tennessee
60	Graves, Rory	T	6-6	295	3	Ohio State
45	Harden, Mike	S	6-1	195	11	Michigan
22	Haynes, Mike	CB	6-2	195	15	Arizona State
61	Hellestrae, Dale	G	6-5	285	4	Southern Methodist
82	Holland, Jamie	WR	6-1	195	4	Ohio State
88	Horton, Ethan	TE	6-4	240	4	North Carolina
98	Hunley, Ricky	LB	6-2	250	7	Arizona
34	Jackson, Bo	RB	6-1	235	4	Auburn
18	Jaeger, Jeff	K	5-11	195	3	Washington
87	Junkin, Trey	TE	6-2	240	8	Louisiana Tech
92	King, Emanuel	LB	6-4	245	6	Alabama
52	King, Linden	LB	6-4	245	13	Colorado State
97	Klostermann, Bruce	LB	6-4	232	4	South Dakota State
25	Land, Dan	CB	6-0	190	3	Albany State
75	Long, Howie	DE	6-5	270	10	Villanova
41	McCallum, Nap.	RB	6-2	215	2	Navy
36	McDaniel, Terry	CB	5-10	175	2	Tennessee
26	McElroy, Vann	S	6-2	195	9	Baylor
65	Montoya, Max	G	6-5	275	12	UCLA
72	Mosebar, Don	C	6-6	280	8	Southern California
42	Mueller, Vance	RB	6-0	215	5	Occidental
43	Patterson, Elvis	CB	5-11	198	7	Kansas
71	Pickel, Bill	NT	6-5	265	8	Rutgers
31	Porter, Kerry	RB	6-1	220	3	Washington State
20	Price, Dennis	CB	6-1	175	3	UCLA
57	Robinson, Jerry	LB	6-2	225	12	UCLA
78	Rother, Tim	T	6-7	280	2	Nebraska
13	Schroeder, Jay	QB	6-4	215	7	UCLA
35	Smith, Steve	RB	6-1	235	4	Penn State
39	Strachan, Steve	RB	6-1	225	6	Boston College
27	Streeter, George	S	6-2	212	2	Notre Dame
93	Townsend, Greg	LB-DE	6-3	255	8	Texas Christian
67	Turk, Dan	C	6-5	275	6	Wisconsin
48	Washington, Lionel	CB	6-0	185	8	Tulane
68	Wilkerson, Bruce	T	6-5	285	4	Tennessee
90	Wise, Mike	DE	6-7	275	4	California-Davis
76	Wisniewski, Steve	G	6-4	280	2	Penn State
66	Wright, Steve	T	6-6	280	8	Northern Iowa

1990 SCHEDULE OF GAMES

September

9	DENVER	1:00
16	at Seattle	1:00
23	PITTSBURGH	1:00
30	CHICAGO	1:00

October

7	at Buffalo (Sun. night)	7:30
14	SEATTLE	1:00
21	at San Diego	1:00
28	*Open date*	

November

4	at Kansas City	12:00
11	GREEN BAY	1:00
19	at Miami (Mon.)	9:00
25	KANSAS CITY	1:00

December

2	at Denver	2:00
10	at Detroit (Mon.)	9:00
16	CINCINNATI	1:00
22	at Minnesota (Sat.)	3:00
30	SAN DIEGO	1:00

1990 DRAFT

Round	Name	Pos.	Ht.	Wt.	College
1.	Smith, Anthony	DE	6-4	257	Arizona
2.	Wallace, Aaron	LB	6-3	236	Texas A&M
4.	Dorn, Torin	CB	6-0	194	North Carolina
5.	Smagala, Stan*	CB	5-9	189	Notre Dame
6.	Wilson, Marcus	RB	6-1	204	Virginia
7.	Lewis, Garry	CB	5-11	175	Alcorn State
8.	Jimerson, Arthur	LB	6-3	214	Norfolk State
9.	Perry, Leon	RB	6-0	227	Oklahoma
11.	Lewis, Ron	WR	6-1	200	Jackson State
11.	Jones, Myron	RB	5-9	189	Fresno State
12.	Harris, Major	QB	6-1	211	West Virginia
12.	Davis, Demetrius	TE	6-3	230	Nevada-Reno

*Smagala was traded to Dallas on the day of the draft.

SAN DIEGO CHARGERS

Address San Diego Jack Murphy Stadium,
 P.O. Box 20666, San Diego, California 92120.
Stadium San Diego Jack Murphy Stadium.
 Capacity 60,750 *Playing Surface* Grass.
Team Colours Navy Blue, White, and Gold.
Head Coach Dan Henning – 2nd year; 6th NFL.
Championships Division 1979,'80,'81; AFL 1963.
History AFL 1960-69, AFC 1970-
 (For 1960 only, they were known as the Los
 Angeles Chargers.)

Offense

After making little progress for some time, the Chargers seem to be on the move. A revamped offensive line saw rookie center Courtney Hall join guards David Richards and Broderick Thompson as the three linemen to start all year. Left tackle Joel Patten moved to the right side to replace Brett Miller for the final two weeks as Joey Howard stepped up at left tackle. It was the kind of stability which the Chargers needed and one which might be disturbed only for the reabsorption of former NFL starters such as guards Dennis McKnight and Larry Williams. Indeed, the calm building of a team confident of future success has become the mood in this southernmost part of California. Miller and James Fitz-Patrick have departed as Plan-B free agents but their places in the scheme of things have been filled by arriving Plan-B free agents Tom Toth and Mike Simmonds, and draftee Leo Goeas. The uncertainties at running back caused by the holdout of Gary Anderson were resolved when he was traded to Tampa Bay during the offseason. It has meant that the pecking order to start as the single running back will probably have Marion Butts leading off with the quartet of Tim Spencer, Darrin Nelson and Plan-B signings Thomas Sanders and Ronnie Harmon on call. There will be competition in the preseason, of course, but a team-leading 683 yards at an average of 4.0 and nine touchdowns should have clinched the starting spot for Butts. The quarterback

situation, too, is much clearer now that Jim McMahon has been released. Billy Joe Tolliver appears to have the lead over Mark Vlasic and David Archer. Vlasic is a tough competitor and, for a time, he appeared to be heading for the starting job before suffering a knee injury which required reconstructive surgery in 1988. The starting wide receivers will be Anthony Miller and either Quinn Early or Wayne Walker, the latter whose mid-season form took him into a starting spot and enabled the Chargers subsequently to trade Jamie Holland. Third-round draftee Walter Wilson begins his apprenticeship. At H-back, Joe Caravello probably will resume while the return of pass receiver Rod Bernstine will be of great value. Arthur Cox, a 16-game starting tight end, is a stalwart of the offense.

Defense

In 1989 there was every indication that the Chargers' defense was another of the AFC's gathering powers. Almost every personnel development was positive, beginning on the three-man line into which rookie defensive end Burt Grossman fitted perfectly. It was to be expected that Pro Bowl left end Lee Williams would grab a hatful of sacks but Grossman's total of ten represents a remarkable achievement. Also encouraging was the form of Joe Phillips, who went through his second season as the starting nose tackle. Without attracting the publicity of Grossman and Williams, he quietly set about closing down the inside lanes. Backups Les Miller and George Hinkle combined for five sacks. But the extra force which gave the Chargers their turbo boost was outside linebacker Leslie O'Neal, whose tremendous fight-back from a critical injury in his rookie year is now complete. Pouring around the end of the line repeatedly, O'Neal led all AFC linebackers with 12.5 sacks. Last year, Billy Ray Smith underlined his status as one of the league's better outside linebackers but, with the arrival of top draftee Junior Seau, there will need to be adjustments. Smith started his NFL career as an inside linebacker but it was only when he switched to the outside that he had the freedom to express the full scope of his powers. Seau is an outside specialist and, if he is to be used fully, it may be that Smith has to shift inside again. The current inside starters are Gary Plummer and Cedric Figaro and it would appear to be the latter who will step down to the role of backup. Plummer led the team in tackles for the second straight year and has become an inspirational force. In the secondary, Gill Byrd led all AFC cornerbacks with seven interceptions. The probability is that Sam Seale, who started at right cornerback before suffering a hamstring injury on Week Fourteen, will also resume. The starting safety pairing of Vencie Glenn and Martin Bayless should be retained, with Lester Lyles as the senior backup.

1990 SCHEDULE OF GAMES	September	
	9 at Dallas	3:00
	16 CINCINNATI	1:00
	23 at Cleveland	1:00
	30 HOUSTON	1:00
	October	
	7 at Pittsburgh	1:00
	14 at New York Jets	1:00
	21 LOS ANGELES RAIDERS	1:00
	28 TAMPA BAY	1:00
	November	
	4 at Seattle	1:00
	11 DENVER	1:00
	18 at Kansas City	12:00
	25 SEATTLE (Sun. night)	5:00
	December	
	2 NEW YORK JETS	1:00
	9 Open date	
	16 at Denver	2:00
	23 KANSAS CITY	1:00
	30 at Los Angeles Raiders	1:00

1990 DRAFT

Round	Name	Pos.	Ht.	Wt.	College
1.	Seau, Junior	LB	6-3	240	Southern California
3.	Mills, Jeff	LB	6-3	227	Nebraska
3.	Goeas, Leo	G	6-3	278	Hawaii
3.	Wilson, Walter	WR	5-10	180	East Carolina
6.	Friesz, John	QB	6-4	209	Idaho
6.	Cornish, Frank	C	6-4	281	UCLA
6.	Pool, David	CB	5-9	188	Carson-Newman
6.	Walker, Derrick	TE	6-0	244	Michigan
7.	Novak, Jeff	G	6-5	279	Southwest Texas State
7.	Staysniak, Joe	T	6-4	290	Ohio State
7.	Lewis, Nate	WR	5-11	197	Oregon Tech
7.	Collins, Keith	CB	5-11	183	Appalachian State
8.	Flannigan, J. J.	RB	5-10	195	Colorado
9.	Goetz, Chris	G	6-2	272	Pittsburgh
10.	Berry, Kenny	S	6-0	180	Miami
11.	Stowers, Tommie	TE	6-2	225	Missouri
12.	Searcy, Elliott	WR	5-8	171	Southern

Special Teams

There will be a changing of the guard in the kicking department with Plan-B signing John Kidd (ex-Buffalo) taking over from the departed Hank Ilesic and John Carney (ex-Tampa Bay) battling Fuad Reveiz (ex-Miami) to succeed Chris Bahr. Ilesic departed as a Plan-B free agent but Bahr was simply released. Starting wide receiver Anthony Miller is a terrific kickoff returner — he averaged 25.4 yards in 1989 and scored a 91-yard touchdown — and one of the draftees will probably take over as the senior punt returner following the release of Phil McConkey.

VETERAN ROSTER

No.	Name	Pos.	Ht.	Wt.	NFL Year	College
15	Archer, David	QB	6-2	208	7	Iowa State
44	Bayless, Martin	S	6-2	212	7	Bowling Green
23	Bennett, Roy	CB	6-2	195	3	Jackson State
82	Bernstine, Rod	TE	6-3	235	4	Texas A&M
58	Brandon, David	LB	6-4	230	4	Memphis State
32	Brooks, Michael	S	6-0	195	1	North Carolina State
35	Butts, Marion	RB	6-1	248	2	Florida State
22	Byrd, Gill	CB	5-11	198	8	San Jose State
46	Caravello, Joe	H-B	6-3	270	4	Tulane
3	Carney, John	K	5-11	160	3	Notre Dame
55	Collins, Jim	LB	6-2	233	10	Syracuse
88	Cox, Arthur	TE	6-2	277	8	Texas Southern
87	Early, Quinn	WR	6-0	190	3	Iowa
51	Figaro, Cedric	LB	6-2	250	3	Notre Dame
25	Glenn, Vencie	S	6-0	192	5	Indiana State
92	Grossman, Burt	DE	6-6	270	2	Pittsburgh
53	Hall, Courtney	C	6-1	269	2	Rice
33	Harmon, Ronnie	RB	6-0	200	5	Iowa
97	Hinkle, George	DE	6-5	269	3	Arizona
79	Howard, Joey	T	6-5	305	2	Tennessee
10	Kidd, John	P	6-3	208	7	Northwestern
24	Lyles, Lester	S	6-3	200	6	Virginia
31	McEwen, Craig	H-B	6-1	220	4	Utah
60	McKnight, Dennis	C-G	6-3	270	8	Drake
36	Mickles, Joe	RB	5-10	221	2	Mississippi
83	Miller, Anthony	WR	5-11	185	3	Tennessee
69	Miller, Les	NT	6-7	293	4	Fort Hays State
20	Nelson, Darrin	RB	5-9	185	9	Stanford
91	O'Neal, Leslie	LB	6-4	259	4	Oklahoma State
85	Parker, Andy	TE	6-5	245	7	Utah
78	Patten, Joel	T	6-7	307	6	Duke
75	Phillips, Joe	NT	6-5	275	5	Southern Methodist
23	Plummer, Bruce	DB	6-1	197	4	Mississippi State
50	Plummer, Gary	LB	6-2	240	5	California
7	Reveiz, Fuad	K	5-11	220	5	Tennessee
65	Richards, David	G-T	6-5	310	3	UCLA
98	Robinson, Gerald	DE	6-3	262	3	Auburn
64	Rodenhauser, Mark	C	6-5	252	3	Illinois State
45	Sanders, Thomas	RB	5-11	203	6	Texas A&M
30	Seale, Sam	CB	5-9	185	7	Western St., Colo.
68	Simmonds, Mike	G	6-4	285	2	Indiana State
54	Smith, Billy Ray	LB	6-3	236	8	Arkansas
43	Spencer, Tim	RB	6-1	223	6	Ohio State
76	Thompson, Broderick	G-T	6-5	295	5	Kansas
11	Tolliver, Billy Joe	QB	6-1	218	2	Texas Tech
73	Toth, Tom	G	6-5	282	5	Western Michigan
13	Vlasic, Mark	QB	6-3	206	3	Iowa
81	Walczak, Mark	TE	6-6	246	4	Arizona
80	Walker, Wayne	WR	5-8	162	2	Texas Tech
77	Williams, Larry	G	6-5	290	4	Notre Dame
99	Williams, Lee	DE	6-5	271	7	Bethune-Cookman
59	Woodard, Ken	LB	6-1	220	9	Tuskegee Institute

Cornerback Gill Byrd was voted Most Inspirational Player by his teammates.

SEATTLE SEAHAWKS

Address 11220 N.E. 53rd Street, Kirkland,
Washington 98033.
Stadium Kingdome, Seattle.
Capacity 64,984 *Playing Surface* AstroTurf.
Team Colours Blue, Green, and Silver.
Head Coach Chuck Knox – 8th year; 18th NFL.
Championships Division 1988.
History NFC 1976, AFC 1977-

Offense

It is surprising that the Seahawks slipped to their first net-losing season since the 1982 strike-shortened campaign. An after-the-event observation makes quite clear the main reason, namely, that the rushing offense dropped off alarmingly. Week after week, we waited for the explosion, but Curt Warner's (almost inevitable) 102-yards-rushing game against the Raiders on Week Four apart, it never came. Warner has departed for the Rams as a Plan-B free agent, leaving John L. Williams as the senior running back. Strangely, we may now see Williams, who is the complete back, rushing, receiving and blocking, at his best. His new starting partner will be one of Elroy Harris, Derrick Fenner or rookie Chris Warren, with the intriguing possibility that James Jones and Bobby Joe Edmonds might have a part to play. The offensive linemen fall into place and, at least, offer the authority which comes with cohesion. Andy Heck has settled in nicely at left tackle and the system will not be disrupted when Ron Mattes, a former starter, moves up to challenge Mike Wilson at right tackle. The guard positions are in the care of Edwin Bailey and Bryan Millard, but there is just a possibility that center Grant Feasel will have to hold off a serious push by 1989 draftee Joe Tofflemire. For the quarterback position Kelly Stouffer had little opportunity to show that he could displace Dave Krieg, a battle-hardened veteran who can have the home fans jeering and cheering in the same breath. Krieg is one of those quarterbacks who can mount the kind of charge which could take him straight into the Hall of Fame and then slump into inexplicable depression. But he's a fighter and has won titles for

Seattle in the past. No longer will he have the peerless Steve Largent at wide receiver but, in Brian Blades, the Seahawks may have another Largent in the making. Indeed, there is a great deal of Largent woven into the fabric of his play. Tommy Kane could come through to start as Blades' partner but he has had knee problems and it may be that Paul Skansi steps up. Travis McNeal is pencilled in to start at tight end but he will be challenged by Plan-B signing Ron Heller.

Defense

Had there been any doubts, the structure of the Seahawks draft, which had defensive players in five of the first six places, indicated the direction in which the club intends to move. Top draftee defensive tackle Cortez Kennedy, a superstar in the making, will start immediately in what is intended to be a four-man defensive line. Kennedy, who comes with the kind of reputation for demanding double-teaming much in the manner of Philadelphia's Reggie White, could bring the best out of defensive end Jacob Green, who has needed top-class help for some time. Jeff Bryant is set to continue at defensive right end and Joe Nash may prefer the extra freedom he receives as a defensive tackle to being overwhelmed as a nose tackle. However, Jethro Franklin will make a bid for playing time and draftee Eric Hayes will be anxious to impress. There could be some changes at linebacker with the prospect of Tony Woods being used more often as a pass-rushing defensive end. The obvious move would see Rufus Porter replace Woods with draftee Terry Wooden starting at right linebacker in place of the departed M. L. Johnson. The probability that Brian Bosworth will not be available leaves Darren Comeaux, Dave Wyman and Plan-B free agent Dave Ahrens competing for the job of middle linebacker. How sad it is that Bosworth, a player of immense powers and no little intelligence, should be lost to the game if, as expected, injuries force his retirement. Draftee Robert Blackmon has arrived to reinforce the defensive secondary, and if he does not start immediately, he should press incumbent strong safety Nesby Glasgow. But the veteran of 11 years who led the team in tackles will not be displaced easily. At free safety, Eugene Robinson will continue to start. Robinson led the Seahawks with five interceptions and is another trusted warrior who has the lifeblood of the northwest surging through his veins. The senior combination at cornerback is not etched in stone. In the contestants, Patrick Hunter, Dwayne Harper and Melvin Jenkins, there is plenty of starting experience but no one has established a distinct superiority and it may be that second-year player James Jefferson comes into the reckoning.

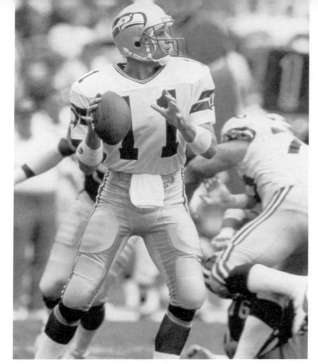

Quarterback Kelly Stouffer awaits his chance to challenge starter Dave Krieg.

1990 DRAFT

Round	Name	Pos.	Ht.	Wt.	College
1.	Kennedy, Cortez	DT	6-1	293	Miami
2.	Wooden, Terry	LB	6-2	232	Syracuse
2.	Blackmon, Robert	DB	5-11	198	Baylor
4.	Warren, Chris	RB	6-1	225	Ferrum, Virginia
5.	Hayes, Eric	DT	6-2	285	Florida State
6.	Bolcar, Ned	LB	6-1	231	Notre Dame
7.	Kula, Bob	T	6-3	282	Michigan State
8.	Hitchcock, Bill	T	6-5	308	Purdue
10.	Morris, Robert	DE	6-5	256	Valdosta State
11.	Reed, Daryl	DB	6-1	186	Oregon
12.	Gromos, John	QB	6-4	210	Vanderbilt

VETERAN ROSTER   NFL

No.	Name	Pos.	Ht.	Wt.	Year	College
50	Ahrens, Dave	LB	6-4	245	10	Wisconsin
65	Bailey, Edwin	G	6-4	273	10	South Carolina State
89	Blades, Brian	WR	5-11	184	3	Miami
55	Bosworth, Brian	LB	6-2	236	3	Oklahoma
64	Brilz, Darrick	G	6-3	270	4	Oregon State
77	Bryant, Jeff	DE	6-5	277	9	Clemson
59	Cain, Joe	LB	6-1	228	2	Oregon Tech
88	Chadwick, Jeff	WR	6-3	190	8	Grand Valley State
84	Clark, Louis	WR	6-0	199	4	Mississippi State
53	Comeaux, Darren	LB	6-1	239	9	Arizona State
3	Donnelly, Rick	P	6-0	190	5	Wyoming
31	Edmonds, Bobby Joe	RB-KR	5-11	186	5	Arkansas
54	Feasel, Grant	C	6-7	279	6	Abilene Christian
44	Fenner, Derrick	RB	6-3	229	2	North Carolina
90	Franklin, Jethro	DE	6-1	258	2	Fresno State
22	Glasgow, Nesby	S	5-10	187	12	Washington
79	Green, Jacob	DE	6-3	254	11	Texas A&M
29	Harper, Dwayne	CB	5-11	174	3	South Carolina State
33	Harris, Elroy	RB	5-9	218	2	Eastern Kentucky
63	Hart, Roy	NT	6-1	279	2	South Carolina
66	Heck, Andy	T	6-6	291	2	Notre Dame
85	Heller, Ron	TE	6-3	235	4	Oregon State
25	Hollis, David	S-PR	6-1	189	4	Nevada-Las Vegas
27	Hunter, Patrick	CB	5-11	185	5	Nevada-Reno
26	Jefferson, James	CB-KR	6-1	199	2	Texas A&I
24	Jenkins, Melvin	CB	5-10	182	4	Cincinnati
9	Johnson, Norm	K	6-2	197	9	UCLA
30	Jones, James	RB	6-2	229	8	Florida
81	Kane, Tommy	WR	5-11	176	3	Syracuse
23	Kaumeyer, Thom	S	5-11	187	1	Oregon
15	Kemp, Jeff	QB	6-0	201	10	Dartmouth
17	Krieg, Dave	QB	6-1	192	11	Milton
70	Mattes, Ron	T	6-6	302	5	Virginia
86	McNeal, Travis	TE	6-3	248	2	Tenn.-Chattanooga
71	Millard, Bryan	G	6-5	281	7	Texas
91	Miller, Darrin	LB	6-1	236	3	Tennessee
72	Nash, Joe	NT	6-2	269	9	Boston College
97	Porter, Rufus	LB	6-1	221	3	Southern
98	Ridgle, Elston	DE	6-5	270	3	Nevada-Reno
41	Robinson, Eugene	S	6-0	186	6	Colgate
5	Rodriguez, Ruben	P	6-2	217	4	Arizona
83	Sandusky, Jim	WR	5-10	180	1	San Diego State
82	Skansi, Paul	WR	5-11	186	8	Washington
11	Stouffer, Kelly	QB	6-3	207	3	Colorado State
56	Tofflemire, Joe	C	6-2	274	1	Arizona
87	Tyler, Robert	TE	6-5	257	2	South Carolina State
74	Wheat, Warren	G	6-6	277	1	Brigham Young
32	Williams, John L.	RB	5-11	228	5	Florida
75	Wilson, Mike	T	6-5	279	13	Georgia
57	Woods, Tony	DE	6-4	264	4	Pittsburgh
92	Wyman, David	LB	6-2	242	4	Stanford

1990 SCHEDULE OF GAMES

September
9	at Chicago	12:00
16	LOS ANGELES RAIDERS	1:00
23	at Denver	2:00

October
1	CINCINNATI (Mon.)	6:00
7	at New England	1:00
14	at Los Angeles Raiders	1:00
21	KANSAS CITY	1:00
28	Open date	

November
4	SAN DIEGO	1:00
11	at Kansas City	12:00
18	MINNESOTA	1:00
25	at San Diego (Sun. night)	5:00

December
2	HOUSTON	1:00
9	vs Green Bay at Milwaukee	12:00
16	at Miami	1:00
23	DENVER (Sun. night)	5:00
30	DETROIT	1:00

Special Teams

Norm Johnson is coming off a moderate season but it is unthinkable that he will be replaced. On the other hand, an off-year by punter Ruben Rodriguez means that he will be joined in camp by Plan-B free agent Rick Donnelly. Bobby Joe Edmonds comes home to Seattle after an absence of one year and could return both kickoffs and punts but there will be healthy competition from last year's specialists, punt returner David Hollis and kickoff returner Jefferson, both of whom did very well indeed.

CHAPTER SEVEN

NATIONAL FOOTBALL CONFERENCE

TEAM RANKINGS

| | OFFENSE | | | | | | DEFENSE | | | | | |
	Total Yds.	Rushing	Passing	Points For	No. Intercepted	No. Sacked	Total Yds.	Rushing	Passing	Points Against	Interceptions	Sacks
Atlanta	12	14	5	12	2	12	14	14	7	14	10	12
Chicago	5	1	11	6	11	2	12	9	11	10 =	3	8 =
Dallas	14	12	14	14	12	3	10	10	8	12	14	14
Detroit	9	4	13	11	10	14	9	7	13	9	12 =	6 =
Green Bay	4	10	4	5	9	11	7	11	5	8	4	10
L.A. Rams	3	7	3	2	6	4	11	5	14	7	6 =	5
Minnesota	8	3	9	7	7 =	6	1	8	1	4	11	1
New Orleans	6	6	6	3 =	7 =	5	6	1	12	5	6 =	3
N.Y. Giants	10	9	12	8	3 =	10	3	4	2	1	5	8 =
Philadelphia	7	2	10	9	3 =	8 =	4	6	4	3	1	2
Phoenix	13	13	8	13	14	13	13	13	10	10 =	12 =	13
San Francisco	1	5	2	1	1	8 =	2	3	3	2	6 =	4
Tampa Bay	11	11	7	10	13	7	8	12	6	13	6 =	1
Washington	2	8	1	3 =	5	1	5	2	9	6	2	6 =

NFC PASSERS

	Att	Comp	% Comp	Yards	Ave Gain	TD	% TD	Long	Int	% Int	Rating Points
Montana, Joe, *S.F.*	386	271	70.2	3521	9.12	26	6.7	t95	8	2.1	112.4
Everett, Jim, *Rams*	518	304	58.7	4310	8.32	29	5.6	t78	17	3.3	90.6
Rypien, Mark, *Wash.*	476	280	58.8	3768	7.92	22	4.6	t80	13	2.7	88.1
Hebert, Bobby, *N.O.*	353	222	62.9	2686	7.61	15	4.2	t54	15	4.2	82.7
Majkowski, Don, *G.B.*	599	353	58.9	4318	7.21	27	4.5	t79	20	3.3	82.3
Simms, Phil, *Giants*	405	228	56.3	3061	7.56	14	3.5	t62	14	3.5	77.6
Miller, Chris, *Atl.*	526	280	53.2	3459	6.58	16	3.0	t72	10	1.9	76.1
Cunningham, Randall, *Phil.*	532	290	54.5	3400	6.39	21	3.9	t66	15	2.8	75.5
Wilson, Wade, *Minn.*	362	194	53.6	2543	7.02	9	2.5	50	12	3.3	70.5
Hogeboom, Gary, *Phoe.*	364	204	56.0	2591	7.12	14	3.8	t59	19	5.2	69.5
Testaverde, Vinny, *T.B.*	480	258	53.8	3133	6.53	20	4.2	t78	22	4.6	68.9
Tomczak, Mike, *Chi.*	306	156	51.0	2058	6.73	16	5.2	t79	16	5.2	68.2
Gagliano, Bob, *Det.*	232	117	50.4	1671	7.20	6	2.6	t75	12	5.2	61.2
Aikman, Troy, *Dall.*	293	155	52.9	1749	5.97	9	3.1	t75	18	6.1	55.7

Non-qualifiers

	Att	Comp	% Comp	Yards	Ave Gain	TD	% TD	Long	Int	% Int	Rating Points
Young, Steve, *S.F.*	92	64	69.6	1001	10.88	8	8.7	t50	3	3.3	120.8
Fourcade, John, *N.O.*	107	61	57.0	930	8.69	7	6.5	t54	4	3.7	92.0
Millen, Hugh, *Atl.*	50	31	62.0	432	8.64	1	2.0	47	2	4.0	79.8
Kramer, Tommy, *Minn.*	136	77	56.6	906	6.66	7	5.1	39	7	5.1	72.7
Harbaugh, Jim, *Chi.*	178	111	62.4	1204	6.76	5	2.8	t49	9	5.1	70.5
Peete, Rodney, *Det.*	195	103	52.8	1479	7.58	5	2.6	69	9	4.6	67.0
Williams, Doug, *Wash.*	93	51	54.8	585	6.29	1	1.1	46	3	3.2	64.1
Walsh, Steve, *Dall.*	219	110	50.2	1371	6.26	5	2.3	46	9	4.1	60.5
Tupa, Tom, *Phoe.*	134	65	48.5	973	7.26	3	2.2	t77	9	6.7	52.2
Ferguson, Joe, *T.B.*	90	44	48.9	533	5.92	3	3.3	t69	6	6.7	50.8

t = Touchdown
Leader based on rating points, minimum 224 attempts

NFC RECEIVERS – Most Receptions

	No	Yards	Ave	Long	TD
Sharpe, Sterling, *G.B.*	90	1423	15.8	t79	12
Carrier, Mark, *T.B.*	86	1422	16.5	t78	9
Monk, Art, *Wash.*	86	1186	13.8	t60	8
Rice, Jerry, *S.F.*	82	1483	18.1	t68	17
Sanders, Ricky, *Wash.*	80	1138	14.2	68	4
Clark, Gary, *Wash.*	79	1229	15.6	t80	9
Rathman, Tom, *S.F.*	73	616	8.4	36	1
Ellard, Henry, *Rams*	70	1382	19.7	53	8
Johnson, Richard, *Det.*	70	1091	15.6	t75	8
Martin, Eric, *N.O.*	68	1090	16.0	t53	8
Byars, Keith, *Phil.*	68	721	10.6	60	0
Carter, Anthony, *Minn.*	65	1066	16.4	50	4
Jackson, Keith, *Phil.*	63	648	10.3	33	3
Smith, J.T., *Phoe.*	62	778	12.5	31	5
Taylor, John, *S.F.*	60	1077	18.0	t95	10
Woodside, Keith, *G.B.*	59	527	8.9	33	0
Collins, Shawn, *Atl.*	58	862	14.9	47	3
Byner, Earnest, *Wash.*	54	458	8.5	27	2
Hilliard, Dalton, *N.O.*	52	514	9.9	t54	5
Holohan, Pete, *Rams*	51	510	10.0	31	2
Hill, Bruce, *T.B.*	50	673	13.5	53	5
Anderson, Neal, *Chi.*	50	434	8.7	t49	4
Craig, Roger, *S.F.*	49	473	9.7	44	1
Hill, Lonzell, *N.O.*	48	636	13.3	46	4
Kemp, Perry, *G.B.*	48	611	12.7	39	2
Martin, Kelvin, *Dall.*	46	644	14.0	46	2
Jones, Ernie, *Phoe.*	45	838	18.6	t72	3
Carter, Cris, *Phil.*	45	605	13.4	42	11
Anderson, Willie, *Rams*	44	1146	26.0	t78	5
Green, Roy, *Phoe.*	44	703	16.0	t59	7
Jones, Hassan, *Minn.*	42	694	16.5	50	1
Clark, Robert, *Det.*	41	748	18.2	69	2
Jones, Keith, *Atl.*	41	396	9.7	46	0
Haynes, Michael, *Atl.*	40	681	17.0	t72	4
Jones, Brent, *S.F.*	40	500	12.5	t36	4
Walker, Herschel, *Dall.-Minn.*	40	423	10.6	52	2
Fontenot, Herman, *G.B.*	40	372	9.3	t38	3

t = Touchdown

NFC RECEIVERS – Most Yards

	Yards	No	Ave	Long	TD
Rice, Jerry, *S.F.*	1483	82	18.1	t68	17
Sharpe, Sterling, *G.B.*	1423	90	15.8	t79	12
Carrier, Mark, *T.B.*	1422	86	16.5	t78	9
Ellard, Henry, *Rams*	1382	70	19.7	53	8
Clark, Gary, *Wash.*	1229	79	15.6	t80	9
Monk, Art, *Wash.*	1186	86	13.8	t60	8
Anderson, Flipper, *Rams*	1146	44	26.0	t78	5
Sanders, Ricky, *Wash.*	1138	80	14.2	68	4
Johnson, Richard, *Det.*	1091	70	15.6	t75	8
Martin, Eric, *N.O.*	1090	68	16.0	t53	8
Taylor, John, *S.F.*	1077	60	18.0	t95	10
Carter, Anthony, *Minn.*	1066	65	16.4	50	4
Collins, Shawn, *Atl.*	862	58	14.9	47	3
Jones, Ernie, *Phoe.*	838	45	18.6	t72	3
Smith, J.T., *Phoe.*	778	62	12.5	31	5
Clark, Robert, *Det.*	748	41	18.2	69	2
Byars, Keith, *Phil.*	721	68	10.6	60	0
Green, Roy, *Phoe.*	703	44	16.0	t59	7
Jones, Hassan, *Minn.*	694	42	16.5	50	1
Haynes, Michael, *Atl.*	681	40	17.0	t72	4
Hill, Bruce, *T.B.*	673	50	13.5	53	5
Jackson, Keith, *Phil.*	648	63	10.3	33	3
Martin, Kelvin, *Dall.*	644	46	14.0	46	2
Hill, Lonzell, *N.O.*	636	48	13.3	46	4
Rathman, Tom, *S.F.*	616	73	8.4	36	1
Kemp, Perry, *G.B.*	611	48	12.7	39	2

t = Touchdown

Sterling Sharpe led the NFL with 90 pass receptions.

NFC RUSHERS

	Att	Yards	Ave	Long	TD
Sanders, Barry, *Det.*	280	1470	5.3	34	14
Anderson, Neal, *Chi.*	274	1275	4.7	73	11
Hilliard, Dalton, *N.O.*	344	1262	3.7	40	13
Bell, Greg, *Rams*	272	1137	4.2	47	15
Craig, Roger, *S.F.*	271	1054	3.9	27	6
Anderson, Ottis, *Giants*	325	1023	3.1	t36	14
Walker, Herschel, *Dall.-Minn.*	250	915	3.7	47	7
Riggs, Gerald, *Wash.*	201	834	4.1	58	4
Fullwood, Brent, *G.B.*	204	821	4.0	38	5
Settle, John, *Atl.*	179	689	3.8	20	3
Cunningham, Randall, *Phil.*	104	621	6.0	51	4
Tate, Lars, *T.B.*	167	589	3.5	48	8
Fenney, Rick, *Minn.*	151	588	3.9	25	4
Toney, Anthony, *Phil.*	172	582	3.4	44	3
Byner, Earnest, *Wash.*	134	580	4.3	24	7
Ferrell, Earl, *Phoe.*	149	502	3.4	t44	6
Byars, Keith, *Phil.*	133	452	3.4	t16	5
Palmer, Paul, *Dall.*	112	446	4.0	t63	2
Delpino, Robert, *Rams*	78	368	4.7	t32	5
Majkowski, Don, *G.B.*	75	358	4.8	20	5
Howard, William, *T.B.*	108	357	3.3	15	1
Morris, Jamie, *Wash.*	124	336	2.7	t12	2
Muster, Brad, *Chi.*	82	327	4.0	20	5
Rathman, Tom, *S.F.*	79	305	3.9	13	1
Aikman, Troy, *Dall.*	38	302	7.9	25	0
Tillman, Lewis, *Giants*	79	290	3.7	19	0
Harbaugh, Jim, *Chi.*	45	276	6.1	t26	3
Woodside, Keith, *G.B.*	46	273	5.9	t68	1
Wilder, James, *T.B.*	70	244	3.5	14	0
Montana, Joe, *S.F.*	49	227	4.6	19	3
Johnston, Daryl, *Dall.*	67	212	3.2	13	0
Jordan, Tony, *Phoe.*	83	211	2.5	15	2
Dozier, D.J., *Minn.*	46	207	4.5	38	0
Jones, Keith, *Atl.*	52	202	3.9	19	6
Gagliano, Bob, *Det.*	41	192	4.7	19	4
Anderson, Alfred, *Minn.*	52	189	3.6	14	2
Higgs, Mark, *Phil.*	49	184	3.8	13	0
Heyward, Craig, *N.O.*	49	183	3.7	15	1
Jordan, Buford, *N.O.*	38	179	4.7	32	3
Sherman, Heath, *Phil.*	40	177	4.4	37	2
Lang, Gene, *Atl.*	47	176	3.7	22	1
Mitchell, Stump, *Phoe.*	43	165	3.8	14	1
Gary, Cleveland, *Rams*	37	163	4.4	18	1
Carthon, Maurice, *Giants*	57	153	2.7	18	0
Peete, Rodney, *Det.*	33	148	4.5	t14	4
Sikahema, Vai, *Phoe.*	38	145	3.8	27	0
Simms, Phil, *Giants*	32	141	4.4	15	1
Stamps, Sylvester, *T.B.*	29	141	4.9	t21	1
Testaverde, Vinny, *T.B.*	25	139	5.6	16	0
Haddix, Michael, *G.B.*	44	135	3.1	10	0
Wilson, Wade, *Minn.*	32	132	4.1	23	1
Flagler, Terrence, *S.F.*	33	129	3.9	t29	1
Drummond, Robert, *Phil.*	32	127	4.0	16	0
Sanders, Thomas, *Chi.*	41	127	3.1	19	0
Young, Steve, *S.F.*	38	126	3.3	22	2
Meggett, Dave, *Giants*	28	117	4.2	18	0
Frazier, Paul, *N.O.*	25	112	4.5	21	1
Dupard, Reggie, *N.E.-Wash.*	37	111	3.0	19	1
Gentry, Dennis, *Chi.*	17	106	6.2	29	0
Paige, Tony, *Det.*	30	105	3.5	16	0
Clark, Jessie, *Phoe.-Minn.*	20	99	5.0	14	0
McGee, Buford, *Rams*	21	99	4.7	15	1
Fourcade, John, *N.O.*	14	91	6.5	14	1
Hogeboom, Gary, *Phoe.*	27	89	3.3	15	1
Hebert, Bobby, *N.O.*	25	87	3.5	11	0
Sargent, Broderick, *Dall.*	20	87	4.4	43	1
Tupa, Tom, *Phoe.*	15	75	5.0	13	0
Green, Gaston, *Rams*	26	73	2.8	9	0

t = Touchdown

NFC SCORING — Kickers

	XP	XPA	FG	FGA	PTS
Cofer, Mike, *S.F.*	49	51	29	36	136
Lohmiller, Chip, *Wash.*	41	41	29	40	128
Karlis, Rich, *Minn.*	27	28	31	39	120
Lansford, Mike, *Rams*	51	51	23	30	120
Jacke, Chris, *G.B.*	42	42	22	28	108
Andersen, Morten, *N.O.*	44	45	20	29	104
Igwebuike, Donald, *T.B.*	33	35	22	28	99
Murray, Eddie, *Det.*	36	36	20	21	96
Davis, Greg, *N.E.-Atl.*	25	28	23	34	94
Butler, Kevin, *Chi.*	43	45	15	19	88
Allegre, Raul, *Giants*	23	24	20	26	83
Del Greco, Al, *Phoe.*	28	29	18	26	82
Zendejas, Luis, *Phil.-Dall.*	33	33	14	24	75
Ruzek, Roger, *Dall.-Phil.*	28	29	13	22	67
McFadden, Paul, *Atl.*	18	18	15	20	63
Nittmo, Bjorn, *Giants*	12	13	9	12	39

NFC SCORING — Touchdowns

	TD	TDR	TDP	TDM	PTS
Hilliard, Dalton, *N.O.*	18	13	5	0	108
Rice, Jerry, *S.F.*	17	0	17	0	102
Anderson, Neal, *Chi.*	15	11	4	0	90
Bell, Greg, *Rams*	15	15	0	0	90
Anderson, Ottis, *Giants*	14	14	0	0	84
Sanders, Barry, *Det.*	14	14	0	0	84
Sharpe, Sterling, *G.B.*	13	0	12	1	78
Carter, Cris, *Phil.*	11	0	11	0	66
Taylor, John, *S.F.*	10	0	10	0	60
Walker, Herschel, *Dall.-Minn.*	10	7	2	1	60
Byner, Earnest, *Wash.*	9	7	2	0	54
Carrier, Mark, *T.B.*	9	0	9	0	54
Clark, Gary, *Wash.*	9	0	9	0	54
Tate, Lars, *T.B.*	9	8	1	0	54
Ellard, Henry, *Rams*	8	0	8	0	48
Johnson, Richard, *Det.*	8	0	8	0	48
Martin, Eric, *N.O.*	8	0	8	0	48
Monk, Art, *Wash.*	8	0	8	0	48
Muster, Brad, *Chi.*	8	5	3	0	48
Craig, Roger, *S.F.*	7	6	1	0	42
Green, Roy, *Phoe.*	7	0	7	0	42
Fenney, Rick, *Minn.*	6	4	2	0	36
Ferrell, Earl, *Phoe.*	6	6	0	0	36
Jones, Keith, *Atl.*	6	6	0	0	36

NFC KICKOFF RETURNERS

	No	Yards	Ave	Long	TD
Gray, Mel, *Det.*	24	640	26.7	57	0
Dixon, James, *Dall.*	47	1181	25.1	t97	1
Howard, Joe, *Wash.*	21	522	24.9	t99	1
Gentry, Dennis, *Chi.*	28	667	23.8	63	0
Meggett, Dave, *Giants*	27	577	21.4	43	0
Sanders, Thomas, *Chi.*	23	491	21.3	t96	1
Johnson, A.J., *Wash.*	24	504	21.0	38	0
Sanders, Deion, *Atl.*	35	725	20.7	72	0
Brown, Ron, *Rams*	47	968	20.6	74	0
Sikahema, Vai, *Phoe.*	43	874	20.3	52	0
Flagler, Terrence, *S.F.*	32	643	20.1	41	0
Shepard, Derrick, *N.O.-Dall.*	27	529	19.6	32	0
Jones, Keith, *Atl.*	23	440	19.1	29	0
Usher, Darryl, *S.D.-Phoe.*	27	506	18.7	33	0
Elder, Donnie, *T.B.*	40	685	17.1	30	0
Workman, Vince, *G.B.*	33	547	16.6	46	0
Ingram, Mark, *Giants*	22	332	15.1	29	0

t=Touchdown
Leader based on average return, minimum 20 returns

Barry Sanders was a danger every time he touched the ball.

Dalton Hilliard led the NFL with 18 touchdowns.

Nfc Punters

	No	Yards	Long	Ave	Total Punts	TB	Blk	Opp Ret	Ret Yds	In 20	Net Ave
Camarillo, Rich, *Phoe.*	76	3298	58	43.4	76	6	0	42	330	21	37.5
Arnold, Jim, *Det.*	82	3538	64	43.1	83	9	1	46	373	14	36.0
Landeta, Sean, *Giants*	70	3019	71	43.1	70	7	0	29	236	19	37.8
Mojsiejenko, Ralf, *Wash.*	62	2663	74	43.0	63	9	1	34	383	21	33.3
Fulhage, Scott, *Atl.*	84	3472	65	41.3	85	9	1	43	460	24	33.3
Saxon, Mike, *Dall.*	79	3233	56	40.9	81	6	2	37	334	19	34.3
Bracken, Don, *G.B.*	66	2682	63	40.6	66	11	0	30	416	17	31.0
Helton, Barry, *S.F.*	55	2226	56	40.5	56	6	1	35	361	13	31.2
Scribner, Bucky, *Minn.*	72	2864	55	39.8	72	8	0	32	300	16	33.4
Barnhardt, Tommy, *N.O.*	55	2179	56	39.6	55	4	0	28	174	17	35.0
Buford, Maury, *Chi.*	72	2844	60	39.5	72	9	0	30	262	21	33.4
Mohr, Chris, *T.B.*	84	3311	58	39.4	86	3	2	54	492	10	32.1
Teltschik, John, *Phil.*	57	2246	58	39.4	57	3	0	29	175	12	35.3
Hatcher, Dale, *Rams*	73	2834	54	38.8	74	7	1	34	315	15	32.1

Leader based on gross average, minimum 40 punts

Nfc Sackers

	No
Doleman, Chris, *Minn.*	21.0
Harris, Tim, *G.B.*	19.5
Millard, Keith, *Minn.*	18.0
Greene, Kevin, *Rams*	16.5
Swilling, Pat, *N.O.*	16.5
Simmons, Clyde, *Phil.*	15.5
Taylor, Lawrence, *Giants*	15.0
Jeffcoat, Jim, *Dall.*	11.5
Noga, Al, *Minn.*	11.5
White, Reggie, *Phil.*	11.0
Brown, Jerome, *Phil.*	10.5
Haley, Charles, *S.F.*	10.5
Holt, Pierce, *S.F.*	10.5
Mann, Charles, *Wash.*	10.0
Marshall, Leonard, *Giants*	9.5
Warren, Frank, *N.O.*	9.5
Ball, Jerry, *Det.*	9.0
Cofer, Mike, *Det.*	9.0
Cotton, Marcus, *Atl.*	9.0
Dent, Richard, *Chi.*	9.0
Manley, Dexter, *Wash.*	9.0
Thomas, Henry, *Minn.*	9.0
Jackson, Rickey, *N.O.*	7.5
McMichael, Steve, *Chi.*	7.5
Fagan, Kevin, *S.F.*	7.0
Harvey, Ken, *Phoe.*	7.0
Pitts, Mike, *Phil.*	7.0
Bruce, Aundray, *Atl.*	6.0
Murphy, Kevin, *T.B.*	6.0
Galloway, David, *Phoe.*	5.5
Howard, Erik, *Giants*	5.5
Moss, Winston, *T.B.*	5.5
Williams, Eric, *Det.*	5.5
Armstrong, Trace, *Chi.*	5.0
Green, Tim, *Atl.*	5.0
Nunn, Freddie Joe, *Phoe.*	5.0
Spielman, Chris, *Det.*	5.0
Wilcher, Mike, *Rams*	5.0
Joyner, Seth, *Phil.*	4.5
Roper, John, *Chi.*	4.5
Stubbs, Danny, *S.F.*	4.5
Banks, Carl, *Giants*	4.0
Coleman, Monte, *Wash.*	4.0
Goff, Robert, *T.B.*	4.0
Marshall, Wilber, *Wash.*	4.0
Perry, William, *Chi.*	4.0
Piel, Mike, *Rams*	4.0
Wilks, Jim, *N.O.*	4.0
Williams, Jimmy, *Det.*	4.0

NFC PUNT RETURNERS

	No	FC	Yards	Ave	Long	TD
Stanley, Walter, *Det.*	36	5	496	13.8	74	0
Meggett, Dave, *Giants*	46	14	582	12.7	t76	1
Sikahema, Vai, *Phoe.*	37	13	433	11.7	53	0
Taylor, John, *S.F.*	36	20	417	11.6	37	0
Drewrey, Willie, *T.B.*	20	2	220	11.0	55	0
Sanders, Deion, *Atl.*	28	7	307	11.0	t68	1
Lewis, Leo, *Minn.*	44	27	446	10.1	65	0
Howard, Joe, *Wash.*	21	18	200	9.5	38	0
Henley, Darryl, *Rams*	28	19	266	9.5	25	0
Williams, Henry, *Phil.*	30	7	267	8.9	24	0
Query, Jeff, *G.B.*	30	7	247	8.2	15	0
Shepard, Derrick, *N.O.-Dall.*	31	2	251	8.1	t56	1
Harris, Rod, *N.O.*	27	7	196	7.3	20	0

t = Touchdown
Leader based on average return, minimum 18 returns

NFC INTERCEPTORS

	No	Yards	Ave	Long	TD
Allen, Eric, *Phil.*	8	38	4.8	18	0
McDonald, Tim, *Phoe.*	7	170	24.3	t53	1
Holmes, Jerry, *Det.*	6	77	12.8	36	1
Hamilton, Harry, *T.B.*	6	70	11.7	30	0
Waymer, Dave, *N.O.*	6	66	11.0	42	0
Gray, Jerry, *Rams*	6	48	8.0	t27	1
Robinson, Mark, *T.B.*	6	44	7.3	16	0
Brown, Dave, *G.B.*	6	12	2.0	12	0
Kinard, Terry, *Giants*	5	135	27.0	t58	1
Reynolds, Ricky, *T.B.*	5	87	17.4	t68	1
Browner, Joey, *Minn.*	5	70	14.0	34	0
Sanders, Deion, *Atl.*	5	52	10.4	22	0
Lott, Ronnie, *S.F.*	5	34	6.8	28	0
Massey, Robert, *N.O.*	5	26	5.2	22	0
Williams, Jimmy, *Det.*	5	15	3.0	9	0
Johnson, A.J., *Wash.*	4	94	23.5	t59	1
Everett, Eric, *Phil.*	4	64	16.0	t30	1
Gordon, Tim, *Atl.*	4	60	15.0	34	0
Stinson, Lemuel, *Chi.*	4	59	14.8	t29	1
Frizzell, William, *Phil.*	4	58	14.5	27	0
Jenkins, Izel, *Phil.*	4	58	14.5	22	0
Walton, Alvin, *Wash.*	4	58	14.5	t29	1
Cooper, Evan, *Atl.*	4	54	13.5	38	0
Davis, Brian, *Wash.*	4	40	10.0	15	0
Mack, Cedric, *Phoe.*	4	15	3.8	9	0
Cook, Toi, *N.O.*	3	81	27.0	t63	1
Johnson, Pepper, *Giants*	3	60	20.0	t39	1
Lynch, Lorenzo, *Chi.*	3	55	18.3	41	0
Irvin, LeRoy, *Rams*	3	43	14.3	18	0
Maxie, Brett, *N.O.*	3	41	13.7	t26	1
Gayle, Shaun, *Chi.*	3	39	13.0	20	0
Brooks, Chet, *S.F.*	3	31	10.3	19	0
Murphy, Mark, *G.B.*	3	31	10.3	20	0
Merriweather, Mike, *Minn.*	3	29	9.7	t15	1
Bowles, Todd, *Wash.*	3	25	8.3	25	0

t = Touchdown

LEFT: Chris Doleman led the NFL in quarterback sacks.

BELOW: A 74-yard run helped Walter Stanley to an NFL-leading, 13.8-yard average on 36 punt returns.

DALLAS COWBOYS

Address Cowboys Center, One Cowboys Parkway, Irving, Texas 75063.
Stadium Texas Stadium, Irving.
Capacity 65,024 *Playing Surface* Texas Turf.
Team Colours Royal Blue, Metallic Silver Blue, and White.
Head Coach Jimmy Johnson – 2nd year.
Championships Division 1970, '71, '73, '76, '77, '78, '79, '81, '85; Conference 1970, '71, '75, '77, '78; Super Bowl 1971, '77.
History NFL 1960-69, NFC 1970-

Offense

Careful trading, the acquisition of several good Plan-B free agents and a specialised draft have helped a Cowboys club which has every prospect of easing out of the NFL's cellar. At the heart of it all, second-year quarterback Troy Aikman should be ready to spread his wings after a learning season and it is to his advantage that the club signed the former Chicago starting wide receiver, Dennis McKinnon, who brings an authority and presence to the pass receiving corps. Add to this the return from injury of Michael Irvin, who has shown himself to be a classy receiver with deep speed, and the selection of Alexander Wright in the second round of the draft, and it would appear that the scramble for backup spots, in which both James Dixon and Kelvin Martin will figure, could be hectic. In what seems likely to be the regular use of a two-tight end formation, Plan-B signing Jay Novacek represents a downfield receiving target with Steve Folsom and Keith Jennings the leading candidates to take the other spot. Again, there is great potential in what is likely to be a new combination at running back. It was seen as a major signing when the Cowboys traded for former San Francisco first-round pick Terrence Flagler, a fine player who languished as a reserve behind Roger Craig. And then in the draft, Dallas traded up to pick Emmitt Smith, a superior athlete with a voracious appetite for yardage and who, importantly, is very durable. Smith, a junior, would have been a strong candidate for the Heisman Trophy had he remained in college. It means that, un-

like many clubs, Dallas has two running backs, each of whom has the capacity to gain 1,000 yards in a season. Laying the foundation for the strike players, the offensive line has been bolstered by Plan-B signing Tony Slaton, the former Rams backup who should settle in at center in place of the retired Tom Rafferty. This would allow Mark Stepnoski to occupy one guard spot with Crawford Ker possibly shifting to the left side. At tackle, last year's starters, Kevin Gogan and Mark Tuinei, and former starting guard Nate Newton have the edge over the rest.

Defense

On defense, one or two players will have to come through if the Cowboys are to present problems for the opposition, and it will be an enormous help if Danny Noonan can resume at full fitness as is expected. Noonan is pencilled in to start at defensive end but that may be contingent upon the emergence of two starters for the defensive tackle positions. Here, the leading candidates are Dean Hamel, Willie Broughton and the talented Mark Walen, whose knee injury kept him out for the whole of last season. The picture is complicated further by the arrival of former San Francisco second-round pick Daniel Stubbs, who played mostly as an outside linebacker for the 49ers but may settle down at defensive end for the Cowboys. Jim Jeffcoat, the club's leading sacker with 11.5 last year, is established at defensive right end. At middle linebacker, Eugene Lockhart is a fixture but head coach Jimmy Johnson regards the outside positions as being open. Ken Norton and Jesse Solomon, the latter who started for Minnesota and came to Dallas as part of the trade which sent running back Herschel Walker to the Vikings, may have the edge. But David Howard is a factor and the use of Jack Del Rio as a combination outside linebacker-defensive end is a possibility. Lockhart, who loves to play an 'attack' form of defense, had a pair of sacks, two interceptions and led the team with 222 tackles in 1989. He has become the heart and soul of the defense. The secondary has been strengthened by the arrival of Plan-B free agent Antonio Gibson, who had started for New Orleans and will challenge Vince Albritton for the strong safety spot. At free safety, James Washington, a former Rams player, will press veteran Ray Horton who is now healthy following arthroscopic knee surgery in March. On the corners, there are plenty of solid players available but none with quite the combination of speed and positional sense to dominate. Certainly, though, former Vikings starter Issiac Holt, who was another component in the Walker trade, has plenty of fire and is the sort to catalyse the entire defensive secondary. Otherwise there is little which separates Holt, Robert Williams, Ron Francis and Manny Hendrix.

1990 SCHEDULE OF GAMES

September

9	SAN DIEGO	3:00
16	NEW YORK GIANTS	3:00
23	at Washington	1:00
30	at New York Giants	1:00

October

7	TAMPA BAY	12:00
14	at Phoenix	1:00
21	at Tampa Bay	1:00
28	PHILADELPHIA	12:00

November

4	at New York Jets	1:00
11	SAN FRANCISCO	
	(Sun. night)	7:00
18	at Los Angeles Rams	1:00
22	WASHINGTON	
	(Thanksgiving)	3:00

December

2	NEW ORLEANS	3:00
9	*Open date*	
16	PHOENIX	12:00
23	at Philadelphia	1:00
30	at Atlanta	1:00

Special Teams

Head coach Johnson is well pleased with both place-kicker Luis Zendejas and punter Mike Saxon, and he now has a wide selection of speedsters for the kick return duties. McKinnon, who has scored three touch-downs on punt returns, will make a bid to displace Der-rick Shepard, whose one touchdown in 1989, ironically, came against Dallas when he played for New Orleans. For high-class consistency over a large number of kick-off returns, Dixon ranks with the very best in the NFL.

1990 DRAFT

Round	Name	Pos.	Ht.	Wt.	College
1.	Smith, Emmitt	RB	5-10	201	Florida
2.	Wright, Alexander	WR	5-11	184	Auburn
3.	Jones, Jimmie	DT	6-4	261	Miami
9.	Gant, Kenneth	DB	5-11	178	Albany State
11.	Harper, Dave	LB	6-1	220	Humboldt State

VETERAN ROSTER   NFL

No.	Name	Pos.	Ht.	Wt.	Year	College
32	Agee, Tommie	RB	6-0	218	3	Auburn
8	Aikman, Troy	QB	6-4	216	2	UCLA
36	Albritton, Vince	S	6-2	214	7	Washington
81	Ankrom, Scott	WR	6-1	194	2	Texas Christian
40	Bates, Bill	S	6-1	199	8	Tennessee
79	Broughton, Willie	DT	6-5	275	4	Miami
75	Carter, Jon	DL	6-4	273	2	Pittsburgh
72	Cheek, Louis	T	6-6	295	3	Texas A&M
58	Cooks, Terrence	LB	6-0	230	2	Nicholls State
	Crockett, Willis	LB	6-3	221	1	Georgia Tech
55	Del Rio, Jack	LB	6-4	236	6	Southern California
86	Dixon, James	WR-KR	5-10	181	2	Houston
	Flagler, Terrence	RB	6-0	200	4	Clemson
85	Folsom, Steve	TE	6-5	240	6	Utah
38	Francis, Ron	CB	5-9	186	4	Baylor
21	Gibson, Antonio	S	6-3	204	5	Cincinnati
66	Gogan, Kevin	T	6-7	309	4	Washington
60	Hamel, Dean	DT	6-3	276	6	Tulsa
17	Harris, Rod	WR	5-10	183	2	Texas A&M
45	Hendrix, Manny	CB	5-10	186	5	Utah
30	Holt, Issiac	CB	6-2	202	6	Alcorn State
20	Horton, Ray	S	5-11	187	8	Washington
99	Howard, David	LB	6-2	230	6	Cal State-Long Beach
88	Irvin, Michael	WR	6-2	202	3	Miami
77	Jeffcoat, Jim	DE	6-5	256	8	Arizona State
84	Jennings, Keith	TE	6-4	251	2	Clemson
67	Johnson, Greg	G	6-4	295	2	Oklahoma
91	Johnson, Walter	LB	6-0	240	4	Louisiana Tech
48	Johnston, Daryl	RB	6-2	234	2	Syracuse
31	Jones, Keith	RB	5-9	182	2	Nebraska
68	Ker, Crawford	G	6-3	285	6	Florida
15	Laufenberg, Babe	QB	6-3	203	5	Indiana
56	Lockhart, Eugene	LB	6-2	233	7	Houston
83	Martin, Kelvin	WR	5-9	162	4	Boston College
81	McKinnon, Dennis	WR	6-1	185	7	Florida State
61	Newton, Nate	G	6-3	318	5	Florida A&M
73	Noonan, Danny	DT	6-4	270	4	Nebraska
51	Norton, Ken	LB	6-2	234	3	UCLA
89	Novacek, Jay	TE	6-4	235	6	Wyoming
	Peterson, Kevin	LB	6-2	227	1	Northwestern
	Robinson, Lybrant	DE	6-5	250	2	Delaware State
39	Sargent, Broderick	RB	5-11	220	4	Baylor
4	Saxon, Mike	P	6-3	198	6	San Diego State
35	Scott, Kevin	RB	5-9	177	3	Stanford
94	Shannon, Randy	LB	6-1	221	2	Miami
87	Shepard, Derrick	WR-PR	5-10	187	3	Oklahoma
65	Slaton, Tony	G-C	6-3	280	7	Southern California
30	Smith, Timmy	RB	5-11	222	3	Texas Tech
57	Smith, Vinson	LB	6-2	230	2	East Carolina
54	Solomon, Jesse	LB	6-0	235	5	Florida State
	Spears, Anthony	DT	6-5	260	1	Portland State
70	Stepnoski, Mark	C	6-2	269	2	Pittsburgh
28	Stewart, Curtis	RB	5-11	208	4	Auburn
	Stubbs, Daniel	DE	6-4	260	3	Miami
25	Tautalatasi, Junior	RB	5-11	208	5	Washington State
92	Tolbert, Tony	DE	6-6	241	2	Texas-El Paso
71	Tuinei, Mark	T	6-5	286	8	Hawaii
95	Walen, Mark	DL	6-5	267	3	UCLA
3	Walsh, Steve	QB	6-2	200	2	Miami
37	Washington, James	S	6-1	196	3	UCLA
78	Widell, Dave	T	6-6	292	3	Boston College
	Williams, Mike	WR	5-10	177	1	Northeastern
23	Williams, Robert	CB	5-10	184	4	Baylor
6	Zendejas, Luis	K	5-9	179	4	Arizona State
76	Zimmerman, Jeff	G	6-3	313	3	Florida

The return of wide receiver Michael Irvin from injury will be welcomed.

NEW YORK GIANTS

Address Giants Stadium, East Rutherford,
   New Jersey 07073.
Stadium Giants Stadium, East Rutherford.
   Capacity 76,891 *Playing Surface* AstroTurf.
Team Colours Blue, Red, and White.
Head Coach Bill Parcells – 8th year.
Championships Division 1986,'89; Conference 1986.
   NFL 1927,'34,'38,'56; Super Bowl 1986.
History NFL 1925-69, NFC 1970-

Offense

With little by way of penetration at running back and a modest passing offense, it says a great deal for the Giants' discipline that they were competitive to the last. Conservatively, they ran the ball three-quarters of the time and 11-year veteran Ottis Anderson thrived, going over 1,000 yards for the sixth time in his career though at a grinding average of 3.1 yards per carry. Anderson may be a factor once again but it is more likely that Joe Morris, whose outside burst can leave opposing defenses in disarray, will return from injury to play the major role. As always, fullback Maurice Carthon will be helping to clear a path and he may be preparing the way for Lewis Tillman and first-round draftee Rodney Hampton, who is a well-balanced runner with a good turn of foot but, having entered the NFL as a junior, may be given a gradual introduction. Quarterback Phil Simms is coming off a subpar year but that should not be taken as indicating that his powers are on the wane. With good arm strength, fine judgement and terrific composure, Simms will be the starter even though the club has hinted at opening the door for backup Jeff Hostetler in camp. The wide receivers are of ample quality and depth, led by probable starters Odessa Turner and Lionel Manuel. Last year, Mark Ingram and Stephen Baker were in backup roles but they, too, easily could step up to start regularly. Complementing the formality of the system, the effervescent Dave Meggett can exploit all the tiny chinks of opportunity in any

defense – last year he averaged 15.6 yards on 34 receptions – and of course, the return of the NFL's most complete tight end, Mark Bavaro, will bring a significant boost. In addition to being an excellent receiver, Bavaro is a fine blocker on the end of a line which has good size and speed. Center Bart Oates may opt for a career in law but 1989 first-rounder Brian Williams could possibly move up to start. The other starters, guards William Roberts and Eric Moore, and tackles John Elliott and Doug Riesenberg, are very solid but the loss of Frank Winters and Damian Johnson has left the club shallow in reserves.

Defense

Week after week, the Giants' defense turned up in force and only twice did the unit give up more than 24 points in a game. It was to their advantage that they had very few serious injuries. The trio on the defensive line had a total of 46 starts out of a possible 48, the secondary had 63 out of a possible 64 and, at linebacker, with three players missing a total of just four starts, the only variations in the opening lineup were those made for tactical reasons, with Pepper Johnson and Johnie Cooks taking care of the inside spot on the right. The defense expected to be good but was improved by the play of eighth-round rookie Myron Guyton, who started 15 games at strong safety and led the team in tackles (99) and fumble recoveries (3). Terry Kinard has departed as a Plan-B free agent but his place at free safety will probably be filled adequately by senior backup Adrian White. On the corners, Mark Collins was unlucky not to gain selection to the Pro Bowl while Perry Williams continued to look comfortable, making three interceptions and defensing 13 passes. The front seven may be the best in the NFL and, with the projected return of Eric Dorsey at defensive left end and John Washington reverting to the role of reserve, increasingly, the defensive line can claim its share of the spoils. Defensive right end Leonard Marshall led all linemen with 9.5 sacks while strong-man nose tackle Erik Howard, who now demands double-teaming, accounted for 5.5. Impressive though the line is, the Giants still can boast the best linebacking quartet in the NFL. Operating on the right side, Lawrence Taylor burns with a fire which was fuelled by a further 15 quarterback sacks as he led the team. However, there is a solid band of experts which contends that left outside linebacker Carl Banks is even better. Banks had only four sacks but he has that knack of petrifying a running back for just long enough to score a hit in the opposing backfield. Gary Reasons is as solid as a rock, as also is Cooks, whose measure is established by the fact that he can share time with a player of Johnson's class.

1990 SCHEDULE OF GAMES

September
9	PHILADELPHIA (Sun. night)	8:00
16	at Dallas	3:00
23	MIAMI	1:00
30	DALLAS	1:00

October
7	*Open date*	
14	at Washington	4:00
21	PHOENIX	4:00
28	WASHINGTON	4:00

November
5	at Indianapolis (Mon.)	9:00
11	at Los Angeles Rams	1:00
18	DETROIT	1:00
25	at Philadelphia	1:00

December
3	at San Francisco (Mon.)	6:00
9	MINNESOTA	1:00
15	BUFFALO (Sat.)	12:30
23	at Phoenix	2:00
30	at New England	1:00

Special Teams

Raul Allegre should return to resume full-time in the position of placekicker held temporarily by Bjorn Nittmo, who has departed as a Plan-B free agent. Allegre has had injury problems and perhaps because of this, Matt Stover was drafted in the 12th round. Punter Sean Landeta is excellent, consistently operating at Pro Bowl level. In 1989 that also was true of Meggett, a dual-purpose exponent who, more for the excitement of his running than his pure statistics, was voted the NFC kick returner in Hawaii.

1990 DRAFT

Round	Name	Pos.	Ht.	Wt.	College
1.	Hampton, Rodney	RB	6-0	217	Georgia
2.	Fox, Mike	DT	6-6	272	West Virginia
3.	Mark, Greg	DE	6-2	252	Miami
4.	Whitmore, David	S	6-0	235	Stephen F. Austin
5.	Kupp, Craig	QB	6-4	230	Pacific Lutheran
7.	Emanuel, Aaron	RB	6-1	230	Southern California
8.	Voorhees, Barry	T	6-3	280	Cal State-Northridge
9.	James, Clint	DE	6-5	265	Louisiana State
10.	Moore, Otis	DT	6-2	270	Clemson
11.	Downing, Tim	DE	6-4	255	Washington State
12.	Stover, Matt	K	5-11	184	Louisiana Tech

VETERAN ROSTER — NFL

No.	Name	Pos.	Ht.	Wt.	Year	College
2	Allegre, Raul	K	5-10	167	8	Texas
24	Anderson, Ottis	RB	6-2	225	12	Miami
85	Baker, Stephen	WR	5-8	160	4	Fresno State
58	Banks, Carl	LB	6-4	235	7	Michigan State
89	Bavaro, Mark	TE	6-4	245	6	Notre Dame
44	Carthon, Maurice	RB	6-1	225	6	Arkansas State
25	Collins, Mark	CB	5-10	190	5	Cal State-Fullerton
98	Cooks, Johnie	LB	6-4	251	9	Mississippi State
87	Cross, Howard	TE	6-5	245	2	Alabama
99	DeOssie, Steve	LB	6-2	248	7	Boston College
77	Dorsey, Eric	DE	6-5	280	5	Notre Dame
76	Elliott, John	T	6-7	305	3	Michigan
	Feggins, Howard	CB	5-10	190	2	North Carolina
29	Guyton, Myron	S	6-1	205	2	Eastern Kentucky
57	Hooten, Mike	LB	6-4	240	1	Wake Forest
15	Hostetler, Jeff	QB	6-3	212	7	West Virginia
74	Howard, Erik	NT	6-4	268	5	Washington State
82	Ingram, Mark	WR	5-10	188	4	Michigan State
47	Jackson, Greg	S	6-1	200	2	Louisiana State
54	Jiles, Dwayne	LB	6-4	245	6	Texas Tech
52	Johnson, Pepper	LB	6-3	248	5	Ohio State
61	Kratch, Bob	G	6-3	288	2	Iowa
5	Landeta, Sean	P	6-0	200	6	Towson State
86	Manuel, Lionel	WR	5-11	180	7	Pacific
70	Marshall, Leonard	DE	6-3	285	8	Louisiana State
30	Meggett, Dave	RB-KR	5-7	180	2	Towson State
60	Moore, Eric	G	6-5	290	3	Indiana
20	Morris, Joe	RB	5-7	195	8	Syracuse
	Mrosko, Bob	TE	6-6	265	2	Penn State
65	Oates, Bart	C	6-3	265	6	Brigham Young
55	Reasons, Gary	LB	6-4	234	7	Northwestern St., La.
72	Riesenberg, Doug	T	6-5	275	4	California
66	Roberts, William	G	6-5	280	6	Ohio State
81	Robinson, Stacy	WR	5-11	186	6	North Dakota State
22	Rouson, Lee	RB	6-1	222	6	Colorado
11	Simms, Phil	QB	6-3	214	12	Morehead State
56	Taylor, Lawrence	LB	6-3	243	10	North Carolina
21	Thompson, Reyna	CB	6-0	193	5	Baylor
	Thornton, Randy	LB	6-4	235	1	Houston
34	Tillman, Lewis	RB	6-0	195	2	Jackson State
83	Turner, Odessa	WR	6-3	205	4	Northwestern St., La.
	Walls, Everson	CB	6-1	193	10	Grambling
73	Washington, John	DE	6-4	275	5	Oklahoma State
36	White, Adrian	S	6-0	200	4	Florida
39	White, Sheldon	DB	5-11	188	3	Miami, Ohio
59	Williams, Brian	C-G	6-5	300	2	Minnesota
23	Williams, Perry	CB	6-2	203	7	North Carolina State

Nose tackle Erik Howard is immensely strong.

PHILADELPHIA EAGLES

Address Veterans Stadium, Broad St. and Pattison Ave., Philadelphia, Pennsylvania 19148.
Stadium Veterans Stadium, Philadelphia.
 Capacity 65,356 *Playing Surface* AstroTurf-8.
Team Colours Kelly Green, Silver, and White.
Head Coach Buddy Ryan – 5th year.
Championships Division 1980,'88; Conference 1980; NFL 1948,'49,'60.
History NFL 1933-69, NFC 1970-

Offense

Under the guidance of head coach Buddy Ryan, the Eagles have improved steadily and there can be little doubt that the 1990 squad is Philadelphia's strongest in the last decade. As the beating heart of the offense, quarterback Randall Cunningham might be expected to generate a big play on any down. As a passer he is better than most and few can match his powers of improvisation. Also, he is a source of calm authority. More remarkable than many of his attributes is that he is the first modern (T-formation) quarterback to lead his club in rushing for three consecutive years. This aspect of his play disguises a Philadelphia weakness, the absence of a consistently productive running back, which some teams would regard as serious. But the demands placed on this aspect of offense are not great and some compensation comes in the form of a major contribution to the passing game. Thus, Keith Byars, while capable of the odd good rushing day, led the team in receptions in 1989. In a deviation from the norm, Byars and nominal fullback Anthony Toney swap positions freely, on occasions stepping aside for the direct running of Robert Drummond and the elusive guile of Heath Sherman. The senior veteran wide receivers, Cris Carter and Mike Quick, are excellent and Ron Johnson ranks as a quality backup. But in the search for long-term continuity, in addition to providing insurance for Quick, classy prospects, led by Mike Bellamy, were selected in rounds two, three and five.

Adding to the array, tight end Keith Jackson is a prolific receiver and has been to the Pro Bowl in each of his two NFL seasons. The argument for continued Philadelphia success is strongly supported by the assembly of an offensive line that has begun to play with decent consistency. Smart trading brought right tackle Ron Heller and right guard Ron Solt. Center David Alexander has developed well after being a 1987 fifth-round pick while left tackle Matt Darwin came in the 1986 fourth round. Left guard Mike Schad, a 1986 first-round pick who could not fit in with the Rams, has settled down well. These days, Philadelphia even has solid, versatile backups in Ben Tamburello, Ken Reeves and Dave Rimington.

Defense

Led by the most feared four-man defensive line in pro football, each year the Eagles take a step closer to total dominance. All three of defensive ends Clyde Simmons (15.5), Reggie White (11) and defensive tackle Jerome Brown (10.5) were in double figures for sacks, and defensive left tackle Mike Pitts had seven. White is the defensive lineman that every team would love to have. He lines up wherever he chooses to and generally creates mayhem, and Simmons must be considered unlucky not to join him in the Pro Bowl. Mike Golic fits into the system smoothly when either tackle needs a breather and Steve Kaufusi appears to have a promising future as a designated pass rusher. At linebacker, the Eagles regard Seth Joyner as the best left side player in the game and they support that assessment by leaving him in for all their variations of defense. Middle linebacker Byron Evans won the job in camp and said, 'Thankyou,' by leading the team with 184 tackles. After a learning year, 1989 second-round pick Jessie Small has been promoted over 11th-year veteran Al Harris to start at right linebacker. The Eagles don't say it but Small may just turn out to be the player who nudges the defense to the level of true greatness. He has an impressive physical presence and a tremendous range of influence. The experienced Harris and Britt Hager, who lacks nothing for intensity, are fine backups. Ryan neither minces his words nor disguises his intentions and those admirable qualities were underlined when he installed first-round draft pick Ben Smith as the starting free safety and he also will be the nickel back. This will force a change in an arrangement which saw former Pro Bowler Wes Hopkins platooning with Terry Hoage and means that Hopkins will be a reserve with Hoage challenging starting strong safety Andre Waters. Pro Bowler Eric Allen, a skin-tight marker who led the NFC with eight interceptions, is unchallenged at right cornerback and the signs are that Izel Jenkins will retain his seniority on the left corner, despite acknowledged technical lapses in 1989.

1990 SCHEDULE OF GAMES

September

9 at New York Giants (Sun. night)	8:00
16 PHOENIX	1:00
23 at Los Angeles Rams	1:00
30 INDIANAPOLIS	1:00

October

7 *Open date*	
15 MINNESOTA (Mon.)	9:00
21 at Washington	1:00
28 at Dallas	12:00

November

4 NEW ENGLAND	1:00
12 WASHINGTON (Mon.)	9:00
18 at Atlanta	1:00
25 NEW YORK GIANTS	1:00

December

2 at Buffalo	1:00
9 at Miami (Sun. night)	8:00
16 GREEN BAY	4:00
23 DALLAS	1:00
29 at Phoenix (Sat.)	2:00

1990 DRAFT

Round	Name	Pos.	Ht.	Wt.	College
1.	Smith, Ben	DB	5-11	183	Georgia
2.	Bellamy, Mike	WR	6-0	196	Illinois
3.	Barnett, Fred	WR	6-0	203	Arkansas State
5.	Williams, Calvin	WR	5-11	181	Purdue
6.	Thompson, Kevin	DB	5-10	191	Oklahoma
7.	Strouf, Terry	T	6-3	285	Wisconsin-LaCrosse
8.	Dykes, Curt	T	6-3	274	Oregon
9.	Gray, Cecil	DT	6-4	264	North Carolina
10.	Adams, Orlando	DT	6-0	303	Jacksonville State
11.	Hudson, John	C	6-2	266	Auburn
11.	Watson, Tyrone	WR	6-4	210	Tennessee State
12.	Garrett, Judd	RB	6-1	209	Princeton

VETERAN ROSTER

No.	Name	Pos.	Ht.	Wt.	NFL Year	College
72	Alexander, David	C	6-3	282	4	Tulsa
21	Allen, Eric	CB	5-10	188	3	Arizona State
49	Bell, Todd	S	6-1	215	9	Ohio State
99	Brown, Jerome	DT	6-2	295	4	Miami
41	Byars, Keith	RB	6-1	238	5	Ohio State
80	Carter, Cris	WR	6-3	198	4	Ohio State
6	Cavanaugh, Matt	QB	6-2	210	13	Pittsburgh
12	Cunningham, Randall	QB	6-4	203	6	Nevada-Las Vegas
78	Darwin, Matt	T	6-4	275	5	Texas A&M
36	Drummond, Robert	RB	6-1	205	2	Syracuse
84	Edwards, Anthony	WR-PR	5-11	195	2	New Mex. Highlands
56	Evans, Byron	LB	6-2	235	4	Arizona
33	Frizzell, William	S	6-3	206	7	N. Carolina Central
67	Gabbard, Steve	T-G	6-4	275	2	Florida State
86	Garrity, Gregg	WR	5-10	175	8	Penn State
83	Giles, Jimmie	TE	6-3	245	14	Alcorn State
90	Golic, Mike	DT	6-5	275	5	Notre Dame
54	Hager, Britt	LB	6-1	222	2	Texas
95	Harris, Al	LB	6-5	245	11	Arizona State
73	Heller, Ron	T	6-6	280	7	Penn State
34	Hoage, Terry	S	6-3	201	7	Georgia
48	Hopkins, Wes	S	6-1	215	7	Southern Methodist
88	Jackson, Keith	TE	6-2	250	3	Oklahoma
46	Jenkins, Izel	CB	5-10	191	3	North Carolina State
85	Johnson, Ron	WR	6-3	190	6	Cal State-Long Beach
59	Joyner, Seth	LB	6-2	248	5	Texas-El Paso
94	Kaufusi, Steve	DE	6-4	274	2	Brigham Young
87	Le Bel, Harper	TE	6-4	251	2	Colorado State
37	Lilly, Sammy	CB	5-9	178	2	Georgia Tech
9	McPherson, Don	QB	6-1	193	1	Syracuse
13	Osborn, William	WR	6-0	188	1	Pittsburgh
74	Pitts, Mike	DT	6-5	277	8	Alabama
82	Quick, Mike	WR	6-2	195	9	North Carolina State
66	Reeves, Ken	T	6-5	270	6	Texas A&M
50	Rimington, Dave	C	6-3	285	8	Nebraska
7	Ruzek, Roger	K	6-1	195	4	Weber State
79	Schad, Mike	G	6-5	290	3	Queens, Canada
51	Shaw, Ricky	LB	6-4	240	3	Oklahoma State
23	Sherman, Heath	RB	6-0	190	2	Texas A&I
96	Simmons, Clyde	DE	6-6	275	5	Western Carolina
68	Singletary, Reggie	G	6-3	285	5	North Carolina State
52	Small, Jessie	LB	6-3	239	2	Eastern Kentucky
65	Solt, Ron	G	6-3	270	6	Maryland
35	Sullivan, Mike	LB	6-0	250	1	Ohio State
61	Tamburello, Ben	G-C	6-3	278	4	Auburn
10	Teltschik, John	P	6-2	210	5	Texas
25	Toney, Anthony	RB	6-0	227	5	Texas A&M
20	Waters, Andre	S	5-11	199	7	Cheyney State
	Werner, Greg	TE	6-4	236	2	DePauw
92	White, Reggie	DE	6-5	285	6	Tennessee

Special Teams

Both placekicker Roger Ruzek and punter John Teltschik are in the Philadelphia mold — athletes who don't mind rolling up their sleeves and tackling the returner if necessary. Entering the preseason, Anthony Edwards is projected to return punts and rookie Calvin Williams will be given the first shot at returning kickoffs, but much will depend on the pressures which emerge when the final roster is taking shape. Come opening day, any one of several fleet-footed backups may be given the nod.

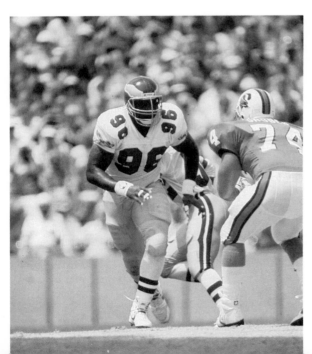

Clyde Simmons led the Eagles with 15.5 sacks.

PHOENIX CARDINALS

Address P.O. Box 888, Phoenix, Arizona 85001-0888.
Stadium Sun Devil Stadium, Tempe, Arizona.
  Capacity 72,000 *Playing Surface* Grass.
Team Colours Cardinal Red, Black, and White.
Head Coach Joe Bugel – 1st year.
Championships Division 1974,'75; NFL 1925,'47.
History NFL 1920-69, NFC 1970-
  (They were known as the Chicago Cardinals until 1960, when they moved to St Louis. In 1988, the franchise, still under the same ownership, was transferred to Phoenix.)

Offense

The Cardinals offense may best be seen as a unit in transition, having had to overcome the loss of quarterback Neil Lomax, injuries and inconsistencies at running back and always with an eye on the need to introduce youth at wide receiver. The quarterback position may not be settled this year. The future lies in the confident expression of Timm Rosenbach, whom the Cardinals obtained in the 1989 supplemental draft, but he may need time to settle. It means that veteran Gary Hogeboom, who'd fancy his chances of retaining the starting spot anyway, probably will open the campaign and even Tom Tupa, who has a strong, if uncultivated, arm may have a say in matters. It will help if the vastly experienced J. T. Smith can come back from injury to start at wide receiver, though it may be that age is catching up on Roy Green, who could be sharing time with Ernie Jones. Third-round draftee Ricky Proehl is not a burner but he does have soft hands and could develop as a medium-range clutch receiver. Most important of all, there is a refreshing look at running back, where second-round draftee Anthony Thompson, holder of the NCAA single-game rushing record (377 yards) is expected to start immediately. Veteran Stump Mitchell is coming back from knee surgery and should play a part but, if he can not reproduce his previous best, it may open the door for Tony Jordan or the speedy Vai Sikahema. Ron Wolfley would be the obvious blocking fullback but Johnny Johnson may make his bid for playing time. Johnson, a seventh-round draftee who brings a range of astonishing talents, was not comfortable with the regime in college but could excel were he to commit himself to the pro game. The offensive line is a strength, starting with Pro Bowler Luis Sharpe at left tackle and on through left guard Joe Wolf, center Derek Kennard, right guard Lance Smith and right tackle Tootie Robbins. Wolf has all the makings of a Pro Bowler, Mike Zandofsky is an excellent backup and further insurance comes with former Raiders center Bill Lewis. At tight end, too, there is good depth, with Walter Reeves expected to come on strongly and challenge starter Robert Awalt.

Defense

The defense has strong points throughout but is not the deepest in the NFL and can not afford injuries at the levels of previous years. The most effective pairing at defensive end would be Freddie Joe Nunn and David Galloway, but Nunn has not regained the fire he breathed before a 1989 suspension for violating the NFL's substance abuse policy. Galloway was in and out with broken thumb and calf injuries. Rod Saddler can play at defensive end but is more comfortable at tackle, probably on the right side, while at left tackle, Bob Clasby, who missed most of last year with a knee injury, is expected back. Happily, 1989 fourth-round pick Jim Wahler survived his baptism and will be a better reserve for the experience of starting nine games at defensive right tackle. At linebacker, all three starters, Ken Harvey, Eric Hill and Anthony Bell, are former first-round picks. None of the trio has emerged as a major star, but they did show signs of forming a cohesive unit last year and can provide the nucleus around which to build. In order they filled the second, third and fourth spots in the tackle list and, as the regular blitzer, Harvey led the team in 1989 with seven sacks. It is in the defensive secondary that the true greatness resides, and that comes in the form of strong safety Tim McDonald. Both for his unquenchable spirit and wide-ranging powers, he has become the team leader, a title confirmed statistically by his seven interceptions and 124 tackles. McDonald took up where he left off in 1988 and roared into a starting spot in the 1990 Pro Bowl. Elsewhere, there will be healthy competition. Left cornerback Cedric Mack intercepted four passes and has seniority over right cornerback Carl Carter, but they will face a determined challenge from Stanley Blair, who comes highly recommended from the CFL. At free safety, Lonnie Young has the edge over Mike Zordich but will need to reconfirm that status in camp. Hovering on the fringes are Jay Taylor and Tracey Eaton, a Plan-B signing who started two games at free safety for Houston in 1989.

1990 DRAFT

Round	Name	Pos.	Ht.	Wt.	College
2.	Thompson, Anthony	RB	5-11	207	Indiana
3.	Proehl, Ricky	WR	5-10	181	Wake Forest
4.	Davis, Travis	DT	6-1	274	Michigan State
5.	Centers, Larry	RB	5-10	203	Stephen F. Austin
6.	Shavers, Tyrone	WR	6-2	205	Lamar
7.	Johnson, Johnny	RB	6-2	212	San Jose State
8.	Washington, Mickey	CB	5-9	187	Texas A&M
9.	Bavaro, David	LB	6-0	231	Syracuse
10.	Elle, Dave	TE	6-4	240	South Dakota
11.	Norman, Dempsey	WR	5-7	178	St Francis, Illinois
12.	Riley, Donnie	RB	5-8	197	Central Michigan
12.	McMichel, Ken	LB	6-0	200	Oklahoma

VETERAN ROSTER

No.	Name	Pos.	Ht.	Wt.	NFL Year	College
80	Awalt, Robert	TE	6-5	244	4	San Diego State
44	Baker, Tony	RB	5-10	190	4	East Carolina
55	Bell, Anthony	LB	6-3	235	5	Michigan State
25	Blair, Stanley	CB	6-0	190	R	S.E. Oklahoma St.
16	Camarillo, Rich	P	5-11	193	10	Washington
45	Carr, Lydell	RB	6-1	228	2	Oklahoma
41	Carter, Carl	CB	5-11	189	5	Texas Tech
79	Clasby, Bob	DT	6-5	276	5	Notre Dame
17	Del Greco, Al	K	5-10	198	7	Auburn
21	Eaton, Tracey	S	6-1	195	3	Portland State
65	Galloway, David	DE	6-3	259	9	Florida
81	Green, Roy	WR	6-0	195	12	Henderson, Ark.
73	Hadd, Gary	DT	6-4	278	3	Minnesota
56	Harvey, Ken	LB	6-2	230	3	California
58	Hill, Eric	LB	6-1	248	2	Louisiana State
5	Hogeboom, Gary	QB	6-4	207	11	Central Michigan
83	Holmes, Don	WR	5-10	177	5	Mesa, Colorado
53	Jax, Garth	LB	6-2	229	5	Florida State
86	Jones, Ernie	WR	5-11	191	3	Indiana
32	Jordan, Tony	RB	6-2	220	3	Kansas State
57	Kauahi, Kani	C	6-2	270	8	Hawaii
70	Kennard, Derek	C	6-3	309	5	Nevada-Reno
52	Kirk, Randy	LB	6-2	231	4	San Diego State
51	Lewis, Bill	C	6-7	280	5	Nebraska
29	Lynch, Lorenzo	DB	5-9	199	3	Cal State-Sacramento
47	Mack, Cedric	CB	6-0	185	8	Baylor
46	McDonald, Tim	S	6-2	209	4	Southern California
54	McKenzie, Reggie	LB	6-1	242	5	Tennessee
30	Mitchell, Stump	RB	5-9	194	10	Citadel
78	Nunn, Freddie Joe	DE	6-4	250	6	Mississippi
89	Reeves, Walter	TE	6-3	249	2	Auburn
43	Robbins, Tootie	T	6-5	307	9	East Carolina
3	Rosenbach, Timm	QB	6-2	210	2	Washington State
72	Saddler, Rod	DE	6-5	280	4	Texas A&M
67	Sharpe, Luis	T	6-4	260	9	UCLA
36	Sikahema, Vai	RB-KR	5-9	184	5	Brigham Young
84	Smith, J.T.	WR	6-2	187	13	North Texas State
61	Smith, Lance	G	6-2	278	6	Louisiana State
27	Taylor, Jay	CB	5-9	170	2	San Jose State
19	Tupa, Tom	QB-P	6-4	220	3	Ohio State
23	Turner, Marcus	DB	6-0	191	2	UCLA
66	Wahler, Jim	DT	6-3	268	2	UCLA
60	Walker, Jeff	T	6-4	289	3	Memphis State
68	Wolf, Joe	T-G	6-5	279	2	Boston College
24	Wolfley, Ron	RB	6-0	222	6	West Virginia
43	Young, Lonnie	S	6-1	191	6	Michigan State
62	Zandofsky, Mike	G	6-2	285	2	Washington
38	Zordich, Mike	S	5-11	197	4	Penn State

1990 SCHEDULE OF GAMES

September

9	at Washington	1:00
16	at Philadelphia	1:00
23	at New Orleans	12:00
30	WASHINGTON (Sun. night)	5:00

October

7	*Open date*	
14	DALLAS	1:00
21	at New York Giants	4:00
28	CHICAGO	2:00

November

4	at Miami	1:00
11	at Buffalo	1:00
18	GREEN BAY	2:00
25	NEW ENGLAND	2:00

December

2	INDIANAPOLIS	2:00
9	at Atlanta	1:00
16	at Dallas	12:00
23	NEW YORK GIANTS	2:00
29	PHILADELPHIA (Sat.)	2:00

Special Teams

The kicking game has a reassuring look, placekicker Al Del Greco combining good leg strength with steady accuracy and Rich Camarillo entering the 1990 campaign with the status of current NFC Pro Bowler. Sikahema wriggled and sped his way to a fine 11.7-yard average on 37 punt returns (it was the fourth-best in the NFL) but was less effective on kickoff returns and may be pressed by draftees Proehl and Dempsey Norman. As usual, Pro Bowl special teamer Wolfley will shift into knock-em-down mode when opponents return kicks and punts.

WASHINGTON REDSKINS

Address Redskin Park, P.O. Box 17247, Dulles
International Airport, Washington, D.C. 20041.
Stadium Robert F. Kennedy Stadium, Washington.
Capacity 55,671 *Playing Surface* Grass (PAT).
Team Colours Burgundy and Gold.
Head Coach Joe Gibbs – 10th year.
Championships Division 1972,'83,'84,'87;
Conference 1972,'82,'83,'87;
NFL 1937,'42; Super Bowl 1982,'87.
History NFL 1932-69, NFC 1970-
(Originally named the Boston Braves for the 1932
season only, they were renamed the Boston
Redskins until, in 1937, they moved to Washington.)

Offense

Washington only just failed to reach the playoffs, ending the 1989 campaign with five straight victories in which quarterback Mark Rypien had his best spell, raising him to a ranking of fifth-best passer in the NFL. A factor in those wins undoubtedly was head coach Joe Gibbs' decision to unleash his trio of wide receivers, Art Monk, Gary Clark and Ricky Sanders, all three of whom topped up to the extent that Washington became only the second club in league history (San Diego was the first in 1980) to have three receivers each catch passes for over 1,000 yards in a campaign. 'The Posse', as they are known collectively, offers a mix of poise, glitter, speed and courage. Nominally, 11th-year veteran Monk is the senior player, but there is little to separate them and, unusually in the NFL, all three expect to see regular action in an offense which has one tight end and one running back. At tight end, Don Warren's blocking keeps him a step ahead of his competition but the challengers are gathering with Terry Orr, Mike Tice, Jimmie Johnson and Plan-B signings John Brandes and Ron Middleton in the shuffle. Interestingly, all except Orr, who has good speed but is not often used, are of similar magnitude – big and strong. There's a similar queue for playing time at running back, giving Gibbs great variety and ranging from the power of Gerald Riggs to the dangerous stealth of Earnest Byner. It was a surprise that Jamie Morris was not protected under Plan B and his will-o'-the-wisp speed has been replaced by the wide-ranging experience of James Wilder, a veteran of nine hard-working years with Tampa Bay. It would not be surprising to see Wilder find an extra yard of pace, given the opportunity of playing behind a mighty offensive line which is undergoing a smooth transition. Injuries to veterans gave opportunities to tackle Ed Simmons and guard Mark Schlereth in particular. Together they took care of the right side in the absence of Joe Jacoby and Mark May. From center Jeff Bostic and on through Russ Grimm and Pro Bowler Jim Lachey, there is tremendous strength and application. Raleigh McKenzie impressed at left guard standing in for Grimm.

Defense

The unit came through a troubled year, notable for the probable *sine die* suspension of Dexter Manley, but by the end was showing signs of its former cohesion. Charles Mann led the team with ten quarterback sacks, while right end Fred Stokes showed himself capable of blunting more than a few of the running plays which came his way. Darryl Grant remains as solid as ever against the run at right tackle and, to his left, rookie Tracy Rocker grabbed the opportunities which opened up when starter Markus Koch was injured. Two Plan-B signings, Milford Hodge (ex-Patriots) and James Geathers (ex-Saints), provide respectable reserve strength for the end positions but, with only Pat Swoopes and Koch on hand for the tackle spots, the Redskins are a little thin. At linebacker, there is a growing unity with Wilber Marshall and Ravin Caldwell flanking Greg Manusky. Marshall, who was a free-range terror with the Bears, has finally adapted to the greater discipline demanded of him by the Redskins' system and is now living up to his true value. Kurt Gouveia and veteran Monte Coleman are the senior reserves, but one kind of help may have arrived in draftee Andre Collins, a player whose great value is his speed for pass coverage. The secondary will be without Barry Wilburn, who has been released, but the former starter was not a significant factor last year. An injury to starting right cornerback Darrell Green and a loss of form by Brian Davis allowed Martin Mayhew and A. J. Johnson to reveal their precocious talents. Mayhew represented a real bargain as a 1989 Plan-B signing. Green should regain his place with three players fighting for the left corner spot. At safety, Alvin Walton and Todd Bowles led the team with 137 and 130 tackles respectively and started in tandem for all but the four games when Walton was injured. Stand-in Clarence Vaughn used his time well, impressing with 52 tackles. Further depth comes with the signing of Plan-B free agent Brad Edwards (ex-Vikings) and the drafting of Rico Labbe.

Gary Clark was one of three Redskins 1,000-yard receivers.

1990 DRAFT

Round	Name	Pos.	Ht.	Wt.	College
2.	Collins, Andre	LB	6-1	224	Penn State
3.	Elewonibi, Mmd.	G	6-4	282	Brigham Young
4.	Conklin, Cary	QB	6-4	215	Washington
4.	Labbe, Rico	S	5-11	202	Boston College
5.	Mitchell, Brian	RB	5-10	198	S.W. Louisiana
6.	Wells, Kent	DT	6-3	291	Nebraska
9.	Moxley, Tim	G	6-6	310	Ohio State
10.	Francisco, D'Juan	CB	5-11	187	Notre Dame
10.	Rayam, Thomas	DT	6-5	286	Alabama
11.	Leverenz, Jon	LB	6-2	226	Minnesota

VETERAN ROSTER

No.	Name	Pos.	Ht.	Wt.	NFL Year	College
61	Adickes, Mark	G	6-4	274	5	Baylor
56	Bonner, Brian	LB	6-1	225	2	Minnesota
53	Bostic, Jeff	C	6-2	260	11	Clemson
23	Bowles, Todd	S	6-2	203	5	Temple
29	Branch, Reggie	RB	5-11	235	6	East Carolina
46	Brandes, John	TE	6-2	251	4	Cameron, Oklahoma
67	Brown, Ray	T	6-5	280	5	Arkansas State
38	Brown, Tom	RB	6-1	228	2	Pittsburgh
24	Bryant, Kelvin	RB	6-2	195	4	North Carolina
21	Byner, Earnest	RB	5-10	215	7	East Carolina
50	Caldwell, Ravin	LB	6-3	229	4	Arkansas
84	Clark, Gary	WR	5-9	173	6	James Madison
51	Coleman, Monte	LB	6-2	230	12	Central Arkansas
34	Davis, Brian	CB	6-2	190	4	Nebraska
26	Davis, Wayne	CB	5-11	180	6	Indiana State
25	Dupard, Reggie	RB	5-11	205	5	Southern Methodist
27	Edwards, Brad	S	6-1	200	3	South Carolina
97	Geathers, James	DE	6-7	290	6	Wichita State
54	Gouveia, Kurt	LB	6-1	227	4	Brigham Young
77	Grant, Darryl	DT	6-1	275	10	Rice
28	Green, Darrell	CB	5-8	170	8	Texas A&I
68	Grimm, Russ	G	6-3	275	10	Pittsburgh
59	Harbour, Dave	C	6-4	265	3	Illinois
90	Hobbs, Stephen	WR	5-11	195	1	North Alabama
75	Hodge, Milford	DE	6-3	278	4	Washington State
80	Howard, Joe	WR	5-8	170	3	Notre Dame
16	Humphries, Stan	QB	6-2	223	2	Northeast Louisiana
66	Jacoby, Joe	T	6-7	310	10	Louisville
47	Johnson, A.J.	CB	5-8	176	2	Southwest Texas St.
88	Johnson, Jimmie	TE	6-2	246	2	Howard
74	Koch, Markus	DE	6-5	275	5	Boise State
79	Lachey, Jim	T	6-6	290	6	Ohio State
8	Lohmiller, Chip	K	6-3	213	3	Minnesota
71	Mann, Charles	DE	6-6	270	8	Nevada-Reno
91	Manusky, Greg	LB	6-1	242	3	Colgate
58	Marshall, Wilber	LB	6-1	230	7	Florida
73	May, Mark	G-T	6-6	295	10	Pittsburgh
35	Mayhew, Martin	CB	5-8	172	2	Florida State
57	McArthur, Kevin	LB	6-2	250	5	Lamar
63	McKenzie, Raleigh	C-G	6-2	270	6	Tennessee
48	Middleton, Ron	TE	6-2	255	5	Auburn
2	Mojsiejenko, Ralf	P	6-2	212	6	Michigan State
81	Monk, Art	WR	6-3	209	11	Syracuse
87	Orr, Terry	TE	6-3	227	5	Texas
35	Profit, Eugene	CB	5-10	175	3	Yale
37	Riggs, Gerald	RB	6-1	232	9	Arizona State
99	Rocker, Tracy	DT	6-3	288	2	Auburn
76	Rutledge, Jeff	QB	6-1	195	12	Alabama
11	Rypien, Mark	QB	6-4	234	3	Washington State
83	Sanders, Ricky	WR	5-11	180	5	Southwest Texas St.
69	Schlereth, Mark	C	6-3	265	2	Idaho
76	Simmons, Ed	T	6-5	300	4	Eastern Washington
89	Stanley, Walter	WR-PR	5-9	180	6	Mesa, Colorado
60	Stokes, Fred	DE	6-3	262	4	Georgia Southern
64	Swoopes, Pat	NT	6-3	280	3	Mississippi State
86	Tice, Mike	TE	6-7	247	10	Maryland
31	Vaughn, Clarence	S	6-0	202	4	Northern Illinois
40	Walton, Alvin	S	6-0	180	5	Kansas
85	Warren, Don	TE	6-4	242	12	San Diego State
82	Whisenhunt, Ken	TE	6-3	240	5	Georgia Tech
32	Wilder, James	RB	6-3	225	10	Missouri

1990 SCHEDULE OF GAMES

September
9	PHOENIX	1:00
16	at San Francisco	1:00
23	DALLAS	1:00
30	at Phoenix (Sun. night)	5:00

October
7	*Open date*	
14	NEW YORK GIANTS	4:00
21	PHILADELPHIA	1:00
28	at New York Giants	4:00

November
4	at Detroit	1:00
12	at Philadelphia (Mon.)	9:00
18	NEW ORLEANS	1:00
22	at Dallas (Thanksgiving)	3:00

December
2	MIAMI	1:00
9	CHICAGO	4:00
15	at New England	4:00
22	at Indianapolis (Sat. night)	8:00
30	BUFFALO	1:00

Special Teams

The Redskins did well when they traded with San Diego for Ralf Mojsiejenko, whose gross average was 43 yards on 62 punts. As for Chip Lohmiller, however, it must be a concern that he kicked only three of 11 field goals in the range, 40-49 yards. Helped by a 99-yard touchdown return, dual-purpose returner Joe Howard averaged 24.9 yards on kickoffs to rank sixth in the NFL. Walter Stanley, the NFL's 1989 leading punt returner, has been signed as a Plan-B free agent and should give the special teams effort a boost.

CHICAGO BEARS

Address Halas Hall, 250 N. Washington,
Lake Forest, Illinois 60045.
Stadium Soldier Field, Chicago.
Capacity 66,949 *Playing Surface* Grass.
Team Colours Navy Blue, Orange, and White.
Head Coach Mike Ditka – 9th year.
Championships Division 1984,'85,'86,'87,'88;
Conference 1985;
NFL 1921,'32,'33,'40,'41,'43,'46,'63;
Super Bowl 1985.
History NFL 1920-69, NFC 1970-
(Before 1922, they were known as firstly the
Decatur Staleys and then the Chicago Staleys.)

Offense

Alarming as it may appear, far from seeking to regain the division title which they surrendered for the first time since 1983, the Bears' first priority is to halt a losing streak which extends back to Week Eleven of last year. Having recognised this, there are several reasons, particularly on offense, for believing that at least the Bears can be competitive. First, they will open with the same offensive line which took them to a Super Bowl title, starting Jim Covert and Keith Van Horne at tackle, Mark Bortz and Tom Thayer at guard and the best center in the NFL, Jay Hilgenberg. Backup tackle Dave Zawatson has been lost to Plan-B free agency but former starting guard Kurt Becker has returned from his one season with the Rams. Taking full advantage of this fine line, Neal Anderson has come close to emulating Walter Payton, not just in his productivity but also by his presence as a running back who is prepared to give his all for the club. Anderson, the NFL's fourth-leading rusher in 1989, led the Bears both in rushing yardage and receptions. As the senior fullback, the time is now right for Brad Muster to make a bigger contribution to the rushing game and, if he is not able to engage a higher gear, it may be a problem since the departure of Plan-B free agent tailback Thomas Sanders leaves Anderson and Muster as the only recognised rushers. At quarterback the competition between the style of Mike Tomczak and the orthodox efficiency of Jim Harbaugh is unresolved. Head coach Mike Ditka has a

leaning towards Tomczak but also he likes to spice the pot and, typically, Florida State quarterback Peter Tom Willis was selected in the third round. The loss of Plan-B free agent Dennis McKinnon took away some depth at wide receiver but it may be that there will be more elbow room for Dennis Gentry, Ron Morris and Wendell Davis. Gentry and Davis do have good hands, and Morris can pose a bustling deep threat, but the Bears' long-passing game doesn't frighten many opponents and is an area of relative weakness. At tight end, James Thornton has an edge on Cap Boso but neither player is the dominant sort.

Defense

It is on defense where the Bears slipped badly, specifically, from 2nd in 1988 to 25th. Scouts identify the major reason as the prolonged absence of premier defensive tackle Dan Hampton, who underwent knee surgery for the tenth time. But only defensive tackle Steve McMichael and middle linebacker Mike Singletary were able to start in all 16 games. Hampton is expected to re-establish his partnership with McMichael and, in addition to bringing the Bears great authority at tackle, the pairing could give defensive end Richard Dent the freedom to go hunting more often. Dent is coming off his lowest sack total, nine, since his rookie season. Reassuringly, Trace Armstrong established himself at defensive left end and, with William Perry perhaps being a factor, in addition to both Fred Washington and Tim Ryan coming in the draft, happy days might not be far away. The draft brought help at linebacker too, with Ron Cox shaping up as a pass-rushing version of Singletary, the team leader who went to his seventh straight Pro Bowl after leading the club with 151 tackles. To Singletary's left, Ron Rivera has established himself and the emergence of rookie John Roper on the right in place of injured veteran Jim Morrissey was a welcome bonus. Mickey Pruitt, Troy Johnson and Dante Jones are the backups. In the defensive secondary, top draftee cornerback Donnell Woolford started well but as he was hit by injuries – a separated shoulder and a broken hand – ended up having a torrid time. Realistically, though, he was a good pick and, on closer inspection, a somewhat-maligned group of players may be better than many fickle sportswriters would accept. Strong safety Dave Duerson has been selected to four Pro Bowls, Shaun Gayle has established himself as a solid free safety and right cornerback Vestee Jackson is a classy performer. On top of this, Lemuel Stinson, who led the team with four interceptions, and Maurice Douglass are above the average as reserves. However, the Bears felt the need to draft USC safety Mark Carrier in the first round and while he may be seen as an eventual replacement for Gayle, it could be that the club will ease the veteran aside in the search for freshness.

1990 SCHEDULE OF GAMES

September
9	SEATTLE	12:00
16	at Green Bay	12:00
23	MINNESOTA	12:00
30	at Los Angeles Raiders	1:00

October
7	GREEN BAY	3:00
14	LOS ANGELES RAMS (Sun. night)	6:30
21	*Open date*	
28	at Phoenix	2:00

November
4	at Tampa Bay	4:00
11	ATLANTA	12:00
18	at Denver	2:00
25	at Minnesota	12:00

December
2	DETROIT	12:00
9	at Washington	4:00
16	at Detroit (Sun. night)	8:00
23	TAMPA BAY	12:00
29	KANSAS CITY (Sat.)	11:30

1990 DRAFT

Round	Name	Pos.	Ht.	Wt.	College
1.	Carrier, Mark	S	6-1	180	Southern California
2.	Washington, Fred	DT	6-2	277	Texas Christian
2.	Cox, Ron	LB	6-2	242	Fresno State
3.	Ryan, Tim	DT	6-3	268	Southern California
3.	Willis, Peter Tom	QB	6-2	188	Florida State
4.	Moss, Tony	WR	5-7	169	Louisiana State
5.	Chaffey, Pat	RB	6-1	218	Oregon State
6.	Mangum, John	CB	5-10	173	Alabama
7.	Anderson, Bill	C	6-3	267	Iowa
8.	Rouse, James	RB	5-11	214	Arkansas
9.	Bailey, Johnny	RB	5-7	176	Texas A&I
10.	Price, Terry	DT	6-4	272	Texas A&M
11.	White, Brent	DE	6-4	245	Michigan
11.	Matusz, Roman	T	6-3	282	Pittsburgh
12.	Cooney, Anthony	S	6-0	204	Arkansas

VETERAN ROSTER

No.	Name	Pos.	Ht.	Wt.	NFL Year	College
35	Anderson, Neal	RB	5-11	210	5	Florida
93	Armstrong, Trace	DE	6-4	259	2	Florida
	Becker, Kurt	G	6-5	280	9	Michigan
62	Bortz, Mark	G	6-6	272	8	Iowa
86	Boso, Cap	TE	6-3	240	4	Illinois
8	Buford, Maury	P	6-0	198	9	Texas Tech
6	Butler, Kevin	K	6-1	204	6	Georgia
94	Chapura, Dick	DT	6-3	275	4	Missouri
74	Covert, Jim	T	6-4	278	8	Pittsburgh
82	Davis, Wendell	WR	5-11	188	3	Louisiana State
95	Dent, Richard	DE	6-5	268	8	Tennessee State
37	Douglass, Maurice	DB	5-11	200	5	Kentucky
22	Duerson, Dave	S	6-1	212	8	Notre Dame
68	Dyko, Chris	T	6-6	295	2	Washington State
67	Fontenot, Jerry	G	6-3	272	2	Texas A&M
23	Gayle, Shaun	S	5-11	194	7	Ohio State
29	Gentry, Dennis	WR-KR	5-8	180	9	Baylor
31	Green, Mark	RB-PR	5-11	184	2	Notre Dame
99	Hampton, Dan	DT	6-5	274	12	Arkansas
4	Harbaugh, Jim	QB	6-3	204	4	Michigan
63	Hilgenberg, Jay	C	6-3	260	10	Iowa
58	Hyche, Steve	LB	6-3	236	2	Livingston
24	Jackson, Vestee	CB	6-0	186	5	Washington
92	Johnson, Troy	LB	6-0	236	3	Oklahoma
53	Jones, Dante	LB	6-1	236	3	Oklahoma
88	Kozlowski, Glen	WR	6-1	205	4	Brigham Young
76	McMichael, Steve	DT	6-2	268	11	Texas
84	Morris, Ron	WR	6-1	195	4	Southern Methodist
51	Morrissey, Jim	LB	6-3	227	6	Michigan State
25	Muster, Brad	RB	6-3	231	3	Stanford
36	Paul, Markus	S	6-2	199	2	Syracuse
72	Perry, William	DT	6-2	330	6	Clemson
52	Pruitt, Mickey	LB	6-1	215	3	Colorado
59	Rivera, Ron	LB	6-3	240	7	California
55	Roper, John	LB	6-1	228	2	Texas A&M
50	Singletary, Mike	LB	6-0	230	10	Baylor
32	Stinson, Lemuel	DB	5-9	159	3	Texas Tech
49	Tate, David	DB	6-0	177	3	Colorado
27	Taylor, Brian	RB	5-10	175	2	Oregon State
57	Thayer, Tom	G	6-4	270	6	Notre Dame
80	Thornton, James	TE	6-2	242	3	Cal State-Fullerton
18	Tomczak, Mike	QB	6-1	198	6	Ohio State
78	Van Horne, Keith	T	6-6	283	10	Southern California
87	Waddle, Tom	WR	6-0	181	2	Boston College
73	Wojciechowski, J.	G	6-4	270	4	Michigan State
21	Woolford, Donnell	CB	5-9	187	2	Clemson

Special Teams

Kevin Butler set an NFL record for consecutive field goals with 24 and has become a fixture while, in the punting department, taking account of the unfavourable conditions in Chicago's early winter and a good 21 punts inside the 20, Maury Buford's gross average of 39.5 is quite respectable. Gentry, who raised his career average to an excellent 23.5 yards, would be a popular choice for best kickoff returner in the NFL. Last year, rookie halfback Mark Green returned most of the punts but he may have to win that job all over again.

Neal Anderson has become the beating heart of the Bears' offense.

DETROIT LIONS

Address Pontiac Silverdome, 1200 Featherstone
  Road – Box 4200, Pontiac, Michigan 48057.
Stadium Pontiac Silverdome.
  Capacity 80,500 *Playing Surface* AstroTurf.
Team Colours Honolulu Blue and Silver.
Head Coach Wayne Fontes – 3rd year.
Championships Division 1983; NFL 1935,'52,'53,'57.
History NFL 1930-69, NFC 1970-
  (Until 1934, they were known as the Portsmouth
  (Ohio) Spartans.)

Offense

Sparkling individual performances and a unique offensive system which some opponents simply could not counter, combined to give the Lions a five-game winning streak to round off the season. The offensive scheme has no tight end and four wide receivers yet the key player is running back Barry Sanders. As a rookie, Sanders established himself as the most dangerous runner in the league, setting a club rushing record with 1,470 yards in leading the NFC. Without doubt, with Sanders in full flow, the Lions might prise open any defense, but behind him there is no reserve strength of comparable quality. Carl Painter rushed for just 64 yards in 1989. However, elsewhere, there is depth ranging from solid to excellent. The Lions did not hesitate to draft Heisman Trophy-winning quarterback Andre Ware, who would appear to be perfect for their 'Silver Stretch' offense. But first he will have to displace the tough Rodney Peete, who too fitted the system well – perhaps he even made it work. Peete does not have Ware's arm strength but he has the kind of scrambling ability which comes in handy when everything is in chaos, and he will not relinquish his starting spot without a scrap. The Lions have found a group of wide receivers to suit their style, with Richard Johnson, who set a club single-season record for receptions by a wide receiver (70) and had the second-most productive yardage total (1,091) in club history, setting the pace. Johnson had big games when he caught passes for 172, 248 and 135 yards, Robert Clark chipped in with 124-

and 141-yard games and Jason Phillips had a 115-yard outing against Tampa Bay. The fourth receiver will emerge from a training camp battle involving John Ford, Mel Gray and Plan-B signings Aubrey Matthews and Terry Greer. As the platform for the entire show, the offensive line is very solid. Tackles Lomas Brown and Harvey Salem can match up to most pairings in the NFL while Kevin Glover has made great progress at center. Eric Sanders is the backup tackle. Eric Andolsek and Mike Utley represent a promising future at guard with solid veteran Ken Dallafior in reserve.

Defense

Head coach Wayne Fontes underlined his commitment to build an awesome defense when he used the draft to improve the defensive end position, an area where normal starters Eric Williams and former Cowboy and Bronco Kevin Brooks are better against the run. Keith Ferguson is a fine specialist pass rusher, but when he was out with injury the charge lost its venom. High draftees Dan Owens and Marc Spindler emerged from the search for aggression. At nose tackle, however, Jerry Ball is coming off a career year in which he had nine sacks and went to his first Pro Bowl. Ball's backup, Lawrence Pete, has too much talent to be ignored and may be tried at defensive end. Hovering behind the line, an outstanding group of linebackers is particularly tough against the run. Even though George Jamison and Dennis Gibson missed substantial playing time with injuries, the quartet held up well under pressure. It gives the club a wide range of options, with inside linebacker Chris Spielman the intense run-stuffer, Jimmy Williams the outstanding cover-man and Mike Cofer, who shared the club lead with nine sacks, the most prominent pass rusher. With everyone healthy, there is an embarrassment of talent. Niko Noga, who is nominally an inside specialist, has a role as a pass rusher in the four-man front and even fourth-round draftee Rob Hinckley may have an input. It would be fair to assert that the defensive secondary has room for improvement but, here again, the club seems to be moving in the right direction. The strength lies in the middle where strong safety William White has a built-in direction finder for action and is regarded as the best tackler. Free safety Bennie Blades, an intimidating athlete with superior instincts and timing, is developing steadily into one of the league's best. The loss of leading interceptor Jerry Holmes was cushioned by the acquisition of Plan-B cornerback William Judson, who has great experience and could form a competent partnership with left cornerback Terry Taylor. Considering the reserve strength, former starter Bruce McNorton is coming off an injury and the club is optimistic about the prospects of last year's rookies, Bruce Alexander, Ray Crockett and John Miller.

1990 DRAFT

Round	Name	Pos.	Ht.	Wt.	College
1.	Ware, Andre	QB	6-2	205	Houston
2.	Owens, Dan	DE	6-3	268	Southern California
3.	Spindler, Marc	DE	6-5	277	Pittsburgh
4.	Hinckley, Rob	LB	6-5	243	Stanford
4.	Oldham, Chris	CB	5-9	183	Oregon
5.	Campbell, Jeff	WR	5-8	170	Colorado
6.	Henry, Maurice	LB	6-0	228	Kansas State
7.	Hayworth, Tracy	LB	6-2	250	Tennessee
8.	Green, Willie	WR	6-2	180	Mississippi
8.	Fortin, Roman	G	6-4	275	San Diego State
9.	Linn, Jack	T	6-4	275	West Virginia
10.	Miller, Bill	WR	5-10	180	Illinois State
11.	Warnsley, Reginald	RB	5-10	224	Southern Mississippi
12.	Claiborne, Robert	WR	5-9	163	San Diego State

VETERAN ROSTER

No.	Name	Pos.	Ht.	Wt.	NFL Year	College
32	Alexander, Bruce	CB	5-9	169	2	Stephen F. Austin
65	Andolsek, Eric	G	6-2	286	3	Louisiana State
6	Arnold, Jim	P	6-3	211	8	Vanderbilt
93	Ball, Jerry	NT	6-1	298	4	Southern Methodist
36	Blades, Bennie	S	6-1	221	3	Miami
97	Brooks, Kevin	DE	6-6	278	6	Michigan
75	Brown, Lomas	T	6-4	287	6	Florida
95	Brown, Mark	LB	6-2	240	8	Purdue
50	Caston, Toby	LB	6-1	243	4	Louisiana State
82	Clark, Robert	WR	5-11	173	3	N. Carolina Central
30	Cocroft, Sherman	S	6-1	190	6	San Jose State
55	Cofer, Michael	LB	6-5	244	8	Tennessee
39	Crockett, Ray	CB	5-9	181	2	Baylor
67	Dallafior, Ken	G-C	6-4	279	6	Minnesota
79	Duckens, Mark	DE	6-4	270	2	Arizona State
77	Ferguson, Keith	DE	6-5	276	10	Ohio State
80	Ford, John	WR	6-2	204	2	Virginia
14	Gagliano, Bob	QB	6-3	196	6	Utah State
98	Gibson, Dennis	LB	6-2	243	4	Iowa State
53	Glover, Kevin	C-G	6-2	282	6	Maryland
23	Gray, Mel	WR-KR	5-9	162	5	Purdue
62	Green, Curtis	DE-NT	6-3	273	10	Alabama State
89	Greer, Terry	WR	6-1	192	5	Alabama State
58	Jamison, George	LB	6-1	228	4	Cincinnati
84	Johnson, Richard	WR	5-6	184	2	Colorado
57	Jones, Victor	LB	6-2	240	3	Virginia Tech
49	Judson, William	CB	6-1	192	9	South Carolina State
90	Karpinski, Keith	LB	6-3	225	2	Penn State
83	Matthews, Aubrey	WR	5-7	165	5	Delta State
29	McNorton, Bruce	CB	5-10	175	9	Georgetown, Kent.
44	Miller, John	S	6-1	195	2	Michigan State
3	Murray, Eddie	K	5-10	180	11	Tulane
51	Noga, Niko	LB	6-1	235	7	Hawaii
26	Painter, Carl	RB	5-9	188	3	Hampton Institute
9	Peete, Rodney	QB	6-0	193	2	Southern California
96	Pete, Lawrence	NT	6-0	282	2	Nebraska
24	Phillips, Jason	WR	5-7	168	2	Houston
73	Salem, Harvey	T	6-6	289	8	California
20	Sanders, Barry	RB	5-8	203	2	Oklahoma State
64	Sanders, Eric	T-G	6-7	286	10	Nevada-Reno
54	Spielman, Chris	LB	6-0	244	3	Ohio State
21	Taylor, Terry	CB	5-10	191	7	Southern Illinois
60	Utley, Mike	G-T	6-6	279	2	Washington State
28	Welch, Herb	S	5-11	180	6	UCLA
35	White, William	S	5-10	191	3	Ohio State
40	Wilkerson, Eric	RB-WR	5-9	185	1	Kent State
76	Williams, Eric	DE	6-4	286	7	Washington State
59	Williams, Jimmy	LB	6-3	225	9	Nebraska
63	Wilson, Curtis	C	6-3	290	1	Missouri

1990 SCHEDULE OF GAMES

September

9	TAMPA BAY	1:00
16	ATLANTA	1:00
23	at Tampa Bay (Sun. night)	8:00
30	GREEN BAY	1:00

October

7	at Minnesota	12:00
14	at Kansas City	12:00
21	Open date	
28	at New Orleans	12:00

November

4	WASHINGTON	1:00
11	MINNESOTA	1:00
18	at New York Giants	1:00
22	DENVER (Thanksgiving)	12:30

December

2	at Chicago	12:00
10	LOS ANGELES RAIDERS (Mon.)	9:00
16	CHICAGO (Sun. night)	8:00
22	at Green Bay (Sat.)	11:30
30	at Seattle	1:00

Special Teams

Even though losing punt returner Walter Stanley to Plan-B free agency, Detroit still has one of the NFL's finest special-teams units. Eddie Murray has a remarkable record for field goal accuracy—he has failed only twice in the last two seasons — and punter Jim Arnold usually is within a decimal point of leading the NFL for gross average. Last year, Gray ranked second in the NFL with a 26.7-yard average on kickoff returns and he has enough top-class experience returning punts to take on a dual role.

GREEN BAY PACKERS

Address 1265 Lombardi Avenue, P.O. Box 10628, Green Bay, Wisconsin 54307-0628.

Stadia Lambeau Field, Green Bay, and Milwaukee County Stadium, Milwaukee.
Capacity (Lambeau Field) 57,095, (Milwaukee County Stadium) 56,051 *Playing Surfaces* Grass, both stadia.

Team Colours Dark Green, Gold, and White.

Head Coach Lindy Infante – 3rd year.

Championships Division 1972;
NFL 1929,'30,'31,'36,'39,'44,'61,'62,'65,'66,'67;
Super Bowl 1966,'67.

History NFL 1921-69, NFC 1970-

Offense

Assuming that the Packers are able to re-sign quarterback Don Majkowski, there would appear to be no reason why they should not maintain their improvement under head coach Lindy Infante. Otherwise, the responsibility would fall on the inexperienced shoulders of Anthony Dilweg. Majkowski's development, unexpected outside Green Bay and most welcome for the fans in that football hotbed, probably has been the key to the club's resurgence. In addition to launching the passing game, also he rushed for a valuable 358 yards and scored five touchdowns. His partnership with wide receiver Sterling Sharpe has become one of the most feared weapons in the NFL and it was a bonus that Perry Kemp was able to take the opportunities created when the opposition weighted their coverages towards the Pro Bowl starter, Sharpe, who led the entire league with 90 receptions. With running backs Keith Woodside and Herman Fontenot making useful contributions, the passing game prospered to the extent that the offense became a little further out of balance than Infante would have liked. And it was in the attempt to provide greater variety that Green Bay used the second of its two first-round options to pick the big, strong Darrell Thompson, who is a larger, slightly faster version of current starter Brent Fullwood. One surprise of the 1989 campaign was that top draftee tackle Tony Man-

darich was unable to displace either of the starters, Ken Ruettgers and Alan Veingrad. Though disappointing in one sense, in another it has to be good news for the team that its veterans show such resilience. Timeless gloss is a quality retained by center Blair Bush, who was felt to be close to retirement but has stayed on for another year. At guard, too, there is stability in Pro Bowl alternate Rich Moran and Ron Hallstrom. And it means that, with former third-round pick Dave Croston and the versatile Keith Uecker returning from injury, the offensive line represents top-class strength in depth. The tight end position does not produce much by way of prolific pass receiving but starter Ed West scored five touchdowns and, in backup Clint Didier, there is all the big-game experience that any club would need.

Defense

On defense, the Packers have not matched the progress of the offense and needs were recognised when two linebackers and a defensive back came amongst the top four options in the draft. Tony Bennett is a pass-rushing specialist and could replace the retired John Anderson at left outside linebacker. The partnership of Bennett and Pro Bowler Tim Harris, who led the team with an outstanding 19.5 sacks and four fumbles forced, could give Green Bay a fearsome pass rush and perhaps is the reason why help was not sought for the defensive end positions. Another factor may be that both Matt Brock and Shawn Patterson will be returning from injury to challenge current starting defensive ends Blaise Winter and Robert Brown. There could be a serious competition at nose tackle, too, when former Rams starter Shawn Miller, a Plan-B free agent, squares off with Bob Nelson. As the second line of defense against the run, inside linebackers Brian Noble and Johnny Holland tied for the team lead with 105 tackles and there is no doubting the class of this pairing. Burnell Dent, Mike Weddington and Scott Stephen are the senior reserves at linebacker. It was probably with pass defense in mind that Green Bay selected Bobby Houston, an outside linebacker with a sprinter's speed and who excels in pass coverage. In the secondary, a replacement needs to be found for departed Plan-B free safety Ken Stills. Chuck Cecil, a ball-hawker who started as a rookie when Stills was injured, would be the obvious successor but draftee LeRoy Butler could jump ahead of him. On the other hand, Butler, who has been described as a slightly slower Deion Sanders, may soon take over from Dave Brown, who is the NFL active leader with 62 career interceptions and is entering his 16th season but, in leading the team with six interceptions last year, he showed no signs of slowing. Otherwise with Mark Lee at left cornerback, Mark Murphy at strong safety and with reserves such as Jerry Holmes, Tiger Greene, Van Jakes and Ron Pitts, the secondary is in good order.

Tackle Tony Mandarich could give the offensive line an extra dimension.

1990 SCHEDULE OF GAMES

September
9	LOS ANGELES RAMS	12:00
16	CHICAGO	12:00
23	KANSAS CITY	12:00
30	at Detroit	1:00

October
7	at Chicago	3:00
14	at Tampa Bay	1:00
21	*Open date*	
28	MINNESOTA at Milwaukee	12:00

November
4	SAN FRANCISCO	12:00
11	at Los Angeles Raiders	1:00
18	at Phoenix	2:00
25	TAMPA BAY at Milwaukee	12:00

December
2	at Minnesota (Sun. night)	7:00
9	SEATTLE at Milwaukee	12:00
16	at Philadelphia	4:00
22	DETROIT (Sat.)	11:30
30	at Denver	2:00

Special Teams

Placekicker Chris Jacke has settled down and enters the season with a sequence of nine straight field goal successes. However, for the punting job, there will be a battle involving incumbent Don Bracken, former Rams punter Dale Hatcher and draftee Kirk Maggio. Wide receiver Jeff Query handles punt returns adequately but, on kickoff returns, there is a need for someone who could better the club's 1989 average of 18 yards.

1990 DRAFT

Round	Name	Pos.	Ht.	Wt.	College
1.	Bennett, Tony	LB	6-2	234	Mississippi
1.	Thompson, Darrell	RB	6-1	220	Minnesota
2.	Butler, LeRoy	DB	5-11	193	Florida State
3.	Houston, Bobby	LB	6-1	230	North Carolina St.
4.	Harris, Jackie	TE	6-3	231	Northeast Louisiana
5.	Wilson, Charles	WR	5-9	178	Memphis State
6.	Paup, Bryce	LB	6-4	238	Northern Iowa
7.	Archambeau, Lester	DE	6-4	265	Stanford
8.	Brown, Roger	CB	5-10	192	Virginia Tech
9.	Baumgartner, Kirk	QB	6-3	203	Wiscon.-Stevens Pt.
10.	Martin, Jerome	S	6-0	210	Western Kentucky
11.	Jackson, Harry	RB	5-10	223	St Cloud, Min'sota
12.	Maggio, Kirk	P	6-0	159	UCLA

VETERAN ROSTER

No.	Name	Pos.	Ht.	Wt.	NFL Year	College
82	Affholter, Erik	WR	5-11	181	1	Southern California
67	Ard, Billy	G	6-3	270	10	Wake Forest
76	Ariey, Mike	T	6-5	285	1	San Diego State
83	Bland, Carl	WR	5-11	182	7	Virginia Union
61	Boyarsky, Jerry	NT	6-3	290	10	Pittsburgh
17	Bracken, Don	P	6-1	211	6	Michigan
62	Brock, Matt	DE	6-4	267	2	Oregon
32	Brown, Dave	CB	6-1	197	16	Michigan
93	Brown, Robert	DE	6-2	267	9	Virginia Tech
51	Bush, Blair	C	6-3	272	13	Washington
63	Campen, James	C	6-3	270	4	Tulane
26	Cecil, Chuck	S	6-0	184	3	Arizona
58	Chubb, Aaron	LB	6-5	235	1	Georgia
55	Clark, Greg	LB	6-1	234	3	Arizona State
92	Cribbs, James	DE	6-3	275	2	Memphis State
60	Croston, Dave	T	6-5	280	2	Iowa
49	Dee, Donnie	TE	6-4	242	3	Tulsa
56	Dent, Burnell	LB	6-1	236	5	Tulane
80	Didier, Clint	TE	6-5	240	9	Portland State
8	Dilweg, Anthony	QB	6-3	215	2	Duke
99	Dorsey, John	LB	6-2	243	6	Connecticut
27	Fontenot, Herman	RB	6-0	206	6	Louisiana State
30	Frazier, Paul	RB	5-8	188	2	Northwestern St., La.
21	Fullwood, Brent	RB	5-11	209	4	Auburn
23	Greene, Tiger	S	6-0	194	6	Western Carolina
35	Haddix, Michael	RB	6-2	227	8	Mississippi State
72	Hall, Mark	DE	6-4	285	2	S. W. Louisiana
65	Hallstrom, Ron	G	6-6	290	9	Iowa
97	Harris, Tim	LB	6-5	235	5	Memphis State
48	Harris, William	TE	6-5	235	3	Texas
5	Hatcher, Dale	P	6-2	220	7	Clemson
50	Holland, Johnny	LB	6-2	221	4	Texas A&M
44	Holmes, Jerry	CB	6-2	172	9	West Virginia
13	Jacke, Chris	K	6-0	197	2	Texas-El Paso
24	Jakes, Van	CB	6-0	190	7	Kent State
88	Johnson, Flip	WR	5-10	185	3	McNeese State
53	Johnson, M.L.	LB	6-3	229	4	Hawaii
81	Kemp, Perry	WR	5-11	170	3	California, Pa.
10	Kiel, Blair	QB	6-0	214	6	Notre Dame
22	Lee, Mark	CB	5-11	189	11	Washington
7	Majkowski, Don	QB	6-2	197	4	Virginia
77	Mandarich, Tony	T	6-5	300	2	Michigan State
98	Miller, Shawn	NT	6-4	270	7	Utah State
41	Mobley, Stacey	WR	5-7	165	2	Jackson State
57	Moran, Rich	G	6-2	275	6	San Diego State
37	Murphy, Mark	S	6-2	201	9	West Liberty
79	Nelson, Bob	NT	6-4	275	3	Miami
91	Noble, Brian	LB	6-3	252	6	Arizona State
96	Patterson, Shawn	DE	6-5	261	3	Arizona State
28	Pitts, Ron	CB	5-10	175	5	UCLA
85	Query, Jeff	WR	5-11	165	2	Millikin
75	Ruettgers, Ken	T	6-5	280	6	Southern California
84	Sharpe, Sterling	WR	5-11	202	3	South Carolina
89	Spagnola, John	TE	6-4	242	11	Yale
54	Stephen, Scott	LB	6-2	232	4	Arizona State
70	Uecker, Keith	G-T	6-5	284	8	Auburn
73	Veingrad, Alan	T	6-5	277	4	East Texas State
87	Weathers, Clarence	WR	5-9	172	8	Delaware State
52	Weddington, Mike	LB	6-4	245	5	Oklahoma
86	West, Ed	TE	6-1	243	7	Auburn
68	Winter, Blaise	DL	6-3	275	6	Syracuse
33	Woodside, Keith	RB	5-11	203	3	Texas A&M
46	Workman, Vince	RB	5-10	193	2	Ohio State
64	Yarno, George	C-G	6-2	270	11	Washington State

MINNESOTA VIKINGS

Address 9520 Viking Drive, Eden Prairie, Minnesota 55344.

Stadium Hubert H. Humphrey Metrodome, Minneapolis. *Capacity* 63,000 *Playing Surface* AstroTurf.

Team Colours Purple, Gold, and White.

Head Coach Jerry Burns – 5th year.

Championships Division 1970, '71, '73, '74, '75, '76, '77, '78, '80, '89; Conference 1973, '74, '76; NFL 1969.

History NFL 1961-69, NFC 1970-

Offense

Even though yet again Minnesota took a few bruises in the regular season and were demolished by San Francisco in the playoffs, it is easy to imagine their retaining the title in the NFC Central. One major reason is the presence of superstar running back Herschel Walker, whose trade from Dallas, thus far, has not looked the best of deals for Minnesota. One difficulty was the requirement to switch from the I-formation favoured by Dallas to the Vikings' pro set. However, with the benefit of a camp, he is expected to begin repaying the high cost of his move. Lining up alongside Walker, fullback Rick Fenney really took the chance which came his way when starter Alfred Anderson was injured. Anderson and Allen Rice will challenge for the fullback position and D. J. Dozier will be on hand for special circumstances. In what was an unsettled year at quarterback, neither Wade Wilson nor Tommy Kramer moved the offense with great panache. Kramer has not been offered a contract and it may be that, with no one breathing down his neck, Wilson will regain the kind of form he showed in 1988 when he won the NFC passing title. One player who can help him along that road is Anthony Carter, a player who needs to be featured more often, both for his breathtaking skills and his self-esteem. Hassan Jones presents a deep threat and can make a circus catch look routine. Again, tight end Steve Jordan is the sort who can turn in a big individual per-

formance. Reserve wide receivers Leo Lewis and Jim Gustafson should stay ahead of Plan-B signing Ira Hillary (ex-Cincinnati) if only because they know the system. It was a good move when the Vikings scouted Arizona State a few years ago. They came back with information which led them to draft both Randall McDaniel and Todd Kalis, who start in the guard positions. Tackles Gary Zimmerman and Tim Irwin are earth movers and, gradually, Kirk Lowdermilk has become accepted as being one of the better centers in the NFC. Chris Foote backs up at center, Dave Huffman provides insurance at tackle and ex-Steeler guard Craig Wolfley was a sensible Plan-B signing.

Defense

It remains a mystery that the Vikings, who ended the season with the top-ranked defense in the NFL, were unable to put pressure on Joe Montana in the playoffs and one explanation could be that several key players were carrying injuries. It means, however, that the defensive right end Chris Doleman, who led the NFL in sacks (21.0), and defensive right tackle Keith Millard, who had 18 sacks and, like Doleman, is an All-Pro, will have something to prove. If, during the regular season, Doleman stole the statistical honours and led on style points, Millard is the emotional destroyer whose mission in life is to crush the opposition. Of the other starters, Henry Thomas is a high-class defensive tackle and Al Noga is yet another hungry pass rusher, but it may be that draftee Marion Hobby begins to share time, say on first downs in circumstances when a rush is implied, freeing Noga for his speciality. The quality extends to the linebacking trio, where Scott Studwell stands firm with Mike Merriweather and Ray Berry at his shoulder. They form an all-action pack, ranging from sideline to sideline, creating disorder and cleaning up the scraps. Local lad Mark Dusbabek, David Braxton and John Galvin are the backups. In the secondary, there will be no immediate change at cornerback, where Carl Lee and Reggie Rutland rule, backed up by Audrey McMillian. Strong safety Joey Browner, who led the team in interceptions as just one measure of his importance to the team, may be the very best in the game. However, since both Travis Curtis and Brad Edwards have departed as Plan-B free agents, he will probably be partnered at free safety by Ken Stills, the former Green Bay starter who was a Plan-B signing. On the other hand, if knowledge of the system counts, the job could go to Darrell Fullington, a solid player who has been the backup for both safety spots. It will be interesting to see how the Vikings use draftee Alonzo Hampton, who can play at both free safety and cornerback. Initially, one imagines his backing up at safety but it could be that he is seen as an eventual replacement for Lee at cornerback.

1990 SCHEDULE OF GAMES

September

9	at Kansas City	12:00
16	NEW ORLEANS	3:00
23	at Chicago	12:00
30	TAMPA BAY	12:00

October

7	DETROIT	12:00
15	at Philadelphia (Mon.)	9:00
21	Open date	
28	vs Green Bay at Milwaukee	12:00

November

4	DENVER (Sun. night)	7:00
11	at Detroit	1:00
18	at Seattle	1:00
25	CHICAGO	12:00

December

2	GREEN BAY (Sun. night)	7:00
9	at New York Giants	1:00
16	at Tampa Bay	1:00
22	LOS ANGELES RAIDERS (Sat.)	3:00
30	SAN FRANCISCO	12:00

1990 DRAFT

Round	Name	Pos.	Ht.	Wt.	College
3.	Jones, Mike	TE	6-3	255	Texas A&M
3.	Hobby, Marion	DE	6-4	277	Tennessee
4.	Hampton, Alonzo	CB	5-10	197	Pittsburgh
5.	Thornton, Reggie	WR	5-10	166	Bowling Green
5.	Smith, Cedric	RB	5-10	223	Florida
7.	Levelis, John	LB	6-1	235	C.W. Post
8.	Schlichting, Craig	DE	6-5	255	Wyoming
9.	Allen, Terry	RB	5-11	202	Clemson
10.	Newman, Pat	WR	5-11	208	Utah State
10.	Smith, Donald	CB	5-11	184	Liberty
12.	Goetz, Ron	LB	6-2	236	Minnesota

VETERAN ROSTER

No.	Name	Pos.	Ht.	Wt.	NFL Year	College
46	Anderson, Alfred	RB	6-1	214	7	Baylor
50	Berry, Ray	LB	6-2	226	4	Baylor
53	Braxton, David	LB	6-1	232	2	Wake Forest
44	Brim, Michael	CB	6-0	186	3	Virginia Union
47	Browner, Joey	S	6-2	223	8	Southern California
82	Burbage, Cornell	WR	5-10	186	4	Kentucky
81	Carter, Anthony	WR	5-11	178	6	Michigan
33	Clark, Jessie	RB	6-0	233	9	Arkansas
71	Clarke, Ken	DT	6-2	281	13	Syracuse
56	Doleman, Chris	DE	6-5	262	6	Pittsburgh
42	Dozier, D.J.	RB	6-0	205	4	Penn State
59	Dusbabek, Mark	LB	6-3	230	2	Minnesota
31	Fenney, Rick	RB	6-1	232	4	Washington
62	Foote, Chris	C	6-4	248	9	Southern California
29	Fullington, Darrell	S	6-1	186	3	Miami
51	Galvin, John	LB	6-3	226	3	Boston College
16	Gannon, Rich	QB	6-3	202	4	Delaware
80	Gustafson, Jim	WR	6-1	174	5	St Thomas, Minnesota
74	Habib, Brian	T	6-6	282	2	Washington
89	Hillary, Ira	WR-PR	5-11	190	4	South Carolina
72	Huffman, David	G	6-6	278	11	Notre Dame
86	Ingram, Darryl	TE	6-2	228	2	California
76	Irwin, Tim	T	6-7	290	10	Tennessee
84	Jones, Hassan	WR	6-0	195	5	Florida State
83	Jordan, Steve	TE	6-4	241	10	Brown
69	Kalis, Todd	G	6-5	284	4	Arizona State
3	Karlis, Rich	K	6-0	180	9	Cincinnati
77	Knight, Shawn	DE	6-6	288	4	Brigham Young
39	Lee, Carl	CB	5-11	184	8	Marshall
87	Lewis, Leo	WR-PR	5-8	166	10	Missouri
63	Lowdermilk, Kirk	C	6-3	264	6	Ohio State
49	Lyons, Robert	S	6-1	195	2	Akron
78	Marrone, Doug	G	6-5	269	2	Syracuse
64	McDaniel, Randall	G	6-3	275	3	Arizona State
26	McMillian, Audrey	CB	6-0	190	5	Houston
57	Merriweather, Mike	LB	6-2	221	8	Pacific
75	Millard, Keith	DT	6-6	264	6	Washington State
18	Newsome, Harry	P	6-0	188	6	Wake Forest
99	Noga, Al	DE	6-1	248	3	Hawaii
85	Novoselsky, Brent	TE	6-2	238	3	Pennsylvania
36	Rice, Allen	RB	5-10	206	7	Baylor
48	Rutland, Reggie	CB	6-1	192	4	Georgia Tech
17	Schillinger, Andy	WR	5-11	183	2	Miami, Ohio
60	Schreiber, Adam	G-C	6-4	288	7	Texas
13	Scribner, Bucky	P	6-0	203	6	Kansas
27	Stills, Ken	S	5-10	186	6	Wisconsin
94	Strauthers, Thomas	DE	6-4	264	6	Jackson State
55	Studwell, Scott	LB	6-2	221	14	Illinois
97	Thomas, Henry	DT	6-2	268	4	Louisiana State
34	Walker, Herschel	RB	6-1	226	5	Georgia
11	Wilson, Wade	QB	6-3	210	10	East Texas State
73	Wolfley, Craig	G	6-1	269	11	Syracuse
65	Zimmerman, Gary	T	6-6	284	5	Oregon

Special Teams

Former Denver placekicker Rich Karlis enjoyed the luxury of working indoors more often and showed it by landing a career-best 31 field goals, including seven in one game to equal the NFL record. Punter Bucky Scribner doesn't have a powerful leg but he is careful and that's what Minnesota seems to prefer. Leo Lewis is a fine punt returner—he ranked equal-eighth in the NFL —and it might make sense were D. J. Dozier, who averaged 21.5 yards, to be kept busy by being used more often on kickoff returns.

All-Pro defensive tackle Keith Millard is a destructive power.

TAMPA BAY BUCCANEERS

Address One Buccaneer Place, Tampa,
Florida 33607.
Stadium Tampa Stadium, Tampa.
Capacity 74,315 *Playing Surface* Grass.
Team Colours Florida Orange, White, and Red.
Head Coach Ray Perkins — 4th year; 8th NFL.
Championships Division 1979,'81.
History AFC 1976, NFC 1977-

Offense

Tampa Bay head coach Ray Perkins reflected, 'Overall it was a disappointing year,' but, if pressed, he might admit that the Bucs did make progress. Certainly, that was true of quarterback Vinny Testaverde, who improved in both touchdown passes, equalling the club record with 20, and throwing only 22 interceptions compared with 35 in 1988. Those apart, his leadership skills are emerging steadily. And it should be recognised that the quality of his passes helped to boost wide receiver Mark Carrier to the NFL's highest echelons. It is unfortunate for Carrier, whose receiving yardage haul (1,422) was the 13th best in NFL history, that he plays in the NFC where most of the star wide receivers reside. Carrier's partner, Bruce Hill, was slightly disappointing following his excellent 1988 season and the development of the passing game was hampered by injuries which restricted rookie Danny Peebles. But tight end Ron Hall contributed a useful 30 receptions and is emerging as a solid blocker despite being bothered by nagging injuries. It is at running back where the Bucs needed a boost and they got it in trading for Gary Anderson, a top-class player who could not reach contractual agreement with San Diego and sat out the whole of last year. Both tough veteran James Wilder and the speedy Don Smith have departed as Plan-B free agents, leaving Lars Tate and William Howard as the veteran stock. Neither is the sort to establish a dominant presence but they may be sparked into action by the arrival of draftee Reggie Cobb, who is an athlete of unlimited potential. The

offensive line is in decent shape, indeed, it is particularly strong at left tackle where the highly disciplined Paul Gruber is a towering force. Right guard John Bruhin started whenever he was healthy and is developing well and it is a source of reassurance when center Randy Grimes swivels the ball in preparation for the snap. Fourth-round draftee center Tony Mayberry should be seen as a two- or three-year project. At left guard, Scott Dill and Tom McHale will be involved in a three-way competition which includes draftee Ian Beckles while right tackle Rob Taylor may feel greater pressure from Harry Swayne.

Defense

Despite a modest contribution to the pass rush, there has been no obvious reinforcement of the defensive line except indirectly with the drafting of Keith McCants, who is widely seen as the best linebacker available. Staying with the three-man line, it certainly is true that defensive end Reuben Davis shows every sign of becoming a force. He had only three sacks but registered 12 tackles for loss and will be helped by the build-up of force at outside linebacker. Nose tackle Curt Jarvis is a willing worker but defensive right end Robert Goff may be challenged by ninth-year veteran John Cannon for playing time. Shawn Lee started three games when Jarvis was injured. At linebacker the picture is much more rosy and there may now be an embarrassment of talent. Last year's top pick, Broderick Thomas, was expected to start but, after a holdout, could not displace either of the in-form veterans, Kevin Murphy and Winston Moss. From the inside positions, both Ervin Randle and Eugene Marve deliver their hammer blows with certainty and led the team with 114 and 106 tackles respectively. It means that the arrival of McCants could create a problem, not least in that it disturbs a quartet which functions well as a unit. The solution may lie in playing one or more outside linebackers as stand-up defensive ends. The secondary did suffer from the lack of a consistent pass rush but can take much of the credit for Tampa Bay's NFL 14th ranking for pass defense. Starting safeties Mark Robinson and Harry Hamilton each had six interceptions to share the club lead while left cornerback Ricky Reynolds returned one of his five interceptions 68 yards for a touchdown. Former first-round pick Rod Jones was the only one of the quartet not to have an interception and he could be pushed by either of Rodney Rice and Eric Everett. Robinson, who, together with a fourth-round draft option, came from Kansas City in 1988 in exchange for quarterback Steve DeBerg, has turned out to be a bargain. In addition to his interceptions, he defensed 22 passes, came third on the team in tackles, forced three fumbles and recovered three.

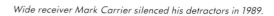
Wide receiver Mark Carrier silenced his detractors in 1989.

1990 DRAFT

Round	Name	Pos.	Ht.	Wt.	College
1.	McCants, Keith	LB	6-4	254	Alabama
2.	Cobb, Reggie	RB	5-11	217	Tennessee
4.	Anderson, Jesse	TE	6-2	240	Mississippi State
4.	Mayberry, Tony	C	6-4	270	Wake Forest
5.	Beckles, Ian	G	6-1	296	Indiana
6.	Douglas, Derrick	RB	5-10	208	Louisiana Tech
7.	Gardner, Donnie	DE	6-3	260	Kentucky
9.	Cook, Terry	DE	6-3	252	Fresno State
10.	Busch, Mike	TE	6-4	249	Iowa State
11.	Anthony, Terry	WR	5-11	193	Florida State
12.	Hammel, Todd	QB	6-0	200	Stephen F. Austin

VETERAN ROSTER

No.	Name	Pos.	Ht.	Wt.	NFL Year	College
	Anderson, Gary	RB	6-0	181	5	Arkansas
56	Anno, Sam	LB	6-2	235	4	Southern California
75	Bax, Carl	G	6-4	290	2	Missouri
11	Bell, Kerwin	QB	6-3	205	3	Florida
55	Bob, Adam	LB	6-2	240	2	Texas A&M
69	Bruhin, John	G	6-3	285	3	Tennessee
78	Cannon, John	DE	6-5	265	9	William & Mary
88	Carrier, Mark	WR	6-0	185	4	Nicholls State
53	Coleman, Sidney	LB	6-2	250	3	Southern Mississippi
23	Cooper, Evan	S	5-11	194	7	Michigan
71	Cooper, Mark	T	6-5	280	8	Miami
79	Davis, Reuben	DE	6-4	285	3	North Carolina
76	Dill, Scott	G	6-5	283	4	Memphis State
87	Drewrey, Willie	WR-PR	5-7	170	6	West Virginia
42	Everett, Eric	CB	5-10	170	3	Texas Tech
12	Ferguson, Joe	QB	6-1	200	18	Arkansas
36	Futrell, Bobby	CB	5-11	190	5	Elizabeth City State
94	Goff, Robert	DE	6-3	270	3	Auburn
65	Graham, Dan	C	6-2	270	1	Northern Illinois
60	Grimes, Randy	C	6-4	275	8	Baylor
74	Gruber, Paul	T	6-5	290	3	Wisconsin
82	Hall, Ron	TE	6-4	245	4	Hawaii
39	Hamilton, Harry	S	6-0	195	7	Penn State
20	Harris, Odie	DB	6-0	190	3	Sam Houston State
84	Hill, Bruce	WR	6-0	180	4	Arizona State
43	Howard, William	RB	6-0	240	3	Tennessee
1	Igwebuike, Donald	K	5-9	190	6	Clemson
95	Jarvis, Curt	NT	6-2	270	3	Alabama
22	Jones, Rod	CB	6-0	185	5	Southern Methodist
38	Lawson, Jamie	RB	5-10	240	2	Nicholls State
97	Lee, Shawn	NT	6-2	285	3	North Alabama
99	Marve, Eugene	LB	6-2	240	9	Saginaw Valley
64	Massaro, Chuck	C	6-2	265	1	North Carolina State
73	McHale, Tom	G	6-4	285	4	Cornell
41	Mitchell, Alvin	RB	6-0	235	2	Auburn
5	Mohr, Chris	P	6-4	220	2	Alabama
58	Moss, Winston	LB	6-3	235	4	Miami
59	Murphy, Kevin	LB	6-2	235	5	Oklahoma
57	Najarian, Pete	LB	6-2	235	3	Minnesota
83	Peebles, Danny	WR	5-11	180	2	North Carolina State
80	Pillow, Frank	WR	5-10	170	3	Tennessee State
54	Randle, Ervin	LB	6-1	235	6	Baylor
29	Reynolds, Ricky	CB	5-11	190	4	Washington State
31	Rice, Rodney	CB	5-8	180	2	Brigham Young
30	Robinson, Mark	S	5-11	200	7	Penn State
98	Seals, Ray	DE	6-3	270	1	None
24	Stamps, Sylvester	RB	5-7	180	7	Jackson State
70	Swayne, Harry	T	6-5	270	4	Rutgers
34	Tate, Lars	RB	6-2	215	3	Georgia
72	Taylor, Rob	T	6-6	290	5	Northwestern
14	Testaverde, Vinny	QB	6-5	215	4	Miami
51	Thomas, Broderick	LB	6-4	245	2	Nebraska
85	Walker, Jackie	TE	6-5	255	5	Jackson State

1990 SCHEDULE OF GAMES

September

9	at Detroit	1:00
16	LOS ANGELES RAMS	1:00
23	DETROIT (Sun. night)	8:00
30	at Minnesota	12:00

October

7	at Dallas	12:00
14	GREEN BAY	1:00
21	DALLAS	1:00
28	at San Diego	1:00

November

4	CHICAGO	4:00
11	at New Orleans	12:00
18	at San Francisco	1:00
25	vs Green Bay at Milwaukee	12:00

December

2	ATLANTA	1:00
9	*Open date*	
16	MINNESOTA	1:00
23	at Chicago	12:00
30	NEW YORK JETS	4:00

Special Teams

In backup wide receiver Willie Drewrey, the Bucs have an elusive punt returner. Last year he averaged 11 yards to rank equal-sixth in the NFL and it may be that he also takes on the vacant role of kickoff returner. Placekicker Donald Igwebuike quietly chipped his way to a new Bucs record with 99 points and, in raising his single-season field goal percentage to a club-record 78.6, equalled his previous best of 22 field goals in a season. However, Chris Mohr may face a challenge after ending up well down the list of NFL punters and having two attempts blocked.

ATLANTA FALCONS

Address Suwanee Road at I-85, Suwanee,
Georgia 30174.
Stadium Atlanta-Fulton County Stadium.
Capacity 59,643 *Playing Surface* Grass (PAT).
Team Colours Red, Black, White, and Silver.
Head Coach Jerry Glanville – 1st year; 6th NFL.
Championships Division 1980.
History NFL 1966-69, NFC 1970-

Offense

Head coach Jerry Glanville builds tough football teams. That's what he has set out to do with Atlanta, and he would be pleased with the decision by the ownership to revert to the Falcons' original jersey colour of black. The major personnel move may turn out to be the trade which brought All-Pro tackle Chris Hinton and potential Pro Bowl wide receiver Andre Rison as part of an arrangement which enabled Indianapolis to select quarterback Jeff George. Without Hinton the line was respectable but with him it could be outstanding. Left tackle Mike Kenn is a former Pro Bowler while right guard Bill Fralic recently had his fourth consecutive selection. Jamie Dukes has come through to start at center and it would seem that Stan Clayton now competes with 1989 holdout John Scully to start at left guard. Atlanta has top-notch reserves in Houston Hoover, Ronnie Lee, Mike Ruether and another former Colts starter, guard Ben Utt. Rison lends astounding agility – the ability to beat several players with one shift – and freshness to any team and he'll break up the pairing of former Northern Arizona teammates Shawn Collins and Michael Haynes, with the latter stepping into the role of senior reserve ahead of Floyd Dixon. Impressive though Rison is, Collins, also who was a rookie last year, out-produced Rison albeit playing in a different system. Yield from the tight end position was a problem exacerbated by the loss of Plan-B free agent Ron Heller and there is no obvious replacement on the horizon. Gargantuan draftee tight end Reggie Redding is essentially a tackle who has some pulling speed and will play purely as a blocker in Glanville's interpretation of the tight end position. The first round of the draft brought yet more excitement and brilliant open-field running in the form of Steve Broussard, whom some scouts regard as the fastest of the serious prospects. Broussard could challenge incumbent John Settle immediately for starting time in partnership with fullback Keith Jones. Catalysing the entire offensive effort, quarterback Chris Miller has rewarded the patience and wisdom of a club which has let him get on with the business of establishing himself. He is not where he'd like to be yet but he's on his way.

Defense

The Falcons are satisfied with the senior players for the defensive line though they hope that Rick Bryan, a five-year starter at defensive right end can come back from injury. He would displace Ben Thomas, to line up alongside nose tackle Tony Casillas and Mike Gann. With Thomas, Tony Bowick and draftee Oliver Barnett as backups, the unit is solid as distinct from overpowering. But its job will be done if it can delay opponents long enough for a fine linebacking corps to join the battle. And here, at linebacker, we may be looking at the force which propels the Falcons to playoff contention. The unit has five players who could start and is joined by a potential sixth in draftee Darion Conner. A little later than expected, both Tim Green and Aundray Bruce have started to play up to first-round draftee status. Together, they form the outside pairing on first downs and logged five and six sacks respectively. Coming in as the specialist pass rusher, the fiery Marcus Cotton led the team with nine sacks. Indeed, everything seems to be coming together, for, in his first full season as a starter, right inside linebacker Jessie Tuggle led the club with 183 tackles while his inside partner, the reliable John Rade, registered the fifth 100-tackle campaign of his six-year career. With the introduction of new personnel, the defensive secondary did show distinct signs of improvement. The most significant change saw the flashy Deion Sanders come through at right cornerback and, despite missing training camp because of a contractual dispute and, as a consequence, starting in only ten games, he led the team with five interceptions. Almost in the manner of the legendary Babe Ruth, who'd sometimes point to where the next home run was going, Sanders has a consummate belief in his own ability and, without question, he is a special kind of player. Tenth-year veteran left cornerback Bobby Butler will be challenged by returning former starter Scott Case. Free safety Tim Gordon did well in his 13 starts and the club is hopeful that Brian Jordan can step up at strong safety. Charles Dimry's speed is put to good use as the nickel back.

1990 SCHEDULE OF GAMES	September	
	9 HOUSTON	4:00
	16 at Detroit	1:00
	23 at San Francisco	1:00
	30 *Open date*	
	October	
	7 NEW ORLEANS	1:00
	14 SAN FRANCISCO	1:00
	21 at Los Angeles Rams	1:00
	28 CINCINNATI (Sun. night)	8:00
	November	
	4 at Pittsburgh	1:00
	11 at Chicago	12:00
	18 PHILADELPHIA	1:00
	25 at New Orleans	12:00
	December	
	2 at Tampa Bay	1:00
	9 PHOENIX	1:00
	16 at Cleveland	1:00
	23 LOS ANGELES RAMS	1:00
	30 DALLAS	1:00

1990 DRAFT

Round	Name	Pos.	Ht.	Wt.	College
1.	Broussard, Steve	RB	5-6	201	Washington State
2.	Conner, Darion	LB	6-3	256	Jackson State
3.	Barnett, Oliver	DE	6-3	285	Kentucky
5.	Redding, Reggie	TE	6-3	280	Cal State-Fullerton
6.	Pringle, Mike	RB	5-8	186	Cal State-Fullerton
8.	Epps, Tory	NT	6-0	280	Memphis State
9.	Jordan, Darrell	LB	6-2	240	Northern Arizona
10.	Salum, Donnie	LB	6-1	233	Arizona
11.	Ellison, Chris	DB	5-10	200	Houston
12.	McCarthy, Shawn	P	6-6	227	Purdue

VETERAN ROSTER

No.	Name	Pos.	Ht.	Wt.	NFL Year	College
82	Bailey, Stacey	WR	6-1	163	9	San Jose State
65	Bingham, Guy	C-G	6-3	260	11	Montana
70	Bowick, Tony	NT	6-2	265	2	Tenn.-Chattanooga
93	Bruce, Aundray	LB	6-5	245	3	Auburn
77	Bryan, Rick	DE	6-4	265	6	Oklahoma
23	Butler, Bobby	CB	5-11	175	10	Florida State
10	Campbell, Scott	QB	6-0	195	6	Purdue
25	Case, Scott	CB	6-0	178	7	Oklahoma
75	Casillas, Tony	NT	6-3	280	5	Oklahoma
74	Clayton, Stan	G	6-3	265	3	Penn State
98	Cline, Jackie	DE	6-5	280	4	Alabama
85	Collins, Shawn	WR	6-2	207	2	Northern Arizona
51	Cotton, Marcus	LB	6-3	237	3	Southern California
5	Davis, Greg	K	5-11	197	4	Citadel
22	Dimry, Charles	DB	6-0	175	3	Nevada-Las Vegas
86	Dixon, Floyd	WR	5-9	170	5	Stephen F. Austin
64	Dukes, Jamie	C	6-1	285	5	Florida State
79	Fralic, Bill	G	6-5	280	6	Pittsburgh
17	Fulhage, Scott	P	5-11	193	4	Kansas State
76	Gann, Mike	DE	6-5	275	6	Notre Dame
41	Gordon, Tim	S	6-0	188	4	Tulsa
99	Green, Tim	LB	6-2	245	5	Syracuse
81	Haynes, Michael	WR	6-0	180	3	Northern Arizona
71	Hinton, Chris	T-G	6-4	300	8	Northwestern
69	Hoover, Houston	T	6-2	285	3	Jackson State
68	Hunter, John	T	6-8	296	2	Brigham Young
43	Johnson, Tracy	RB	6-0	230	2	Clemson
28	Johnson, Undra	RB	5-9	199	2	West Virginia
38	Jones, Keith	RB	6-1	210	2	Illinois
40	Jordan, Brian	S	6-1	205	2	Richmond
78	Kenn, Mike	T	6-7	277	13	Michigan
33	Lang, Gene	RB	5-10	206	7	Louisiana State
63	Lee, Ronnie	T	6-3	277	12	Baylor
6	McFadden, Paul	K	5-11	166	7	Youngstown State
7	Millen, Hugh	QB	6-5	218	3	Washington
12	Miller, Chris	QB	6-2	200	4	Oregon
36	Paterra, Greg	RB	5-11	211	2	Slippery Rock
49	Primus, James	RB	5-11	196	3	UCLA
59	Rade, John	LB	6-1	240	8	Boise State
95	Reid, Michael	LB	6-2	235	4	Wisconsin
80	Rison, Andre	WR	6-0	191	2	Michigan State
56	Ruether, Mike	C	6-4	275	5	Texas
21	Sanders, Deion	CB-PR	6-0	187	2	Florida State
61	Scully, John	G	6-6	270	9	Notre Dame
44	Settle, John	RB	5-9	207	4	Appalachian State
37	Shelley, Elbert	S	5-11	180	4	Arkansas State
53	Thaxton, Galand	LB	6-1	242	2	Wyoming
72	Thomas, Ben	DE	6-3	275	5	Auburn
89	Thomas, George	WR	5-9	169	2	Nevada-Las Vegas
58	Tuggle, Jessie	LB	5-11	230	4	Valdosta State
66	Utt, Ben	G	6-6	293	9	Georgia Tech
87	Wilkins, Gary	TE	6-2	235	4	Georgia Tech

Special Teams

Scott Fulhage took over the punting duties in 1989 and should continue after ending up fifth in the NFC with a respectable 41.3-yard gross average. Placekicker Greg Davis, who came back to Atlanta after a spell with New England, replaced the injured Paul McFadden with whom he now competes for a spot on the roster. On both kickoff and punt returns, Sanders is a threat to break free at any time. Last year, in addition to his 68-yard punt return for a touchdown, he had kickoff returns of 72 and 60 yards while a 96-yarder was called back for a penalty.

Marcus Cotton led the team with nine sacks.

LOS ANGELES RAMS

Address 2327 West Lincoln Avenue, Anaheim,
   California 92801.
Stadium Anaheim Stadium, Anaheim.
   Capacity 69,008 *Playing Surface* Grass.
Team Colours Royal Blue, Gold, and White.
Head Coach John Robinson – 8th year.
Championships Division 1973, '74, '75, '76, '77, '78,
   '79, '85; Conference 1979; NFL 1945,'51.
History NFL 1937-69, NFC 1970-
   (Until 1946, they were known as the Cleveland Rams.)

Offense

It is still difficult to believe that the mighty Rams were dismissed with such ease by San Francisco in the NFC Championship Game, and we should not forget that it was the Rams who handed the 49ers one of their two defeats of the season. They begin the campaign with an offensive line which, though not up to historic levels, still is good enough. Irv Pankey and Jackie Slater are the tackles, Tom Newberry and Duval Love start at guard and Doug Smith still holds the fort at center. Gradually, however, depth has become a problem and, with the departures of Plan-B free agents Kurt Becker and Tony Slaton, this may now have reached emergency proportions. Other than top draftee center Bern Brostek, veterans Robert Cox and Plan-B signing Joe Milinichik are the only reserves. However, elsewhere, there is ample, perhaps even an embarrassment of depth. At running back, it is difficult to see how Plan-B signing Curt Warner can find much playing time in a group led by Greg Bell and including Cleveland Gary, Mel Farr and Gaston Green. On the other hand, a completely healthy Warner is a nightmare for any defense. The fullback position is in fine shape with the immensely promising Robert Delpino and Buford McGee vying for seniority. At quarterback, too, the Rams are in excellent condition with Jim Everett regarded as one of the NFL's premier passers. Last year he rated better than 100 in seven games, all of which the Rams won except a close loss to San Francisco on Week Fourteen. Entering the season, Everett's backup is Mark Herrmann, but Chuck Long, who was a 1986

first-round pick of Detroit but did not fit that club's plans, could be transformed by his new environment. As wide receivers, Henry Ellard and Willie (Flipper) Anderson are as good as most starting pairs in the league. Each man can dominate a game. Backup Aaron Cox is a deep threat and draftee Tim Stallworth might just play a useful part in things. The Rams use one tight end, Damone Johnson backed up by Pat Carter, primarily as a blocker, and another as an H-back. In the latter role, Pete Holohan is a key member of the receiving unit.

Defense

On the surface of it, the Rams do look a little thin for the defensive line and the position was not helped by the departure of Plan-B free agent Shawn Miller, who was a starter at defensive tackle. However, both Doug Reed and 1989 first-round pick Bill Hawkins are coming back from injury and, out of the group completed by Alvin Wright, Mike Piel, and backups Brian Smith and Sean Smith, there should emerge a competitive trio. Further help for the line emerges naturally from a gameplan in which nominal outside linebackers Kevin Greene and, to a lesser extent, Mike Wilcher, often serve as pass rushers. Greene, who does this 'par excellence', led the team in 1989 with 16.5 sacks ahead of Wilcher (5) with the swashbuckling Brett Faryniarz ranking equal-fourth on the team with three sacks from his limited opportunities. There is a solid core of defense at inside linebacker, where Larry Kelm and Fred Strickland are the starters ahead of Frank Stams and Mark Messner. Certainly, opponents do not fancy rushing against a defense which, in this category, ranked fifth in the NFL last year. However, when it comes to pass defense, the Rams are coming off one of the worst years in their history. They were rated last in the league. The reasons for this are not immediately obvious but limited pressure from the defensive line and injuries may have been factors. Even so, opposing teams did find ways of isolating, hence rendering vulnerable, Rams defensive backs, who were beaten on long passes too often for comfort. One player who played up to form and will continue so to do is All-Pro cornerback Jerry Gray, who led the club with six interceptions and a huge 23 passes defensed. With the departure of LeRoy Irvin, Gray will have a new starting partner, probably Clifford Hicks, who started seven games in 1989 and has an edge on Bobby Humphery, Darryl Henley and Alfred Jackson. Draftee Pat Terrell was a free safety at Notre Dame and, while he is not expected to displace either of incumbent Vince Newsome and strong safety Michael Stewart, he is a real ballhawker with a love for collisions. Completing the reserve strength, Anthony Newman is a former second-round draft choice.

<table>
<tr><td colspan="3">1990 SCHEDULE
OF GAMES</td><td colspan="2">September</td></tr>
</table>

1990 SCHEDULE OF GAMES

September
9	at Green Bay	12:00
16	at Tampa Bay	1:00
23	PHILADELPHIA	1:00
30	*Open date*	

October
7	CINCINNATI	1:00
14	at Chicago (Sun. night)	6:30
21	ATLANTA	1:00
29	at Pittsburgh (Mon.)	9:00

November
4	HOUSTON	1:00
11	NEW YORK GIANTS	1:00
18	DALLAS	1:00
25	at San Francisco	1:00

December
2	at Cleveland	1:00
9	NEW ORLEANS	1:00
17	SAN FRANCISCO (Mon.)	6:00
23	at Atlanta	1:00
31	at New Orleans (Mon.)	7:00

Special Teams

Draftee Kent Elmore and ex-Charger Hank Ilesic will compete for the job of punter which became vacant when Plan-B free agent Dale Hatcher was signed by Green Bay. There will be a change, too, returning kick-offs, where Delpino is challenged by Humphery following the departure of Ron Brown for the Raiders. Henley showed himself to be a fine punt returner, averaging 9.4 yards without the boost of a big gain. The reliable Mike Lansford comes back for a ninth year to take care of the placekicking.

1990 DRAFT

Round	Name	Pos.	Ht.	Wt.	College
1.	Brostek, Bern	C	6-3	300	Washington
2.	Terrell, Pat	S	6-0	195	Notre Dame
3.	Berry, Latin	RB	5-9	196	Oregon
6.	Stallworth, Tim	WR	5-9	177	Washington State
7.	Elmore, Kent	P	6-2	180	Tennessee
8.	Savage, Ray	LB	6-1	238	Virginia
8.	Crawford, Elbert	C	6-3	271	Arkansas
9.	Lomack, Tony	WR	5-8	179	Florida
10.	Bates, Steve	DE	6-3	249	James Madison
11.	Goldberg, Bill	DT	6-2	255	Georgia
12.	Lang, David	RB	5-10	198	Northern Arizona

VETERAN ROSTER

No.	Name	Pos.	Ht.	Wt.	NFL Year	College
83	Anderson, Willie	WR	6-0	172	3	UCLA
42	Bell, Greg	RB	5-11	210	7	Notre Dame
57	Bethune, George	LB	6-4	240	2	Alabama
59	Butcher, Paul	LB	6-0	230	4	Wayne State
88	Carter, Pat	TE	6-4	250	3	Florida State
84	Cox, Aaron	WR	5-10	178	3	Arizona State
72	Cox, Robert	T	6-5	285	4	UCLA
39	Delpino, Robert	RB	6-0	205	3	Missouri
80	Ellard, Henry	WR	5-11	182	8	Fresno State
11	Everett, Jim	QB	6-5	212	5	Purdue
34	Farr, Mel	RB	6-0	223	2	UCLA
51	Faryniarz, Brett	LB	6-3	235	3	San Diego State
43	Gary, Cleveland	RB	6-0	226	2	Miami
25	Gray, Jerry	CB	6-0	185	6	Texas
44	Green, Gaston	RB	5-11	192	3	UCLA
91	Greene, Kevin	LB	6-3	250	6	Auburn
70	Hawkins, Bill	DT	6-6	268	2	Miami
20	Henley, Darryl	CB-PR	5-9	170	2	UCLA
9	Herrmann, Mark	QB	6-4	202	10	Purdue
28	Hicks, Clifford	CB	5-10	188	4	Oregon
81	Holohan, Pete	TE	6-4	232	10	Notre Dame
48	Humphery, Bobby	CB-KR	5-10	180	7	New Mexico State
8	Ilesic, Hank	P	6-1	210	2	None
31	Jackson, Alfred	CB	6-0	177	2	San Diego State
86	Johnson, Damone	TE	6-4	250	5	Cal Poly-SLO
21	Johnson, Johnnie	S	6-1	183	11	Texas
52	Kelm, Larry	LB	6-4	240	4	Texas A&M
1	Lansford, Mike	K	6-0	190	9	Washington
	Long, Chuck	QB	6-4	221	6	Iowa
67	Love, Duval	G	6-3	287	6	UCLA
90	McDonald, Mike	LB	6-1	235	6	Southern California
24	McGee, Buford	RB	6-0	210	7	Mississippi
60	Messner, Mark	LB	6-2	256	2	Michigan
71	Milinichik, Joe	G	6-5	283	4	North Carolina State
66	Newberry, Tom	G	6-2	285	5	Wisconsin-LaCrosse
26	Newman, Anthony	S	6-0	199	3	Oregon
22	Newsome, Vince	S	6-1	185	8	Washington
58	Owens, Mel	LB	6-2	240	10	Michigan
75	Pankey, Irv	T	6-5	295	11	Penn State
95	Piel, Mike	DT	6-4	263	2	Illinois
93	Reed, Doug	DT	6-3	265	7	San Diego State
78	Slater, Jackie	T	6-4	285	15	Jackson State
96	Smith, Brian	LB	6-6	242	2	Auburn
56	Smith, Doug	C	6-3	272	13	Bowling Green
97	Smith, Sean	DT	6-4	275	4	Grambling
50	Stams, Frank	LB	6-2	240	2	Notre Dame
23	Stewart, Michael	S	6-0	195	4	Fresno State
53	Strickland, Fred	LB	6-2	250	3	Purdue
21	Warner, Curt	RB	5-11	205	7	Penn State
54	Wilcher, Mike	LB	6-3	245	8	North Carolina
99	Wright, Alvin	DT	6-2	285	5	Jacksonville State

Tight end Pete Holohan is a key part of the pass receiving corps.

NEW ORLEANS SAINTS

Address 1500 Poydras Street, New Orleans, Louisiana 70112.
Stadium Louisiana Superdome, New Orleans. *Capacity* 69,548 *Playing Surface* AstroTurf.
Team Colours Old Gold, Black, and White.
Head Coach Jim Mora – 5th year.
Championships None.
History NFL 1967-69, NFC 1970-

Offense

Confidence-building wins in the last three games of the 1989 season enable the Saints to march into the 1990 campaign in what is the NFL's toughest division. A quick reference to the club's Plan-B signings and a draft list which shows defensive players being selected in the first four rounds indicates without question that the club is comfortable with its existing offensive personnel. And why should this not be true? For in Dalton Hilliard New Orleans has last season's league-leading touchdown scorer, the NFC's third-best rusher and its most productive dual-purpose back. The anticipated return of Rueben Mayes, who is a rusher of wide-ranging talents, together with solidity at fullback in the form of Buford Jordan, backed up by Craig (Ironhead) Heyward and Bobby Morse, should give the rushing offense every option it needs. Hilliard's value can not be overstated. He's not likely to produce mammoth rushing days but only rarely is he going to be stopped cold. On the one occasion when this happened in 1989 – he rushed for just nine years on ten carries against San Francisco on Week Five – he caught nine passes for 77 yards. The offensive line has a settled look with rookie Kevin Haverdink having established himself at left tackle alongside the veterans, Jim Dombrowski, Joel Hilgenberg, Steve Trapilo and Stan Brock. Brad Edelman, who has started in the past, is one of the league's better backups but, following the departures of Plan-B free agents Doug Marrone and Jeff Walker, center Steve Korte and tackle Glenn Derby complete

the reserve strength. The quarterback position has not been settled but, having started the final three games of the 1989 campaign and doing particularly well in those victories, John Fourcade has an advantage over Bobby Hebert, the former starter who was openly disgruntled and indicated his desire to be traded. The wide receivers are led by Eric Martin, a flowing deep threat who improves each year and now is expected to gain over 1,000 yards. The other starter, Lonzell Hill, is developing steadily but could be overtaken by Brett Perrimen, who rounded off the season with a minor flourish. At tight end, both Hoby Brenner and his backup, John Tice, are becoming an endangered species in that they can both block and catch passes.

Defense

The Saints are committed to maintaining the quality of their defense, in particular the defensive line for which the pass rushing of draftees Renaldo Turnbull and Joel Smeenge will be invaluable. Defensive left end Frank Warren had a tremendous year with 9.5 sacks, but he is under suspension and the other 1989 starter, James Geathers, has been lost to Plan-B free agency. It means that nose tackle Jim Wilks will have last year's first-round pick, Wayne Martin, to his right and either Michael Simmons or one of the draftees on his left. Wilks is now a seasoned veteran and, behind him at inside linebacker, he will have the reassuring presence of Pro Bowlers Sam Mills and Vaughan Johnson, who led the team with 95 and 83 tackles respectively and accounted for four sacks. For much of his nine-year career, Rickey Jackson has been one of the best outside linebackers in the game, a status underlined by his career (unofficial) sack total of 79.5 and four selections to the Pro Bowl. At right outside linebacker, Pat Swilling enjoyed his best campaign and, with a team-leading 16.5 sacks in 1989, finally gave the Saints a complete Pro Bowl set. There should be room for all three of veteran Brian Forde and newcomers DeMond Winston and James Williams, both of whom were taken in the top half of the draft. Considering the defensive secondary, the fact that New Orleans ranked a poor 26th in yardage given up to the pass may say more about the quality of the club's run defense, in which it led the NFL, than indicating a weakness against the pass. Quite simply, many opponents discarded the rush as an option. Even so, with the departure of Plan-B free agent safeties Antonio Gibson and Dave Waymer, it was a wise move to draft Vince Buck. 1989 leading interceptor Waymer will be replaced by Buck or veteran Brett Maxie, while Gene Atkins comes in for Gibson. Left cornerback Robert Massey had a fine rookie campaign, grabbing five interceptions and defensing a team-high 18 passes. The other starter will be the much-improved Toi Cook at right cornerback.

Linebacker Vaughan Johnson is a model of concentration in preseason training camp.

Special Teams

Morten Andersen missed going to his fifth straight Pro Bowl after showing himself to be human by missing a few field goals in 1989. He is top class but punter Tommy Barnhardt could use an extra yard on his gross average of 39.6. When it comes to returning kickoffs and punts the Saints aren't that hot. By the end of the year, Bobby Morse had moved up to return both punts and kickoffs, the latter in which he scored a 99-yard touchdown.

SAN FRANCISCO 49ers

Address 4949 Centennial Boulevard, Santa Clara, California 95054.
Stadium Candlestick Park, San Francisco. *Capacity* 65,701 *Playing Surface* Grass.
Team Colours Forty Niners Gold and Scarlet.
Head Coach George Seifert – 2nd year.
Championships Division 1970, '71, '72, '81, '83, '84, '86, '87, '88, '89; Conference 1981,'84,'88,'89; Super Bowl 1981,'84,'88,'89.
History AAFC 1946-49, NFL 1950-69, NFC 1970-

Offense

With only two pauses along the way, the 49ers moved serenely to their fourth Super Bowl title and they have every prospect of becoming the first team since the inception of the Super Bowl to 'threepeat', a word coined just for them. At quarterback, Joe Montana now has reached levels of perfection and certainty which suggest that he really could run the team blindfolded. While he may not be the greatest quarterback in NFL history – as some scouts insist he is on the basis of his career passer rating alone – he is perfect for the system which was tailored to his skills. Behind him, San Francisco has Steve Young, who may be the best reserve in the game. The only doubt arises when Young thinks of being traded to run his own show rather than simply being part of a winning team. No club, except perhaps the Washington Redskins, has a group of wide receivers to match the quartet of Jerry Rice, John Taylor, Mike Wilson and Mike Sherrard. Rice is on his way to owning the NFL record book and, were he not on the 49ers' roster, Taylor could be burning that trail himself. Wilson, a valuable third receiver for the times when the 49ers find themselves needing a clutch reception, is highly respected and the evidence is that, given opportunities, Sherrard can operate at the highest levels. Tight end Brent Jones revels in the freedom which, inevitably, comes his way when teams are obliged to double-cover other strike players. At running back, the strength is so deep that the club felt able to trade Terrence Flagler, who might start for many other teams but was not likely to displace the great Roger Craig, who seems to save his high-stepping heroics for the big games. Strangely, though, the 49ers then went and drafted running back Dexter Carter. Fullback Tom Rathman has an immense presence, running and catching as he pleases. The main surprise of the playoff series was an offensive line which had been good but became sensational. The group formed by Harris Barton, Bruce Collie, Terry Tausch, Jesse Sapolu, Guy McIntyre, Bubba Paris and Steve Wallace, all of whom played their parts, now can claim its place in history.

Defense

On defense also the 49ers approached perfection in a playoff series when even the awesome Vikings, most often reminiscent of their forbears who ravaged coastal Europe, were made to look like any other group of Norsemen out for a boating trip. It seems that just about everyone who dons a San Francisco jersey becomes Superman. The playbook has a variety of three- and four-man defensive lines to suit the occasion. The nominal starters are Pierce Holt and Kevin Fagan at defensive end, with Michael Carter at nose tackle. Larry Roberts plays a key role providing extra pressure against the pass. Again, this talent-laden club could afford to trade away Daniel Stubbs, who was a reserve both at defensive end and outside linebacker. And with Carter possibly not regaining his full powers following a lengthy absence through injury and Jim Burt coming to the end, the club dipped into the Plan-B free-agent pie and came out with Fred Smerlas, a former Pro Bowler who'll probably play like he did in his prime. Yet more help came in the form of draftee Dennis Brown. The linebackers didn't yield very much to opposing rushers, not least because of the evergreen former Raider, Matt Millen, who came as a free agent. Michael Walter underlined his reputation with an non-stop display which saw him lead the team with 103 tackles. Charging in from an outside position, Charles Haley had 10.5 sacks to share the team lead with Holt. At right outside linebacker both Keena Turner and Bill Romanowski do not normally blitz the passer and look more comfortable in pass coverage rather than against the run. An outstanding defensive secondary led by perennial All-Pro Ronnie Lott doesn't normally need assistance and, in 1989, played a major part in the collective effort. Lott is of priceless value and the development of hard-tackling strong safety Chet Brooks has been a revelation. On the corners, Don Griffin and Darryl Pollard start, with former Pro Bowler Eric Wright joined by Hanford Dixon and Dave Waymer as the unit's experienced backups. Draftee Eric Davis will fill the spot vacated by an unsettled Tim McKyer.

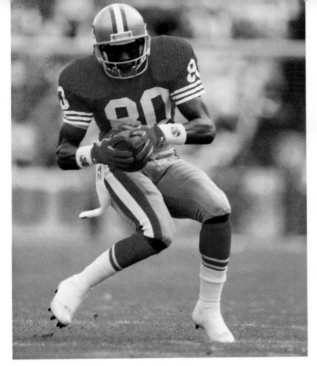

Jerry Rice has the capacity to become the most prolific wide receiver in NFL history.

1990 DRAFT

Round	Name	Pos.	Ht.	Wt.	College
1.	Carter, Dexter	RB	5-8	168	Florida State
2.	Brown, Dennis	DT	6-4	308	Washington
2.	Davis, Eric	CB	5-10	176	Jacksonville State
3.	Lewis, Ron	WR	5-11	172	Florida State
4.	Caliguire, Dean	C	6-3	265	Pittsburgh
6.	Pollack, Frank	T	6-4	286	Northern Arizona
8.	Pickens, Dwight	WR	5-10	170	Fresno State
9.	Haggins, Odell	DT	6-1	261	Florida State
10.	Harrison, Martin	DE	6-4	233	Washington
11.	Shelton, Anthony	S	6-0	185	Tennessee State

VETERAN ROSTER

No.	Name	Pos.	Ht.	Wt.	NFL Year	College
79	Barton, Harris	T	6-4	280	4	North Carolina
13	Bono, Steve	QB	6-4	215	6	UCLA
65	Bregel, Jeff	G	6-4	280	4	Southern California
31	Brooks, Chet	S	5-11	191	3	Texas A&M
64	Burt, Jim	NT	6-1	260	10	Miami
95	Carter, Michael	NT	6-2	285	7	Southern Methodist
6	Cofer, Mike	K	6-1	190	3	North Carolina State
69	Collie, Bruce	G	6-6	275	6	Texas-Arlington
38	Cox, Greg	S	6-0	223	3	San Jose State
33	Craig, Roger	RB	6-0	214	8	Nebraska
59	DeLong, Keith	LB	6-2	235	2	Tennessee
28	Dixon, Hanford	CB	5-11	195	10	Southern Mississippi
75	Fagan, Kevin	DE	6-4	265	4	Miami
55	Fahnhorst, Jim	LB	6-4	230	7	Minnesota
98	Goss, Antonio	LB	6-4	228	2	North Carolina
29	Griffin, Don	CB	6-0	176	5	Middle Tennessee St.
94	Haley, Charles	LB-DE	6-5	230	5	James Madison
9	Helton, Barry	P	6-3	205	3	Colorado
30	Henderson, Keith	RB	6-1	220	2	Georgia
56	Hendrickson, Steve	LB	6-0	245	2	California
78	Holt, Pierce	DE	6-4	280	3	Angelo State
40	Jackson, Johnny	S	6-1	204	2	Houston
84	Jones, Brent	TE	6-4	230	4	Santa Clara
42	Lott, Ronnie	S	6-0	200	10	Southern California
62	McIntyre, Guy	G	6-3	265	7	Georgia
54	Millen, Matt	LB	6-2	245	11	Penn State
16	Montana, Joe	QB	6-2	195	12	Notre Dame
77	Paris, Bubba	T	6-6	299	8	Michigan
26	Pollard, Darryl	CB	5-11	187	4	Weber State
76	Putzier, Rollin	NT	6-4	279	3	Oregon
57	Radloff, Wayne	C	6-5	277	6	Georgia
44	Rathman, Tom	RB	6-1	232	5	Nebraska
80	Rice, Jerry	WR	6-2	200	6	Mississippi Valley St.
91	Roberts, Larry	DE	6-3	275	5	Alabama
53	Romanowski, Bill	LB	6-4	231	3	Boston College
61	Sapolu, Jesse	C	6-4	260	5	Hawaii
71	Shannon, John	NT	6-3	270	3	Kentucky
88	Sherrard, Mike	WR	6-2	187	5	UCLA
72	Smerlas, Fred	NT	6-3	288	12	Boston College
24	Sydney, Harry	RB	6-0	217	4	Kansas
66	Tausch, Terry	G	6-5	276	9	Texas
82	Taylor, John	WR	6-1	185	4	Delaware State
60	Thomas, Chuck	C-G	6-3	280	5	Oklahoma
23	Tillman, Spencer	RB	5-11	206	4	Oklahoma
58	Turner, Keena	LB	6-2	222	11	Purdue
74	Wallace, Steve	T	6-5	276	5	Auburn
89	Walls, Wesley	TE	6-5	246	2	Mississippi
99	Walter, Michael	LB	6-3	238	8	Oregon
51	Washington, Chris	LB	6-4	240	7	Iowa State
43	Waymer, Dave	S	6-1	188	11	Notre Dame
81	Williams, Jamie	TE	6-4	245	8	Nebraska
85	Wilson, Mike	WR	6-3	215	10	Washington State
21	Wright, Eric	CB	6-1	185	9	Missouri
8	Young, Steve	QB	6-2	200	6	Brigham Young

1990 SCHEDULE OF GAMES

September
10	at New Orleans (Mon.)	8:00
16	WASHINGTON	1:00
23	ATLANTA	1:00
30	Open date	

October
7	at Houston	12:00
14	at Atlanta	1:00
21	PITTSBURGH	1:00
28	CLEVELAND	1:00

November
4	at Green Bay	12:00
11	at Dallas (Sun. night)	7:00
18	TAMPA BAY	1:00
25	LOS ANGELES RAMS	1:00

December
3	NEW YORK GIANTS (Mon.)	6:00
9	at Cincinnati	1:00
17	at Los Angeles Rams (Mon.)	6:00
23	NEW ORLEANS	1:00
30	at Minnesota	12:00

Special Teams

Placekicker Mike Cofer does not have a powerful leg but he failed on only one field goal attempt from inside the 42-yard line and is unchallenged. Again, the club is satisfied with punter Barry Helton, who had only one attempt blocked and averaged a respectable 40.5 gross yards. Returning punts, the elegant John Taylor coasted effortlessly to an NFL fifth-best average of 11.6 yards and, with the departure of Flagler, the hard-running Spencer Tillman may become the senior kick-off returner.

CHAPTER EIGHT

1990 NATIONAL FOOTBALL LEAGUE SCHEDULE

(All times local)

FIRST WEEK
Sunday, September 9 — **Kickoff**

Denver at Los Angeles Raiders	1:00
Houston at Atlanta	4:00
Indianapolis at Buffalo	4:00
New York Jets at Cincinnati	4:00
Miami at New England	4:00
Minnesota at Kansas City	12:00
Philadelphia at New York Giants	8:00
Phoenix at Washington	1:00
Pittsburgh at Cleveland	4:00
Los Angeles Rams at Green Bay	12:00
San Diego at Dallas	3:00
Seattle at Chicago	12:00
Tampa Bay at Detroit	1:00

Monday, September 10

San Francisco at New Orleans	8:00

SECOND WEEK
Sunday, September 16

Atlanta at Detroit	1:00
Buffalo at Miami	1:00
Chicago at Green Bay	12:00
Cincinnati at San Diego	1:00
Cleveland at New York Jets	1:00
Houston at Pittsburgh	8:00
New England at Indianapolis	12:00
New Orleans at Minnesota	3:00
New York Giants at Dallas	3:00
Los Angeles Raiders at Seattle	1:00
Los Angeles Rams at Tampa Bay	1:00
Phoenix at Philadelphia	1:00
Washington at San Francisco	1:00

Monday, September 17

Kansas City at Denver	7:00

THIRD WEEK
Sunday, September 23

Atlanta at San Francisco	1:00
Dallas at Washington	1:00
Detroit at Tampa Bay	8:00
Indianapolis at Houston	12:00
Kansas City at Green Bay	12:00
Miami at New York Giants	1:00
Minnesota at Chicago	12:00
New England at Cincinnati	1:00
Philadelphia at Los Angeles Rams	1:00
Phoenix at New Orleans	12:00
Pittsburgh at Los Angeles Raiders	1:00
San Diego at Cleveland	1:00
Seattle at Denver	2:00

Monday, September 24

Buffalo at New York Jets	9:00

FOURTH WEEK
Sunday, September 30
Open Date: 4 NFC West teams

Chicago at Los Angeles Raiders	1:00
Cleveland at Kansas City	3:00
Dallas at New York Giants	1:00
Denver at Buffalo	1:00
Green Bay at Detroit	1:00
Houston at San Diego	1:00
Indianapolis at Philadelphia	1:00
Miami at Pittsburgh	1:00
New York Jets at New England	4:00
Tampa Bay at Minnesota	12:00
Washington at Phoenix	5:00

Monday, October 1

Cincinnati at Seattle	6:00

FIFTH WEEK
Sunday, October 7
Open Date: 4 NFC East teams

Cincinnati at Los Angeles Rams	1:00
Detroit at Minnesota	12:00
Green Bay at Chicago	3:00
Kansas City at Indianapolis	12:00
Los Angeles Raiders at Buffalo	7:30
New Orleans at Atlanta	1:00
New York Jets at Miami	1:00
San Diego at Pittsburgh	1:00
San Francisco at Houston	12:00
Seattle at New England	1:00
Tampa Bay at Dallas	12:00

Monday, October 8
Cleveland at Denver 7:00

SIXTH WEEK
Sunday, October 14
Open Date: 4 AFC East teams
Cleveland at New Orleans 12:00
Dallas at Phoenix 1:00
Detroit at Kansas City 12:00
Green Bay at Tampa Bay 1:00
Houston at Cincinnati 1:00
Los Angeles Rams at Chicago 6:30
New York Giants at Washington 4:00
Pittsburgh at Denver 2:00
San Diego at New York Jets 1:00
San Francisco at Atlanta 1:00
Seattle at Los Angeles Raiders 1:00

Monday, October 15
Minnesota at Philadelphia 9:00

SEVENTH WEEK
Thursday, October 18
Open Date: 4 NFC Central teams
New England at Miami 8:00

Sunday, October 21
Atlanta at Los Angeles Rams 1:00
Dallas at Tampa Bay 1:00
Denver at Indianapolis 12:00
Kansas City at Seattle 1:00
Los Angeles Raiders at San Diego 1:00
New Orleans at Houston 12:00
New York Jets at Buffalo 1:00
Philadelphia at Washington 1:00
Phoenix at New York Giants 4:00
Pittsburgh at San Francisco 1:00

Monday, October 22
Cincinnati at Cleveland 9:00

EIGHTH WEEK
Sunday, October 28
Open Date: 4 AFC West tesms
Buffalo at New England 1:00
Chicago at Phoenix 2:00
Cincinnati at Atlanta 8:00
Cleveland at San Francisco 1:00
Detroit at New Orleans 12:00
Miami at Indianapolis 1:00
Minnesota vs. Green Bay at Milwaukee 12:00
New York Jets at Houston 12:00
Philadelphia at Dallas 12:00
Tampa Bay at San Diego 1:00
Washington at New York Giants 4:00

Monday, October 29
Los Angeles Rams at Pittsburgh 9:00

NINTH WEEK
Sunday, November 4
Atlanta at Pittsburgh 1:00

Buffalo at Cleveland 1:00
Chicago at Tampa Bay 4:00
Dallas at New York Jets 1:00
Denver at Minnesota 7:00
Houston at Los Angeles Rams 1:00
New England at Philadelphia 1:00
New Orleans at Cincinnati 1:00
Phoenix at Miami 1:00
Los Angeles Raiders at Kansas City 12:00
San Diego at Seattle 1:00
San Francisco at Green Bay 12:00
Washington at Detroit 1:00

Monday, November 5
New York Giants at Indianapolis 9:00

TENTH WEEK
Sunday, November 11
Open Date: 4 AFC Central teams
Atlanta at Chicago 12:00
Denver at San Diego 1:00
Green Bay at Los Angeles Raiders 1:00
Indianapolis at New England 1:00
Miami at New York Jets 1:00
Minnesota at Detroit 1:00
New York Giants at Los Angeles Rams 1:00
Phoenix at Buffalo 1:00
San Francisco at Dallas 7:00
Seattle at Kansas City 12:00
Tampa Bay at New Orleans 12:00

Monday, November 12
Washington at Philadelphia 9:00

ELEVENTH WEEK
Sunday, November 18
Chicago at Denver 2:00
Dallas at Los Angeles Rams 1:00
Detroit at New York Giants 1:00
Green Bay at Phoenix 2:00
Houston at Cleveland 1:00
Minnesota at Seattle 1:00
New England at Buffalo 1:00
New Orleans at Washington 1:00
New York Jets at Indianapolis 4:00
Philadelphia at Atlanta 1:00
Pittsburgh at Cincinnati 8:00
San Diego at Kansas City 12:00
Tampa Bay at San Francisco 1:00

Monday, November 19
Los Angeles Raiders at Miami 9:00

TWELFTH WEEK
Thursday, November 22
Denver at Detroit 12:30
Washington at Dallas 3:00

Sunday, November 25
Atlanta at New Orleans 12:00
Chicago at Minnesota 12:00
Indianapolis at Cincinnati 1:00

Kansas City at Los Angeles Raiders	1:00
Los Angeles Rams at San Francisco	1:00
Miami at Cleveland	1:00
New England at Phoenix	2:00
New York Giants at Philadelphia	1:00
Pittsburgh at New York Jets	4:00
Seattle at San Diego	5:00
Tampa Bay vs. Green Bay at Milwaukee	12:00

Monday, November 26

Buffalo at Houston	8:00

THIRTEENTH WEEK
Sunday, December 2

Atlanta at Tampa Bay	1:00
Cincinnati at Pittsburgh	1:00
Detroit at Chicago	12:00
Green Bay at Minnesota	7:00
Houston at Seattle	1:00
Indianapolis at Phoenix	2:00
Kansas City at New England	1:00
Los Angeles Raiders at Denver	2:00
Los Angeles Rams at Cleveland	1:00
Miami at Washington	1:00
New Orleans at Dallas	3:00
New York Jets at San Diego	1:00
Philadelphia at Buffalo	1:00

Monday, December 3

New York Giants at San Francisco	6:00

FOURTEENTH WEEK
Sunday, December 9

Open Date: 4 1989 fifth-place teams

Buffalo at Indianapolis	1:00
Chicago at Washington	4:00
Cleveland at Houston	12:00
Denver at Kansas City	3:00
Minnesota at New York Giants	1:00
New Orleans at Los Angeles Rams	1:00
New England at Pittsburgh	1:00
Philadelphia at Miami	8:00
Phoenix at Atlanta	1:00
San Francisco at Cincinnati	1:00
Seattle vs. Green Bay at Milwaukee	12:00

Monday, December 10

Los Angeles Raiders at Detroit	9:00

FIFTEENTH WEEK
Saturday, December 15

Buffalo at New York Giants	12:30
Washington at New England	4:00

Sunday, December 16

Atlanta at Cleveland	1:00
Chicago at Detroit	8:00
Cincinnati at Los Angeles Raiders	1:00
Green Bay at Philadelphia	4:00
Houston at Kansas City	12:00
Indianapolis at New York Jets	1:00

Minnesota at Tampa Bay	1:00
Phoenix at Dallas	12:00
Pittsburgh at New Orleans	12:00
San Diego at Denver	2:00
Seattle at Miami	1:00

Monday, December 17

San Francisco at Los Angeles Rams	6:00

SIXTEENTH WEEK
Saturday, December 22

Detroit at Green Bay	11:30
Los Angeles Raiders at Minnesota	3:00
Washington at Indianapolis	8:00

Sunday, December 23

Cincinnati at Houston	12:00
Cleveland at Pittsburgh	1:00
Dallas at Philadelphia	1:00
Denver at Seattle	5:00
Kansas City at San Diego	1:00
Miami at Buffalo	1:00
New England at New York Jets	1:00
New Orleans at San Francisco	1:00
New York Giants at Phoenix	2:00
Los Angeles Rams at Atlanta	1:00
Tampa Bay at Chicago	12:00

SEVENTEENTH WEEK
Saturday, December 29

Kansas City at Chicago	11:00
Philadelphia at Phoenix	2:00

Sunday, December 30

Buffalo at Washington	1:00
Cleveland at Cincinnati	1:00
Dallas at Atlanta	1:00
Detroit at Seattle	1:00
Green Bay at Denver	2:00
Indianapolis at Miami	1:00
New York Giants at New England	1:00
New York Jets at Tampa Bay	4:00
Pittsburgh at Houston	7:00
San Diego at Los Angeles Raiders	1:00
San Francisco at Minnesota	12:00

Monday, December 31

Los Angeles Rams at New Orleans	7:00

Postseason

Saturday, Jan. 5	AFC and NFC First Round Playoffs
Sunday, Jan. 6	AFC and NFC First Round Playoffs
Saturday, Jan. 12	AFC and NFC Second Round Playoffs
Sunday, Jan. 13	AFC and NFC Second Round Playoffs
Sunday, Jan. 20	AFC and NFC Championship Games
Sunday, Jan. 27	Super Bowl XXV at Tampa Stadium, Tampa, Florida
Sunday, Feb. 3	AFC-NFC Pro Bowl at Honolulu, Hawaii

INTERPRETING THE ALL-TIME
HEAD-TO-HEAD CHART
(See inside back cover)

1. Identify a team from the left (vertical) column. The status of this team's games is set out in the horizontal row which corresponds with the team name. Buffalo's results appear along the very top horizontal row.

2. The rectangles are colour coded to show a team's status in the all-time head-to-head series as follows:

    A green rectangle if the team is leading the series.

    A red rectangle if the team is trailing in the series.

    A yellow rectangle if the series is tied.

3. Examples using the Buffalo Bills:

    The Bills hold a 14-10-1 won-lost-tied advantage in all games against the Denver Broncos.

    The Bills are behind 13-34-1 in all games against the Miami Dolphins.

    The Bills are tied 19-19-1 in all games against the Indianapolis Colts.

ALL-TIME HEAD-TO-HEAD RESULTS

	Buffalo	Indianapolis	Miami	New England	N.Y. Jets	Cincinnati	Cleveland	Houston	Pittsburgh	Denver	Kansas City	L.A. Raiders	San Diego	Seattle
Buffalo		19-19-1	13-34-1	26-33-1	31-28-0	6-11-0	2-8-0	12-18-0	5-6-0	14-10-1	15-12-1	12-13-0	9-17-2	1-3-0
Indianapolis	19-19-1		13-28-0	17-22-0	21-19-0	6-5-0	7-13-0	6-5-0	4-10-0	2-7-0	3-6-0	3-4-0	5-6-0	2-0-0
Miami	34-13-1	28-13-0		27-21-0	25-23-1	9-3-0	5-4-0	10-11-0	8-5-0	5-2-1	7-9-0	4-15-1	6-9-0	3-2-0
New England	33-26-1	22-17-0	21-27-0		27-32-1	7-4-0	2-7-0	16-14-1	3-6-0	12-15-0	7-11-3	13-13-1	13-12-2	6-3-0
N.Y. Jets	28-31-0	19-21-0	23-25-1	32-27-1		8-5-0	4-9-0	11-15-1	1-10-0	11-10-1	13-14-1	11-13-2	8-14-1	3-7-0
Cincinnati	11-6-0	5-6-0	3-9-0	4-7-0	5-8-0		20-19-0	23-18-1	19-20-0	6-9-0	9-10-0	5-13-0	8-11-0	6-3-0
Cleveland	8-2-0	13-7-0	4-5-0	7-2-0	9-4-0	19-20-0		26-14-0	48-32-0	4-12-0	6-5-2	2-10-0	5-6-1	3-8-0
Houston	18-12-0	5-6-0	11-10-0	14-16-1	15-11-1	18-23-1	14-26-0		14-28-0	19-11-1	13-22-0	12-22-0	14-17-1	4-3-0
Pittsburgh	6-5-0	10-4-0	5-8-0	6-3-0	10-1-0	20-19-0	32-48-0	28-14-0		6-10-1	12-5-0	6-9-0	10-5-0	4-3-0
Denver	10-14-1	7-2-0	2-5-1	15-12-0	10-11-1	9-6-0	12-4-0	11-19-1	10-6-1		24-35-0	19-39-2	30-29-1	15-11-0
Kansas City	12-15-1	6-3-0	9-7-0	11-7-3	14-13-1	10-9-0	5-6-2	22-13-0	5-12-0	35-24-0		24-35-2	27-31-1	13-10-0
L.A. Raiders	13-12-0	4-3-0	15-4-1	13-13-1	13-11-2	13-5-0	10-2-0	22-12-0	9-6-0	39-19-2	35-24-2		38-21-2	11-15-0
San Diego	17-9-2	6-5-0	9-6-0	12-13-2	14-8-1	11-8-0	6-5-1	17-14-1	5-10-0	29-30-1	31-27-1	21-38-2		10-12-0
Seattle	3-1-0	0-2-0	2-3-0	3-6-0	7-3-0	3-6-0	8-3-0	3-4-0	3-4-0	11-15-0	10-13-0	15-11-0	12-10-0	
Dallas	3-1-0	6-3-0	2-5-0	6-0-0	4-0-0	2-2-0	9-16-0	4-2-0	11-13-0	3-2-0	2-2-0	1-3-0	3-1-0	3-1-0
N.Y. Giants	2-2-0	3-7-0	0-1-0	2-1-0	3-3-0	0-3-0	16-26-2	3-0-0	41-26-3	4-2-0	5-1-0	2-3-0	4-2-0	4-2-0
Philadelphia	4-1-0	5-5-0	2-4-0	4-2-0	4-0-0	0-5-0	11-30-1	4-0-0	43-25-3	4-2-0	1-0-0	3-3-0	2-3-0	3-1-0
Phoenix	3-2-0	5-4-0	0-5-0	4-1-0	2-1-0	1-3-0	10-31-3	3-2-0	21-29-3	0-2-1	1-3-1	1-2-0	1-4-0	3-0-0
Washington	3-2-0	6-15-0	2-5-0	3-1-0	4-0-0	3-2-0	8-32-1	2-3-0	41-27-3	3-3-0	1-2-0	2-5-0	5-0-0	4-1-0
Chicago	3-1-0	15-21-0	1-4-0	3-3-0	2-1-0	2-2-0	3-7-0	2-3-0	15-4-1	4-4-0	3-1-0	3-3-0	1-4-0	1-4-0
Detroit	1-1-1	16-17-2	1-2-0	2-2-0	2-3-0	2-3-0	13-4-0	2-3-0	13-10-1	2-4-0	3-3-0	2-4-0	3-2-0	1-3-0
Green Bay	1-3-0	18-18-1	0-6-0	2-2-0	1-4-0	2-4-0	8-5-0	2-3-0	16-11-0	1-3-1	2-2-1	1-5-0	3-1-0	3-2-0
Minnesota	4-2-0	6-12-1	1-5-0	2-2-0	1-3-0	3-3-0	7-3-0	3-2-0	6-5-0	3-2-0	2-2-0	2-5-0	3-3-0	1-3-0
Tampa Bay	4-1-0	1-4-0	1-3-0	0-3-0	1-3-0	1-3-0	0-4-0	1-3-0	0-4-0	0-2-0	2-4-0	0-2-0	0-3-0	0-2-0
Atlanta	3-2-0	0-10-0	1-4-0	3-3-0	2-3-0	1-5-0	1-7-0	4-2-0	1-7-0	3-4-0	0-2-0	2-4-0	2-1-0	0-4-0
L.A. Rams	3-2-0	16-20-2	1-4-0	2-3-0	4-2-0	2-3-0	7-9-0	3-2-0	13-4-2	3-3-0	3-0-0	2-4-0	2-2-0	4-0-0
New Orleans	2-2-0	2-3-0	1-4-0	1-5-0	2-4-0	3-3-0	2-8-0	3-2-1	5-4-0	1-4-0	2-2-0	1-3-1	1-3-0	2-2-0
San Francisco	2-2-0	16-21-0	2-4-0	5-1-0	5-1-0	6-1-0	5-8-0	4-2-0	6-7-0	3-4-0	3-1-0	2-4-0	2-3-0	3-1-0